Legends of Irish Rugby

Forty Golden Greats

JOHN SCALLY

MAINSTREAM
PUBLISHING
EDINBURGH AND LONDON

This edition, 2006

First published in Great Britain in 2005 by
MAINSTREAM PUBLISHING COMPANY (EDINBURGH) LTD
7 Albany Street
Edinburgh EH1 3UG

ISBN 1 84596 108 0

A catalogue record for this book
is available from the British Library

Typeset in Meta and Times

Printed and bound in Great Britain by
Cox & Wyman Ltd

ACKNOWLEDGEMENTS

THOSE WHO CAN DO. THOSE WHO CAN'T TALK AND WRITE about it.

I am very grateful to the many rugby legends, past and present, who shared their memories and personal anecdotes with me. It was a case of the who's who of Irish rugby sharing with the 'Who's he?' of Irish rugby.

My thanks in particular to Willie Anderson, Peter Clohessy, Victor Costello, Noel Coughlan, Gordon D'Arcy, Paul Dean, Girvan Dempsey, the late Mick Doyle, Mick English, Ciaran Fitzgerald, Mick Galwey, Simon Geoghegan, Jim Glennon, Tom Grace, Ray Gravell, Rob Henderson, Denis Hickie, David Humphreys, Moss Keane, Jack Kyle, Donal Lenihan, Willie John McBride, Jim McCarthy, Barry McGann, Paul McNaughton, Hugo MacNeill, Philip Matthews, Eric Miller, Johnny Moloney, Geordan Murphy, Des O'Brien, Phil O'Callaghan, Paul O'Connell, Brian, Frank, Geraldine and John O'Driscoll, Ronan O'Gara, Eddie O'Sullivan, Phil Orr, Colin Patterson, Paddy Reid, John Robbie, Fergus Slattery, David Wallace, Tony Ward and Pat Whelan.

I am also grateful to Niall Barry, Gerry Casey, Suzanne Costello, Carmel Dempsey, Helen Glennon, Suzanne O'Connell, Dara O'Neill of Seafield Golf Club and Judy Rooney for help with pictures.

The courageous Ian McCall has provided practical help as well as ongoing inspiration.

Special thanks to Mick Quinn for his supply of stories and to the wonderfully kind and enthusiastic Angie Henderson for her practical assistance.

Very special thanks to Ollie Campbell for agreeing to write the foreword and, more importantly, for his friendship down the years.

Thanks to Bill Campbell, Graeme Blaikie, Claire Rose, Emily Bland and all at Mainstream for their enthusiastic support of this book.

CONTENTS

FOREWORD

ON MY LIFE, AS ON THAT OF MANY ANOTHER INTERNATIONAL, rugby has had a defining influence.

In 1948, six years before I was even born, Ireland, captained by Karl Mullen of Old Belvedere, won the Grand Slam for the first, and so far only, time when they beat Wales in Ravenhill by six points to three.

My dad, James Oliver (Ollie) Campbell, attended that game and I was weaned on the exploits of that infamous team, particularly the immortal and revered Jackie Kyle, my dad's all-time sporting hero.

In December 1963, my dad brought me to Lansdowne Road for the first time, to see Ireland take on the mighty All Blacks.

The All Blacks won 6–5 and I was hooked, on rugby and on Ireland. My everlasting fascination with the All Blacks was also born on that day.

In early 1964, I saw my first-ever live match on TV – in Karl Mullen's house. It was Ireland against England at Twickenham and I was a birthday guest of schoolmate Karl Mullen junior, who was celebrating his tenth birthday. I was then playing my first season at out-half, with the Belvedere College Under-10s. That day, I saw Mike Gibson play his first game for Ireland, in the number 10 jersey. Inspired by the immaculate Gibson, Ireland had a historic victory, winning 18–5, and I instantly had my own personal rugby idol.

Twelve years later, on 17 January 1976, I won my first cap, against Australia at Lansdowne Road, with Mike Gibson in the centre outside me. By that time, he had of course metamorphosed into Cameron Michael Henderson Gibson.

Then, in 1982, I was privileged to be on Ciaran Fitzgerald's Ireland team, which won the Triple Crown for the first time in 33 years, and for the first time ever at Lansdowne Road, when we beat Scotland 21–12.

Although by now retired, I was of course at Lansdowne Road again in 1985 to witness Ciaran Fitzgerald lead Ireland to our second Triple Crown in four years when Michael Kiernan kicked that never-to-be-forgotten drop-goal against England in the dying minutes to win 13–10.

Nineteen years later, in 2004, I was fortunate to see at first hand another famous day in Irish rugby, when Brian O'Driscoll led Ireland to victory over Scotland by 37–16 to win only our seventh-ever Triple Crown. Of course, it was also very sweet to see Ireland beat England in 2006 to claim our eighth.

These unforgettable and personally enriching days apart, Irish rugby has of course known many other magnificent days. Unfortunately, we have also experienced many disappointing and very forgettable days in our 130-year history.

However, the one constant theme throughout the years of fluctuating fortunes has been the appearance of many brilliant individual players, and unique and colourful characters who have worn the emerald-green jersey of Ireland.

In this book, John Scally, who is as passionate about sport as any man I have ever met, recalls some, if not all, of these legendary players and gives an insight into their personalities and backgrounds that otherwise might never have seen the light of day.

That idol of mine, the incomparable Cameron Michael Henderson Gibson, once eloquently wrote that 'rugby is like love, it is a game of touch and of feel and of instinct'.

I have no doubt that John has written this book, his 21st, with those same qualities of love, touch, feel and instinct. I hope you enjoy it as much as I did.

Seamus Oliver (Ollie) Campbell

INTRODUCTION

TO BE OR NOT TO BE? THAT WAS THE QUESTION FOR HAMLET BUT
for this scribe, the question was to include or to exclude. The most
difficult part of writing this book was deciding which 40 players to
feature. Any collection that is literally bookended by Brian O'Driscoll
and Jack Kyle is an obvious celebration of great Irish rugby talent. I
was spoilt for choice and acutely conscious that no matter what route I
took I was not going to please everybody. To come close to cataloguing
all the great players who have lined out for Ireland, I would need five
books, not one. I am not claiming that the 40 legends in this book are
the greatest Irish players. Several of them certainly are among those but
pundits may query some of my choices. In that respect, I follow in the
tradition of the Irish selectors!

The task I set myself was twofold: to pay homage to the legends of
Irish rugby and to write an entertaining book. In doing so, I may have
stretched the definition of 'legend' to get as much diversity and colour
into the profiles as possible. I also wanted to honour some of the Irish
players who have attained legendary status more for their activities off
the pitch than for anything they ever did on it! Were I to include all the
players in this category, I would have more chapters than the Bible! It
does mean that some of the stories told in the book are more folklore
than fact.

There is of course a case for extending 'legends' to people who have
made a great contribution to Irish rugby in capacities other than as
players. The late, much missed RTÉ radio commentator Tom Rooney,

11

who will always be remembered for his legendary commentary on Noel Mannion's famous try against Wales in 1989 (when the big Connacht number 8 got in the way of Bleddyn Bowen's fly-kick and ran 70 yards to secure Ireland's 19–13 win), is just one person who falls into this category, which would also include coaches like Eddie O'Sullivan. However, in this book I restrict myself to those who have worn the green shirt with distinction.

While I had many doubts about which players to include/exclude, the one selection decision that was never in doubt was the people to dedicate the book to: the aforementioned Tom Rooney and the late John McCall, who died so tragically and shockingly on 27 March 2004 on the field of play during Ireland's game against New Zealand in the Under-19 World Cup in Durban, South Africa. Just two weeks previously, he had captained Royal School Armagh to victory in the Ulster Schools Cup. On the same day, Ireland won their first Triple Crown in 19 years. Poignantly, John's uncle, Brian, was a substitute on Ireland's last Triple Crown-winning team of 1985.

Death always sends a chill through the bones. Each death is a painful reminder of the ultimate and unwelcome end for us all. It is all the more harrowing when a young person dies and all the promise of a young life is denied. John's death left the Irish rugby community in a state of numbed disbelief. Of course, the death was devastating for his family: his father, Ian; mother, Carolyn; brother, James and sister, Rebecca. As Ian observed to me, 'My dad, who is 85 now, often said, "The old people used to say your own trouble is your own trouble." I thought I knew what he meant but with John's death, we now know all too well. Grief is very personal and can't be shared or given away. We are now only starting to feel the depth of our loss. John, as I'm sure you would know, took up a lot of space in our home. However, we are sure we'll all be together again some day and the way we feel, we would rather it was sooner than later.'

May he rest in peace.

1

THE LIFE OF BRIAN

'THEY CALL HIM GOD. WELL, I RECKON HE'S A MUCH BETTER player than that.'

Thus spoke Stuart Barnes during the Sky Sports commentary on one of the all-time great tries. In his first Test for the Lions in 2001, Brian O'Driscoll left the world champions, Australia, looking as slow as growing grass as he ran half the field and scythed through their defence to score one of the greatest individual tries ever seen, the very signature of genius. Following his vintage displays for the Lions, O'Driscoll continued his dizzying ascent to become one of the very biggest names in world rugby. The French rugby legend Philippe Sella said of him, 'Brian is like a locomotive.' Tony Ward frequently refers to him as 'He Who Walks on Water'. Matt Williams said, 'Brian O'Driscoll was touched by God to run with the ball.' His stunning tries against England and France in the 2005 Six Nations confirm that analysis. He is to the rugby aficionado what Nureyev was to the ballet enthusiast.

Fear can keep you a prisoner; hope can set you free. From his earliest days, O'Driscoll approached each international as if he expected to win, regardless of the opposition. This can-do philosophy was a breath of fresh air in Irish rugby.

Yet in real life, Brian O'Driscoll plays down any talk of stardom. He presents a powerful combination of charm, alert intelligence and lively spirit. A sense of habitual calm is communicated by the soft voice in which he speaks his well-constructed sentences and the expression of amiable serenity that is usually on his face. Although he possesses arguably the greatest arsenal of gifts the country has ever seen, he is not keen to speak at length about his achievements. On the pitch, he makes his own truth. He seems to be more at home there than anywhere else. It is to the fans' benefit that he found himself articulate in such a wonderful language. His courage, like his endearing warmth and honesty, is in the inviolable core of his nature. Since making his international debut for Ireland in June 1999, against Australia in Brisbane, he has slowly come to terms with his celebrity status.

'The thing about the media is that they tend to build you up into something you are not. And they do it early, before you've actually achieved anything. So just for a while at the start of my career, I was a little hesitant. I'm more relaxed now, after a couple of seasons at the top level.'

FAMILY TIES

O'Driscoll has been in thrall to the game of rugby for as long as he can remember. It helps that his father, Frank, played for Ireland and that his cousins, Barry and John, also played for Ireland. Indeed, John went on to play for the Lions and starred on Ireland's Triple Crown-winning team in 1982. A kind, passionate but polite, thoroughly delightful man, Frank recalls Brian's introduction to rugby with pure and undiluted happiness.

'I can remember as if it were yesterday going to see Brian playing his first Schools match. I think he scored four tries on that day. After the game, people were asking, "Who is this new kid on the block?" Having been fortunate enough to play for Ireland myself, I always felt that if Brian got the breaks he would go on and play for the national team. I never had any doubt about whether he had the talent but in the past, the most talented players haven't always made it, for a variety of reasons, like injury.

'One of the proudest days for me was when Brian played his first game for Ireland at schoolboy level. I remember saying to my wife, Geraldine, on the way to the match, "Do you realise that only 14 other sets of parents in Ireland are going to experience what we are going to experience today?" I was so proud of him that day. Although he has done a lot of great things on the field, I am particularly proud of him because of his discipline. He never lets his social life interfere with his rugby. It's always the other way round.'

O'Driscoll honed his craft in Ireland's most famous rugby nursery,

Blackrock College, having first made his mark at its feeder school, Willow Park.

'During primary school, I played Gaelic football for my school, Belgrove in Clontarf. I also played tennis and soccer. My hero as a child was Mark Hughes. I was a big Manchester United fan and when things weren't going well for them you could rely on Hughes to do something special. I was in awe of the fact that he scored so many spectacular goals and I admired his aggressiveness and competitiveness. I didn't have too many rugby idols but if I did have to pick one it would be New Zealand's Michael Jones. I think he was ahead of his time in the sense that he was able to mix the hard stuff of the forwards and the silky skills of the backs. He was a very graceful runner and he had a huge amount of skill.

'Everything changed for me when I went to Willow Park when I was 12. In my first-ever training session, I was put in the second row. Needless to say, I wouldn't be the biggest player in the world, so it wasn't until I was moved to the backs that I really cemented my position. I was pushed onto the B team and then the A team within a few weeks. As a 12 year old, I was quite fast; people's legs grew quicker than mine in the following years but eventually I caught up with them.'

At Blackrock, he was noticed by a man who would have a significant impact on his international career a decade later – future Ireland coach Eddie O'Sullivan. In conversation with this writer, O'Sullivan recalled his early impressions of the brightest star in Irish rugby: 'Brian O'Driscoll burst onto the scene in pretty explosive style. I remember seeing him at school in Blackrock College when I worked there for a while. He was quite small then but suddenly got this great growth spurt and turned into a fine athlete. He has something special. He's very gifted in terms of athleticism and in terms of football skills but he's also a very intelligent guy. He's got that key thing that makes him different from everyone else, in that he can perform at the highest level under the greatest pressure and still come through. That's the biggest test for any athlete.'

At Blackrock College, O'Driscoll paraded all the fluent skills that would characterise his international career: great speed and an almost unique combination of attacking and defensive qualities. Those talents brought him to the attention of the international selectors.

'My debut for Ireland came in June 1999. I had been brought on the tour of Australia having sat on the bench for one of the Six Nations games. I played a few games on the tour before I was selected to play in the centre with Kevin Maggs in the First Test in Brisbane. I was lucky to play for Ireland when I was so young. It was a huge honour for me and something that I had always hoped to rise to at some stage of my career but to have it come at such an early age was incredible for me and something I really cherished. I had mixed emotions, because we got a bad beating but at the same time I'd won my first cap. I probably got to enjoy my Second Test more, because we really pushed the Aussies all the way. I had heard people say that your first cap always goes by so quickly that you can't really take it all in and enjoy it. That was my experience too.

'At the start, things weren't going so well for Ireland. The low point was probably losing to Argentina in the World Cup back in Lens in 1999. That defeat was crushing. I think we panicked as a team towards the end and our 13-man lineout probably showed we were a bit short of ideas.

'It was just as bad when we lost so heavily to England the following year. After that, a lot of changes were made, the team started to improve and we started to win again. When you have bad losses as well as great victories, you become very philosophical and realise that when you are down, the team is probably not as bad as people say you are and that when you win, you are not the world-beaters that everybody says you are.'

THE FRENCH CONNECTION

Happier times were around the corner and in 2000 O'Driscoll dramatically announced his arrival on the world stage with a stunning performance in Paris, culminating in his three tries.

'When we went to play France, nobody expected us to even challenge the French, which probably took a lot of weight off our shoulders. I look back at the pictures and see the joy on our faces for having achieved something that Irish teams had failed to do for 28 years. We were overwhelmed at the end and it was really a fantastic feeling. For me to have scored three tries was a nice bonus!

'The third try sticks out most of all. What most people probably don't realise is that I shouldn't have been where I was when I got the ball. I was just trying to catch a breather before I got back into position but the ball squirted out in front of me and I went for the gap. That try took us to within two points of them and convinced us that we could win the game. A lot of people have remarked that Émile Ntamack didn't make a great effort to tackle me and I'm only glad he didn't come crashing into me!'

O'Driscoll is fortunate in having a temperament that gets energised rather than drained by the big occasion. The bigger the occasion the more he likes it; in fact, where Brian is least relaxed is watching a game he is not playing in.

'I know some people will probably feel this is strange but I was far more nervous watching the 1997 Lions tour of South Africa when I was back home in Dublin staring at the television set than I was on the field in Brisbane for the First Test in 2001. When you're playing, you have no time to dwell on things. Mind you, I was aware of the crowd at the Gabba. Just looking up into that sea of red as we ran out was enough to put us on our toes, but when the Wallabies appeared and the boos drowned out the cheers it was just unbelievable.'

O'Driscoll looks back on the tour with mixed feelings.

'If we had gone on to win the series that First Test would probably have been a major highlight of my career but because we lost the series, it doesn't have the same glow in my memory. We were fairly surprised at what we achieved in the opening 50 minutes of the First Test in particular but all the gaps were closed up for the next two Tests. When you are a part of a tour like that, every result counts in terms of morale and encouragement. The First Test gave us a big lift but losing the other two was a crushing blow.'

There is a limit to the amount of resolution you can muster from your own resources. When things hit a rocky patch, you need the example and inspiration of others to help sustain your will to fight the good fight. O'Driscoll is fortunate to have the support of such a united family behind him, particularly as he is now so much in the public eye. Ours is an age in thrall to an almost mystical concept of celebrity. Brian's mother, Geraldine, is all too aware of this.

'The France game in 2000, when he scored the three tries, changed everything for Brian and indeed for us. I first realised that when I was introduced to someone after the match and they said, "This is Geraldine O'Driscoll. She used to be Frank O'Driscoll's wife. Now she's Brian O'Driscoll's mother!"

'That game was on a Sunday and shortly after the match, we had to rush for the train to be home for work the next day. One of our daughters was in Australia at the time and she rang us on the mobile.

She said, "Mum, after Brian's three tries I'm now a minor celebrity here!"

'Probably the most interesting experience of all came in Australia during the Lions tour. After the First Test when Brian scored the famous try, Frank and I got on the bus with a gang of Lions supporters. We sat at the back of the bus and nobody knew who we were. Then the crowd burst into song. They started singing "Waltzing O'Driscoll". Frank and I said nothing. We just nodded at each other but it was actually very emotional.'

One of his squadmates, Austin Healey, was somewhat less respectful, throwing chips at O'Driscoll in Manly High Street, which led to him being dive-bombed by seagulls.

CAPTAIN SENSIBLE

A major landmark in O'Driscoll's career came in March 2004 when he captained Ireland to their first Triple Crown in 19 years.

'In the Scotland game, we had to wear them down a bit. These Six Nations aren't easy and a lot of the time you mightn't pull away till the end, which was the case in this one. There was another agenda in this game. [Former Leinster coach] Matt Williams was coming back to Lansdowne Road. He had a point to prove because Scotland's campaign up to then had been disastrous. Added to the mix there was the fact that he literally knows the way the wind blows in the Lansdowne from his time as Leinster and Ireland A coach and his intimate knowledge of so many of the players he once coached on the Irish team. There had to be an element of proving the critics wrong.

'We weren't second-guessing what was going on in his mind. We were concentrating on playing to the best of our ability and we felt that if we were to do that, we could and would win the game.'

The high point of his career came when he was chosen to captain the 2005 Lions tour to New Zealand. It was the best of times. It was the worst of times. O'Driscoll's tour came to an abrupt and controversial end when he was the victim of a tackle of 'questionable sportsmanship' by Tana Umaga and Kevin Mealamu in the first minute of the First Test, sustaining a dislocated shoulder.

Rugby has opened a lot of doors for O'Driscoll.

'I loved the chances to play for the Barbarians because they play a seven-man game with fifteen players on the team. That's the way I'd describe it. My first experience was very exciting, even the build-up was thrilling, playing with people you'd not normally have the opportunity to work with was very special. Just to experience it was incredible. Training with Carlos Spencer, who was a childhood hero of mine, was great. Seeing the tricks he was doing in training left me flabbergasted but I had to pretend to be taking everything he was doing in my stride!'

Which rugby player would he most like to be compared with?

'If I had to be compared with anyone, I suppose I would like to be compared with Australia's Tim Horan. He could mix his game a huge amount and was in the World Cup-winning side of 1991 at a very young age. The fact that he could mix running skills and hard tackling makes him the complete rugby player and a lot of his skills I tried to emulate.'

O'Driscoll is aware that his status within the game is something of a mixed blessing.

'Rugby is a different kind of world than it was in Ollie Campbell's time. With the onset of professional rugby, people are interested in what rugby players are doing when they are not playing or training. They are interested in what we are doing socially and now, to a degree, who we are dating. At times this can get a bit frustrating and annoying but I guess it is part and parcel of the game. For the most part, it is great but there is an element of people prying into your life too much. I am happy to have people judging me on my rugby but I think my private life should be private.

'The commercial side of rugby has really taken off. My dad is my agent, if you like, though he prefers the term "manager". He is able to continue in his medical practice and it is great that he is able to look after my affairs because I know I can trust him.'

Brian still has unfinished rugby business.

'The Heineken Cup is a fantastic competition which I would like to win with Leinster. People don't realise just how difficult it is in terms of what you have to do to win. You have to win at least eight out of nine games and you have to keep going till the season ends with the final at the end of May. It's caught the imagination of the public, especially since so many of the games are televised. In the past everyone thought that the Super 12 in the southern hemisphere was the ultimate but as the Heineken Cup has established itself as a major competition it has narrowed the gap in standard between the northern and southern hemispheres because it means that players here now consistently play club rugby at a very high level.

'Some years, the way the fixtures fall – as in a World Cup year, a lot of Test matches – takes its toll on the body. The Celtic League is useful because when the provinces have lost players due to international duty, the teams need a practice match to get the players reintegrated again before they play a big game in the Heineken Cup. The League is perfect for that, as well as the opportunity to blood new players.'

The downside of the number of games is that the chances of getting seriously injured have increased dramatically.

'You have insurance in your contract but at the same time a huge number of professional players take out their own personal insurance in case something happens to them that ends their career prematurely. Every year, more and more people are having to retire early because there are more career-finishing injuries. The hits are bigger in professional rugby. I always remember my grandfather telling me that anybody who went into a tackle trying to mind themselves always came out worse in the end and if you have that mindset, you will put your body on the line.'

O'Driscoll has already achieved so much. What does he still hope to achieve?

'I suppose I've reached the stage where I've got a bit selfish. A few years ago, I just wanted to play for Ireland. Now I want to play on an Irish side that can win things or make a serious challenge for honours.'

He pauses for reflection when asked what advice he would give any young player today.

'Whatever you decide to do, give it your best shot. If you play a team sport, always remember that your first obligation is not to yourself but to your team.

'The best piece of advice I've ever been given was from my old coach at UCD [University College Dublin], Lee Smith. Lee always wrote out a couple of sentences on a piece of paper for each player before a match telling you what he wanted you to do and what your role on the team was but when he came around to me, he said, "Just go out and play your own game." Such a small thing made a big difference, and inspired me and gave me a lot of confidence to go out and play well, because I thought very highly of Lee and I still do.'

A GOOD WALK SPOILED

Never was O'Driscoll's ability to play his own game more tellingly illustrated than in his decisive break in the last minute of the 2006 Championship match against England to set up the try that saw Ireland claim its second Triple Crown under his captaincy. As a keen golfer, meanwhile, Brian has a high-profile association with Seafield Golf Club. He enjoys the story of the two Mexican detectives who were investigating the murder of Juan Gonzalez.

'How was he killed?' asked one detective.

'With a golf gun,' the other detective replied.

'A golf gun?! What the heck is a golf gun?'

'I'm not certain, but it sure made a hole in Juan!'

2

MR D'ARCY

WELCOME TO THE WORLD OF GORDON D'ARCY.
10 p.m., 10 November 2004. Twelve hours earlier, it has been announced in the national media that he is one of the elite Irish sports personalities who has been chosen for a prestigious Texaco Sportstars Award. Every hour, on the hour, the story has been told on every radio station in the country. I ring the reigning IRB Northern Hemisphere Player of the Year to congratulate him on his award. He has no idea what I'm talking about. As he digests the information, his reaction is instructive. While he is happy to be honoured, there is no hint of euphoria or elation. His instinct is not to look back on former glories but to look to the future and how he can make his contribution to Irish rugby in the years ahead by becoming an even better player.

Few dreams come true. Rugby dreamers tend to see a terrific rainbow every time it rains, so when a new sensation's limitations are exposed, it is a crushing let-down. Dreamers are forever assuring themselves that the next truly great player is on the horizon, but, like the skyline, he never comes any closer, remaining always just out of reach. The problem is easily identified – much more difficult to remedy. Gordon D'Arcy was to change all that.

Few players have ever announced their arrival on the Six Nations stage with a louder blare of trumpets than D'Arcy in 2004. If there is one moment that will forever define his impact that season, it came in the last minute of the match against Scotland which sealed Ireland's Triple Crown. Eddie O'Sullivan was making a bench clearance and

D'Arcy was one of the players to be called ashore. He had scored two tries and consistently tormented the Scottish defence with his powerful and intelligent running; the cheer for him nearly raised the rafters.

From the start of that campaign, Irish rugby followers took to him with extraordinary warmth, not just because of the subtlety and invention and spirit of adventure that enabled him to terrorise opposing defenders; above all, they loved his all-action style, like a mighty atom, and relentless pursuit of every opportunity to take off on an incisive run. Allied to this, his creativity on the ball, his genius for penetration and his killing finish commanded their respect. His fusion of great commitment and dazzling skills was the stuff of cult status and instant sporting legend. It had not always been clear, though, that he was destined to light up the rugby landscape so dramatically.

'My next-door neighbour Peter Redmond got me into rugby. To this day, he still claims that he taught me everything I know about rugby but not everything he knows! He's a gas lad. I also played a lot at home with my brother, Ian. He remains the hardest player I ever had to play against and many's the time his crunching tackles left me bruised and battered. When I went to Clongowes, I started as a hooker and played there until I was 14. Then I moved to out-half, which was a pretty major positional switch!

'The late Vinny Murray was a huge influence on me as I came through schoolboy level. As a coach he was able to get the most out of me. I can look back now and think, "That's what he was trying to achieve when he did that." It would have been great if he'd been around to see the fruits of his labour, even though I made him work hard for it!

'Of course, my dad has been a great influence on me. He knows very little about rugby but thinks he knows everything about the game! My dad has always been my harshest critic. I made the World Cup squad in '99 but didn't get a game. After that, for years, he would ring me before the Irish squad was due to be announced and say, "Don't be disappointed if you don't get picked." I would think, "Of course I'll be picked." Up to 2004, I generally wasn't picked. I swear to God, to this day, every time the Irish squad is picked my heart is pounding and I'm silently praying, "Just let me be in it." It never gets any easier.'

WILD THING?

Before 2004, there had been a number of hints in newspaper articles that D'Arcy had a problem with his attitude. How accurate was that perception?

'When I first started playing rugby, I had a very blasé approach. I was enjoying playing rugby but I was carrying that casual attitude into my preparation and training, and it just gave off the wrong vibe. It took me a while to realise that more commitment was needed. When you have established yourself as a consistently top-class player, you don't have to be too worried about the vibe you give off but when you are trying to break into a new team it is important, because other people make judgements about you on the basis of that rather than what you can do on the pitch. It took me a while to adjust to that.'

Some sports personalities are in the business of self-justification. When the former Chelsea player Adrian Mutu was asked why he tested positive for cocaine, he replied, 'I got into this situation because of some complicated matters with my soul.' D'Arcy is refreshingly candid.

'I don't think saying I had a bad attitude is the most accurate way of portraying it. I just had my own way. When I look back at it now, I came straight out of school and into a professional set-up. I probably wasn't given the direction initially. I probably should have been put into an Under-21 squad or on a regimented programme where someone said, "You are a stone and a half overweight, you need to lose that, then we will work on your fitness etc." Instead it was very haphazard. I was here and there working with different people but nobody was actually telling me what to do. When I look back at it now, I think I wasted a lot of time then. It wasn't that I was resisting anybody or had a bad attitude, because people like that don't last in sport.

'What amazed me was that certain people in the media were looking for a story to latch on to and a story about Matt Williams, my coach at Leinster at the time, finding me drunk got legs and started turning up everywhere. My attitude, though, was that one incident doesn't sum me up as a person. I was doing things my way. I was playing exciting rugby in my eyes, like running the ball from my own five-metre line – sometimes it came off, sometimes it didn't. As a 19 year old, the consequences of your actions aren't all that relevant. People say, "He was a crazy, crazy kid." I wasn't. I was just a regular 19 year old.'

MATT-ER OF FACT

What then is his assessment of Matt Williams?

'Mattie has his pros and cons. He gave me a little correction and he said I wasn't professional enough. I thought I was but I wasn't. I didn't see the need to kick, because I thought I could run my way out of trouble but he said, "No – you have to be able to kick with both feet."

'Mattie probably did more for the set-up at Leinster in general than for any player in particular. There was a lot of talk that he resurrected Reggie Corrigan's and Victor Costello's careers but I don't think that's true. There's a great saying that when you are down and out and on the ground nobody can pick you up. People can hold out their hand but in the end you have to pick yourself up off the floor. Matt gave us a lot of the tools we needed to help ourselves. When he first came, he brought in revolutionary changes, like us having a sports massage every Monday morning. At the time, we were all saying, "That's crazy." Now we have two a week and we don't even think about it. He revolutionised Leinster rugby and fought hard for the players. He told us that he would shout and curse at us behind closed doors but in public, he would defend us to the hilt. In fairness to him, that's exactly what he did.'

HOME AND AWAY

D'Arcy was controversially omitted from the Irish World Cup squad in 2003.

'That will go down as one of the low points of my life. I always said when I made the first World Cup in '99 that I would like to play in four World Cups. I might still play in 2011 but if so, it will be my third and not my fourth. It was between Paddy Wallace and myself for the one spot. It was a call that had to be made, and you live and die by those calls. There have been calls that have gone my way since, like when Brian (O'Driscoll) was injured before the France game in 2004.

'I remember I was inconsolable when I heard I had missed out on the squad. I was talking to a schoolteacher friend of mine and I asked in a wailing tone, "What's going to happen to me now?" He calmly said, "Well, you're going to be able to play eight games at full-back for Leinster and you're always saying that you want to play at full-back." It helped me to start thinking positively again.'

The popular perception was that his omission from the World Cup squad was the catalyst D'Arcy needed to finally get his act together and fulfil his true potential. Not for the first time in his career, the real story was more complex.

'It was easy for people to write that missing out on the World Cup was what spurred me on to perform in 2004 but that is not the case. When I wasn't getting picked for Ireland, I lost my enjoyment of playing rugby and I lost the things I enjoyed about the game, like beating a man one-on-one or putting in a good tackle. During the World Cup, I started to enjoy my rugby again. At Leinster, Gary Ella had replaced Matt Williams as coach. I got on brilliantly with him and my career flourished once more. He gave me a free role. I asked him before one game, "Is there anything you want me to do?" and he said, "If you see it, do it."

'"Is there anything you don't want me to do?"

'"No, not really, mate."

'"OK."

'I was just smiling after a game and I was training well because I was so looking forward to playing again, and that was what re-energised me. I didn't consciously say, "I'm going to get my place on the Irish team" or "I'm going to train harder". I was just enjoying it more.'

His international redemption came almost by accident.

'There wasn't much cover in either Leinster or Ireland for the centre positions. During the run-up to a Leinster game, Gary Ella casually asked me one day, "Do you want to go 13?" It really was as casual as that. We were walking onto the pitch and we were having a little banter.

'I replied, "Well, do you want me to play 13?"

'"Well, what do you think?"

'"Yeah, OK. We'll see how it goes."

'It seemed to work for Leinster, and Eddie O'Sullivan gave it a try against France.'

PARISIAN ADVENTURE

Brian O'Driscoll's injury allowed D'Arcy to take his place on the Irish team for the opening Six Nations fixture in Paris. Yet some shook their heads and said that playing for the national team in the cauldron atmosphere of such a match would be too big a leap. It was an extraordinary burden for such an inexperienced player to carry but, driven by a fierce determination and that most magical of qualities, a big-match temperament, D'Arcy refused to buckle under the pressure.

'I had five caps before I started the Six Nations game against France in 2004. The experience of those caps and of being in and out of the Irish squad probably helped me for a start.'

He came into a side with a clear mission.

'People said we were a "nearly team" before we won the Triple Crown. I remember Brian O'Driscoll saying when we beat Australia in

2002, "Let's not be the nearly team, let's not get the good win now and again; let's strive to beat the big guns consistently." I think we did that winning the Triple Crown. We had beaten France in 2000, England in 2001 and Australia in 2002 but we hadn't strung enough good results together against top opposition. Winning the Triple Crown took that monkey off our back and gave us a base to build on. When we went on to tour to South Africa, a good performance was no longer losing by only ten points. A good performance was nothing less than a win.'

Five years after winning his first cap against Romania in the '99 World Cup, D'Arcy was finally to stamp his distinctive mark on international rugby.

'There were a few moments before the France game that stand out for me. You train for the start of week with a squad of 30. Then, on the Wednesday, a squad of 22 was announced. I was in the 22 and I thought "Wow. I'm going to be on the bench." I presumed they were going to go for a different combination in the centre but I was pretty sure that I would win another cap at some stage in the match by coming on as a replacement.

'Then the team was called out. I heard "D'Arcy 13". I was in a state of shock. After that, we went to training. Eddie [O'Sullivan] said to me, "Relax, play your game and when you get the ball, run hard." It was the best advice I ever got.

'The other thing I remember is arriving at the Stade de France before the match. I had heard a lot about it but never been in it. I remember when we turned a corner on the team bus there it stood in front of us and I actually couldn't see as far as the top of it because it was so huge. I walked out with Malcolm O'Kelly to throw the ball around. You had to look almost straight up to see the sunlight.

'As the game started, I just wanted the ball. From the kick-off, we went straight at them but two defensive mistakes, two simple things, cost us fourteen points and the game. I went to [the well-known Irish pub] Kitty O'Shea's afterwards and met my brothers and sisters who had travelled over for the match, and that was great.

'For me, the Wales game was massive. It was my first start at home for Ireland and I felt really in the zone. Your first home game is amazing and it was also Brian's first game back from his injury. Playing with Brian makes my job a lot easier. Everyone knows he is a great player but I honestly think people don't fully appreciate how good he is and all the things he does on the pitch. People remember the flashy stuff he does, like the tries, but they don't see the amount of bread-and-butter stuff he gets through in a match. If people only knew the amount of work he does on the pitch, they would be in awe. From a selfish point of view, his great value is that he creates more space for me. He actually creates more time on the ball for you. Hopefully, a time will come when I can repay him and create as much space for him as he has for me.

'The English game was special. All week, everybody was "locked and loaded" as Eddie likes to put it. The great thing was that the squad, players and staff had gelled together so well, and our play on the field reflected that. Brian made a throwaway comment that he hoped Ireland might make the Twickenham crowd "choke on their prawn sandwiches". Of course, the English media whipped up a storm about it but we didn't let it faze us in the slightest.

'Before the game, we did a warm-up and you could feel the energy running through the side. Rog [Ronan O'Gara] was playing so well, and was able to give Brian and myself the type of ball we needed – that made a huge difference. A big part of the game plan for that match was for Rog to throw wide, flat passes to Brian and myself. When we came in at half-time, the question was asked, "Is anybody tired?" The answer was an emphatic "No" from everyone. These are the world champions and we are going to win. They can't beat us. The try we scored from our own 22 was my favourite Ireland team try ever. I remember speaking to Eddie that evening and saying, "I'd say that put a smile on your face."

'"What?"

'"That try was exactly what you were getting us to do during the week."

'"Yeah."

'He wasn't saying it in a smug way, he was just satisfied that everybody had done exactly what they were supposed to do.

'I know I got two tries in the Scotland game but, going on the stats, my best game was against England, in terms of ball-carrying and so on. I was more satisfied with my performance in the England game than in the Scotland game. I was 14 the last time Ireland had won at Twickenham, in 1994, when Simon Geoghegan got that try in the corner. I was jumping up and down, and I didn't even like rugby then! So that was a big one to win.

'The England game was the critical one that season. From 1 to 22, we believed that we were going to win that game. The preparation had gone well all week, the self-belief was there, which was a huge thing. The popular view was that we were the underdogs but in the squad, not a single one of us believed that. We felt we were as good as them.

'The problem with the Scottish game was that they were like a cornered dog. It was going to be a five-game whitewash for them, so we knew it was going to be a tough game. Down through the years, one of the things that's always bugged me about Irish sport is that we're not comfortable about being favourites. We're much happier as underdogs, grinding out a result. You have to get used to being favourites. People say it is a weight around your neck; I think it's time we saw it the other way, as something you wear on your shoulders to make you feel taller. We need to develop that mentality. Up to the last 20 minutes against Scotland, we were grinding away with them. Finally, we pulled away from them. Winning the Triple Crown was something I hadn't even dreamed about because it happens so seldom.'

What is his personal highlight from that magical season?

'My second try against Scotland was the last nail in the coffin and effectively sealed the Triple Crown but it was my first try that day that was the most satisfying for me because it was a much better score.'

After the match, though, D'Arcy was to find himself involved in a memorable moment off the pitch.

THE RIGHT HOOK

Irish sport has been blessed with television pundits like John Giles, Eamon Dunphy, Pat Spillane, Colm O'Rourke and Ger Loughnane, who have been informing and entertaining for years. More recently, a new triumvirate has been created on RTÉ television: Tom McGurk, George Hook and Brent Pope. What makes the dynamic between them so intriguing is that the viewer is never too clear as to whether Tom and George like each other.

It is not overstating things to say that Hook's style is unique. Asked why Leinster lost to Perpignan in the Heineken Cup in 2003, he replied, 'It's in Mrs Beeton's cookery book – recipe, chicken soup. First, catch your chicken. This team has not caught their chicken since this championship started; today that chicken has come home to roost. That's why they're in the manure they're in.' He does not spare people's sensibilities: 'If Frankie Sheahan was playing William Tell, his son would have an arrow in his chest and not in his apple.' After Ireland's surprise capitulation to the Scots in 2001, the Right Hook observed, 'Scotland are . . . I nearly said the nymphomaniacs . . . of course I mean kleptomaniacs of world rugby.'

Brent Pope, too, can get a good barbed comment in. Noticing that the Irish captain was carrying a few spare pounds around his waistline, he said, 'Brian O'Driscoll's been going to the same gym as George Hook.'

Hook recognises one of the most important things about the job of an analyst: that they are part of the entertainment business. It is great that in Ireland people take sport so seriously, because it often seems that Bill Shankly's famous remark about sport – that it's much more important than a matter of life and death – seems if anything a little bland. But Hook is one of the people who appreciate that you need a bit of craic as well. This was most evident after Ireland won the Triple Crown by beating Scotland. After the previous game when Ireland beat Italy, George took a dig at Ireland's national treasure Brian O'Driscoll for taking full advantage of his post-match interview to slug out of a highly visible Powerade bottle after every answer he gave to RTÉ. After the Scots game, O'Driscoll recruited his centre partner D'Arcy to join him in drinking from their Powerade bottles while they were being interviewed by Michael Lyster, presumably as payback for George's little dig. Hook responded with a great stroke. He had prepared his own drink and while answering questions he was busy knocking back 'Hook's Hooch'. Tom McGurk and Brent Pope were laughing so hard they had to take an ad break.

FAST EDDIE

His past experiences ensure that D'Arcy always keeps his feet on the ground. To be chosen as the player of the Six Nations would be more than enough for most players – but it was not enough for D'Arcy.

'Unfortunately, it was only a good six months. I was injured for most of the second half of the year. I came back from injury in the autumn and played two games for Leinster in the Heineken Cup against Treviso and Bath. I was happy with the way I was playing against Bath, when I ripped my groin completely. That was very annoying because I felt I hadn't proved all the things people were saying about me. They were saying nice things but it was based on my form in the Six Nations. When you are injured, you don't get the opportunity to play and I was anxious to move it along.'

If there are caveats to his view of his own 2004, there are no ambiguities when he is asked about the Irish coach.

'Eddie has been a great help to me since I made the transition to regular international rugby in 2004, in ways nobody will ever see. It's just the way he gives me a kick in the ass when I need it, like the week before the France game in 2004 when I did an interview for a newspaper article which I shouldn't have done. Eddie had a few words with me about it but I know that he made his comments because he was looking out for my best interests.

'In 2003, on the summer tour to Australia, he said to me, "You have an X-factor in your play which all the great attacking players have. The problem with you is that you can either win a game or lose a game. You are a little too much at either end of the spectrum for me." That was hard to hear then. I was playing well for Leinster at the time and there were Leinster supporters saying I should be on the Irish team. When I look back, objectively there was no reason for me to be on the Irish team.

'Eddie wasn't far off the mark when he spoke to me on the Australian tour. He told me that I did good things and I did bad things, but it wasn't a case of if I was doing eight things well and six things badly, I would be picked for the team, because it doesn't work like that. Any time I ask Eddie an honest question, he will give me an honest answer. In his unique way, he's always looking out for me. I can't speak highly enough of him.'

THE FAMOUS FIVE

Injury disrupted D'Arcy's Six Nations in 2005 and his rapier-like attacking instincts were sorely missed in the France and Wales games in particular. However, proof of his impact on the world stage came in October 2004 when he was one of five players, with France's Serge Betsen, Australia's Matt Giteau and South Africa's Marius Joubert and Schalk Burger, nominated for the International Rugby Board (IRB) Player of the Year award.

Further confirmation of D'Arcy's status in the game came when he was selected to tour with the Lions to New Zealand in 2005. The trip did not go as well as he would have wished, though in the penultimate game of the tour against Auckland he showed the rugby world his true class in a storming display. Given the disruption of his season through injury, just making the Lions squad was an achievement in itself. The impact of his new-found fame on his life has been profound.

'It has changed my life in the sense that if I'm sitting down having a cup of coffee in a coffee shop people come up to me and shake my hand, which is very nice. I also get asked to visit schools and rugby clubs a lot more. Kids tell you that you're their favourite rugby player and that brings a responsibility you have to rise to. The rugby fan feels that they want to have a piece of you, whether it's to shake your hand or buy you a beer on the occasional times when you can have a drink, so that's part and parcel of life.'

D'Arcy shows an unexpected talent, launching into a wonderful impersonation of his former Leinster coach Declan Kidney as he puts these changes in perspective.

'During the Six Nations, I was a little overwhelmed with all the calls I was getting. At one stage, I was sitting down with Declan Kidney talking about something else when I asked him, "How do you deal with all this attention?" In his unique schoolteacher way, Declan replied, "Well, Gordon, there's an easy way to figure out who's who. How many of these were ringing you to say hard luck when you weren't selected for the World Cup in Australia?" That summed it up.

'On the pitch, you are a marked man. Brian is probably the best example in world rugby of this. He came flying onto the international stage, with a series of amazing performances for Ireland and the Lions. He became such a star so quickly that opposing teams came up with special strategies to try and curb him; but he was still able to rise above these. He had to rise to the first level playing international rugby and then he had to rise to another level again, which he did brilliantly and he has continued to improve.'

D'Arcy was at the heart of Ireland's almost-miracle recovery against France in the 2006 Six Nations. He has clear ambitions for Ireland's future.

'There's no point in setting goals that are easily achievable. The goal we set is for us to be a top-four side in the 2007 World Cup. If we continue to turn out new talent like Paul O'Connell, who has been a revelation since he burst on the scene, or Johnny O'Concrete [O'Connor] and Jerry Flannery, I don't think a top-four position is out of the question at all.'

When asked about his personal ambitions, he is more circumspect.

'I want to enjoy playing rugby. If I can do that and play as well as I know I can, then anything is possible.'

THE FUN FACTORY

D'Arcy rejoices in the camaraderie of the Irish squad.

'Guy Easterby's a great character. He drags fun out of everybody. He is the judge, essentially, and if somebody is acting the maggot or arrives in with a new, flash car or has a new girlfriend, he will give them a hard time. Himself and Donncha O'Callaghan are comedians, really. When you get them behind closed doors, both Brian O'Driscoll and Geordan Murphy are real fun guys as well. As Brian is captain, he has to be very careful with his public image because any little incident will be reported in the press and transformed into a major event. In the safety of the team hotel, when he can relax with the lads and drop his guard, he is great fun.

'The memories of our great victories will always be there but what lingers in the mind is the stuff nobody sees. It is not so much what happens on the field but the little things that happen off it. I was talking with some of the lads recently and someone asked if anybody had a photo of the Triple Crown team and nobody had. There will be time for that when the career is over. The players live in each other's pockets and that creates a special bond between us.

'To take a specific example, before the France game in Paris in 2004, just as we walked out the tunnel, Malcolm O'Kelly turned to me and said, "Get ready for this." The noise from the cheering was like having someone strike you with a bat on the back of the head as you walked onto the pitch. I stood beside Mal for the anthems that day and at all the matches after that because there's something comforting about having that giant put his arm around you. Mal probably has forgotten that moment in Paris and has his own special memory but it is one I will always treasure.

'After beating England that season, when all the madness had died down, I went to meet my dad and my uncle. Almost all the fans had gone home but there was an Irish fan who had flown in especially for the game from somewhere in Africa and was on his way back. He recognised me and came over to us and said, "Thanks very much." It is little things like that which stay in the mind forever because you could tell it meant so much to him. You just can't put a price on an experience like that.'

3

THE LIMERICK LEADER

ONE OF THE MOST STRIKING THINGS ABOUT SPENDING AN HOUR in Paul O'Connell's company is the number of times he uses the word 'lucky' about himself. Another insight into his character is furnished by his initial reservations about being interviewed for this book – he does not accept that he is a legend of Irish rugby. His generous and humane sensibility is also indicated by the way the litany of coaches who helped him on the way are all mentioned by name and spoken of with genuine affection and respect. His innate modesty is also revealed when he is asked if he has any interest in a career in the media after rugby now that he has dipped his toes into punditry as a match analyst with the *Irish Independent*: 'I don't think I have the boyish good lucks for a career as a TV pundit!'

HOOKERS AND SWINGERS

Rugby was not O'Connell's first love.

'Swimming was my main sport between the ages of five and fourteen. I was training before school, after school, and on Saturday and Sunday mornings. Apart from the discipline it gave me, which stood me in good stead later on, it engrained good habits in me. The mantra I learned from all my coaches was that success only comes from dedication, application and working hard.

'Then I kind of swapped swimming for golf. I wasn't bad at golf but I knew I was never going to be really great. I also played Gaelic football and hurling for South Liberties, which is the club J.P. McManus supports and

34

is chairman of. In fact, when I was 11 or 12, I caddied for him and he gave me £50 sterling for it. In my innocence, I thought it was fake money!

'I played rugby in my school, Ard Scoil Rís. Rugby only started in the school in 1982, through the initiative of Des Harty. We are not one of the traditional powers in Schools rugby, like Pres Cork, and only won our first Munster Schools Cup two years ago.

'My dad's sport was rugby. He started playing with Sunday's Well in Cork but when he moved to Limerick, he became a big Young Munster man in every respect, as a player and on the committee.

'My brother, Justin, won a Munster Senior Cup with Sunday's Well in 1994, which was a huge thing for my dad. Justin was probably my hero when I was growing up. As I was very involved in swimming, Gary O'Toole was another hero after he won a silver medal in the European Championships in Bonn. Given my interest in golf, I also admired Philip Walton, especially when he "won" the Ryder Cup. I am an Everton supporter and if there was an Irish guy doing well, I always supported him. In recent years, the two people I look up to the most are Roy Keane and Padraig Harrington.

'When I was sixteen, I decided to concentrate on rugby and two years later I was selected for the Irish Schools side. We beat Wales and Scotland but lost to England. Gordon D'Arcy was the undisputed star of our team. It was a big thing to be selected for Ireland and it opened a lot of doors for me in rugby. I then progressed to the Munster Under-20s, then on to the Ireland Under-21s and the All-Ireland League with Young Munster. I was lucky enough to break into the Munster team then, and seven months after I turned professional, I picked up my first cap when Malcolm O'Kelly was injured.'

THE MASTER

Learning his craft in the second row, O'Connell could not have served his apprenticeship with a more skilled instructor beside him playing with Mick 'Gallimh' Galwey for both Munster and Ireland.

'I think every player on the Munster team has a bit of a Mick Galwey in him. Gallimh was very similar to Peter Clohessy in that he was old school. He liked his pints, wasn't very fond of training but when it come to Saturday, there was nobody who put themselves on the line more or gave more on the pitch. He was a great guy to talk to players and get them up for a match. When you saw a man who had accomplished so much get so emotional and be so committed for every

Munster game, it did inspire you to give of your best. He always knew exactly which buttons to push to get the best out of every guy on the team on every occasion.

'In that respect, I see his influence now in Anthony Foley. Frankie Sheahan is the same and so is Rog. When we go scrummaging, Frankie will pull us in together and say a few words to the forwards, and that is straight out of the Gallimh manual. Gallimh's legacy lives in all of us. When I played for Ireland Under-21s, I was coached by Ciaran Fitzgerald and he was very Gallimh-like. Ciaran was very passionate and a great motivator.

'I learned a lot from Gallimh and the Claw [Clohessy] because they knew every trick in the game and every short cut there was to know. Gallimh had a very good tight game. He was clever, tactically astute and, above all, a great leader. When I first came into the Munster squad, Mick O'Driscoll was in the second row for us and he was brilliant in the lineout. I learned so much about lineout play from him. I was lucky enough to get his place on the team and he was so helpful.

'"Woodie" [Keith Wood] was a great leader as well. When he pointed his finger at you and said he needed a big game from you, you wanted to give it to him, because he was one of the greatest players in the world and had done it all himself.

'"Drico" [Brian O'Driscoll] has a different style of captaincy from either Gallimh or Woodie but when he asks you to do something you know that whatever he asks you to give, he himself will give more. Some players give a hundred per cent but Drico gives a million per cent. He puts his body on the line every time and I love that about him. He's not a Fancy Dan by any means.'

THE FIRST CUT IS THE DEEPEST

O'Connell made his debut for Ireland against Wales in the Six Nations in 2002 at Lansdowne Road. It was also Ireland's first match under Eddie O'Sullivan's tenure as Irish coach. The young player made an excellent start and thoroughly deserved his debut try but left the field injured and in tears after only half an hour.

'I think I scored the try after about 20 minutes but I got concussed in about the fifth minute. I don't remember anything after that. I was basically on autopilot. It was a weird thing. I was doing everything I normally would but I just can't remember any of it.

'There were seven Munster forwards in the pack, plus Simon

Easterby of Llanelli, so I felt right at home. Normally after your first cap, everybody gets you a drink and you end up smashed. As I was concussed, that didn't happen to me. My parents were up for the game and as my dad is such a massive rugby fan, it was a big day for him.'

Just as O'Connell got his taste of the big time, his career ran into problems.

'Up to winning my first cap, my career had the ideal trajectory: one upward step after another. While that day against Wales was brilliant, it triggered off a series of injuries for me which I thought would never end. Having got a concussion in the Wales match, I played for my club two weeks later to see if I would be fit for the next international against Scotland. The problem was that I had an abscess in my tooth and while I did play in the match, I was sick all the way home. I picked up a shoulder injury playing for Munster in the run up to the Heineken Cup semi-final against Castres. The morning of the match, I had to do a fitness test. That is a test I will never forget, because my shoulder was standing up well and I was hitting a tackle bag which Declan Kidney was holding. The problem was that I hit it so hard at one stage, I knocked out one of Declan's teeth! He was due to give an interview three-quarters of an hour later so he had to go to the dentist to get it stuck back in. The shoulder was fine but I probably wasn't 100 per cent fit. We won the game but in a warm-up match before the Heineken Cup final, I damaged my ankle ligaments. I did manage to play against Leicester in the final but with my shoulder and ankle problems, I didn't play well.

'That summer, I made the tour to New Zealand but in the First Test, I damaged the same shoulder again and had to miss the Second Test. On the plane home, I ruptured a disc in my back, which I had to have an operation on. I was out for four months. I got back and had played four games for Munster when I broke a bone in my thumb. I made my comeback as a sub in the Grand Slam decider against England in 2003. My proper rehabilitation only came with the tour to Australia, Tonga and Samoa. It was a tough tour. Tonga is a very poor country and we played in dreadful conditions. Samoa wasn't much better but at least we had a nice hotel.'

In August 2003, he scored two tries in the warm-up game against Wales before the World Cup. He was one of the stars of the Rugby World Cup later that year.

'Overall, the World Cup went well for me personally. It was horribly disappointing to lose to Australia. Although sometimes the media didn't believe us, we felt we had a good team. The days when moral victories mattered for us are over. We knew that if we won that game, a lot of things could happen for us. We didn't play fabulously well against France but a couple of defensive mistakes cost us dearly. I have been homesick on tours before, but not on that one, because it was such a carnival of rugby. For two weeks, we were staying in a hotel outside Sydney by the beach, going surfing every day and swimming in the sea after training as part of our recovery. We were in Melbourne at the time of the Melbourne Cup and there was massive hysteria about it. The whole experience was the kind of stuff you dream of.'

In the absence of Brian O'Driscoll, O'Connell led Ireland in their opening 2004 Six Nations game against France in Paris.

'It was a great thrill to be selected as captain but the experience was spoilt by the fact that we lost. We paid for a few defensive errors. Thankfully my second outing as Irish captain against Scotland in the 2005 Six Nations had a happier outcome.'

There was a lot of criticism of the side after that French defeat. Was that hard to take at the time?

'We knew that we had a lot of potential in the side and that's why talk of "brave old Ireland" has no interest for us. We want to win and are not satisfied any more to play heroically but to lose. I think criticism is brilliant. It only makes you a better player if you are mentally strong enough to take it. If someone has a go at me personally in the press and I respect him, I think I can learn from that. If you don't respect him but he's speaking the truth, you have to take it on board; but if you know it's not the truth, you just ignore it.'

It is a potent testimony to O'Connell's stature in the game that he was considered one of the leading contenders to captain the Lions on their ill-fated tour to New Zealand in 2005. He was to discover on the 'tour de farce' the reason for the joke:

Q: What's the difference between Iraq and the All Blacks?

A: The All Blacks really do have weapons of mass destruction.

O'Connell played in all three Tests and took over as captain when Gareth Thomas went off injured in the final Test. Unlike some of his illustrious teammates, he was not found wanting at any stage in the commitment, character or courage departments.

GENTLE GIANT
O'Connell has the sort of weight problem that most people would kill for.

'All of my family are naturally tall but slim, so I've had to do a lot of work in the gym to build up my weight. I am 17½ st. now but making the weight is tough for me.'

Yet his towering frame and his fierce commitment on the pitch mask his gentle nature off it.

'I have had a huge amount of good luck to get where I am. To take one example, when I was playing in the trial for the Irish Schools, I didn't play that well but I was lucky because the guy who was lifting me lifted me by the legs and the guy who was opposite me was getting lifted by the shorts, so I had two feet on him straight away. I robbed a few lineouts off him and so I was picked. If he had been picked, it could be him doing this interview now and not me.'

He has no plans yet for life after rugby.

'I studied computer engineering at the University of Limerick but I have deferred for the moment. I'll probably go back and finish my course at some stage but I can't see myself spending the rest of my life in front of a computer. I'm not sure what I will do though.'

For the moment, he is happy to enjoy the adventure and the friendships.

'On the Irish team, the Munster lads get on great but there's none of the guys you wouldn't get on with. They are all characters in their own way. To take just one example, Reggie Corrigan is Leinster's answer to Gallimh. There are great guys like Simon Easterby everywhere you look. You wouldn't be worried when you go to dinner where you'll sit. You just walk in and pick up your plate and take the next available place.

'Donncha O'Callaghan is a great character but also a fabulous player and really aggressive on the pitch. He has a reputation as a messer and, to be fair, he deserves it! Off the pitch and away from the training ground, there's no bigger messer and when he's around you know there's a prank on its way but when it comes to playing, training, diet or getting the proper rest, there is nobody more dedicated. He is a contradiction in some ways but if you ask anyone within the squad, they will tell you that he's the most focused and dedicated of us all.'

TAKE A CHANCE ON ME

Ireland's two most famous coaches, Declan Kidney and Eddie O'Sullivan, feature prominently on O'Connell's most-admired list.

'I am forever indebted to Declan Kidney. He gave me my first big break with Munster. I had a bit of a discipline problem when I was younger and I suppose I was lucky that he took a chance on me. I was getting too many yellow cards and if you are doing that, you don't get picked and if you don't play for your club, you don't get selected for Ireland and your career goes nowhere.

'Declan is a good motivator. He is always looking for the psychological edge. I remember at one stage in Munster, we were conceding too many penalties and the odd soft try because of a lapse in concentration. Declan got white t-shirts for us to wear in training with "Concentration" written on the front and "Discipline" written on the back. You couldn't escape the message wherever you looked on the training pitch.

'My favourite story about him, though, goes back to 2000, before I joined the Munster squad. On the way to the Heineken Cup final against Northampton, Munster had to play Saracens away. Saracens were a club without a tradition and they brought in marketing people to tell them how to attract the crowds. One of the things they did was to play the *Rocky* music whenever there was a fight or a row; when the team came onto the pitch, they played the *A Team* music; when the opposition came on, they played "The Teddy Bears' Picnic"; when the Saracens place-kicker faced up to a penalty, the crowd put on fez hats and had a little routine to guide the ball over the bar, and the tee came on in a remote-controlled car. To play against Saracens, you have to face a lot of distractions. Before Munster played them, the Munster squad were watching a Saracens match as part of their video analysis. With about two minutes to go on the video, Declan turned on a ghetto-blaster and had the *A Team* music blaring, put on his fez hat and started playing with the remote control and the lights. After a minute or so, Declan turned off the television, took off his hat and turned off the ghetto-blaster, and he asked, "What happened in the last 60 seconds of the Saracens game?"

'Nobody knew because they had all been watching him. Point made.'

O'Connell also clearly has great admiration for the current Ireland coach.

'Eddie gets the best out of players. He is very good tactically and bucks the Irish trend in terms of preparation. He is always thinking about the game and coming up with new tactical ploys. He is trying new things in training all the time. When things are not to his liking, he has a meeting and he will let a few things be known.'

ABSOLUTION

One of the stories told about O'Connell goes back to the aftermath of Ireland's triumph over South Africa in autumn 2004. Before the game, the Springboks coach Jake White became the *bête noire* of Irish rugby when he publicly stated that Brian O'Driscoll was the only Irish player who would get into the Springboks side, although he reluctantly conceded that the second rows, Paul O'Connell and Malcolm O'Kelly, would be contenders. How significant were White's comments for the Irish players?

'We had lost two Test games in South Africa that summer because we didn't do the basics right. We beat them that autumn for two reasons: we did the basics right and we had special players on the day like "Shaggy" [Shane Horgan] and Drico who could make ground and put them on the back foot. We were aware of Jake White's comments. We slagged each other about it and made a few jokes. There was no need for Eddie to say anything about it to motivate us. If you can't motivate yourself after someone insults you like that, there's something wrong with you.'

According to legend, O'Connell went to confession a month after the game and confessed to the priest, 'I lost my temper and said some bad words to one of my opponents.'

'Ahhh, that's a terrible thing for an Irish international to be doing,' the priest said. He took a piece of chalk and drew a mark across the sleeve of his coat.

'That's not all, Father. I got mad and punched one of my opponents.'

'Saints preserve us!' the priest said, making another chalk mark.

'There's more. As I got out of a ruck, I kicked two of the other team's players in the . . . in a sensitive area.'

'Oh, Jesus, Mary and Joseph!' the priest wailed, making two more chalk marks on his sleeve. 'Who in the world were we playing when you did these awful things?'

'South Africa.'

'Ah, well,' said the priest, wiping his sleeve, 'boys will be boys.'

For years, O'Connell has been spoken of as the new Martin Johnson. With his imperious performances in the 2006 Six Nations, notably against England, the giant Munster man showed such comparisons are redundant. He has now eclipsed Johnson's playing abilities.

OLD SCHOOL

Winning his first cap will forever hold a special place in O'Connell's memory chest. Waking as a boy on Christmas morning was like this – the sleepy thrill before remembering its source. International rugby also gave him a chance to meet some of his heroes. He loves stories of the 'old school', before rugby went professional, and the way players combined drinking and other 'extra-curricular' activities and playing. It was an aspect of another time and place. For O'Connell, the players from that era allow him to glimpse another kind of rugby life. He got a taste of it when he spent a week with Peter Clohessy.

'I used to travel up with the Claw for internationals because we were both Young Munster and both of us lived in Annacotty. The Claw was such a legend at the time that he roomed alone but as it was my first cap, he was asked to room with me for the week. It was a week I will never, ever forget!

'At the moment, I am rooming with Anthony Foley and we knock off at 11 p.m. and go to sleep. We eat a proper breakfast of muesli and scrambled eggs, and drink lots of water. We also take protein shakes after training. We do our weights but go for a nap during the day to ensure that we are getting the proper rest. After having a good dinner, we might do some video analysis but then we're in bed early.

'My week with the Claw was very different! He was old school. On the way up to Dublin, we stopped off at a petrol station. I had a tuna sandwich with no butter and a pint of milk. The Claw had a sausage sandwich with plenty of butter and lashings of brown sauce, and cups of tea with shovels of sugar.

'When we were in our hotel room he was smoking fags the whole day. We'd be getting room service up all day, every day, with various not particularly healthy dishes like mayonnaise sandwiches. I would go to sleep about eleven and he'd still be up watching the TV. I'd wake up about two to go to the toilet. The Claw wouldn't be one for bringing water into the room. The TV would still be on and I would knock it off. I'd wake back up at four and the TV would be back on! I'd knock it off again. Then I would wake up again at seven. The Claw would be sitting up in bed, smoking a fag and watching the TV.

'On our afternoon off, the Dublin lads would go home to their families but we didn't have that luxury because the journey was too far. We were staying in the Glenview Hotel and we drove up to the Wicklow mountains and went to a café for a healthy meal of rhubarb tart, ice-cream and custard!

'He did everything differently and yet before the match, he was the one with the tear in his eye and he would get more up for the game than anyone else. He was the best player on the pitch against Wales by a mile. His understanding of professionalism was very different but he had a bigger heart than everyone else and that's why everybody loved him and still loves him.'

4

THE GEORGE BEST OF RUGBY

DURING THE BUILD-UP TO THE 2003 WORLD CUP, RUGBY PUNDITS throughout the world predicted that Geordan Murphy was destined to become one of stars of the tournament and one of the giants of world rugby. Tragically, injury intervened and Murphy, who had emerged as the star of the previous Six Nations, missed out on the world stage his rich talents deserved. It was a catastrophic setback to Ireland's chances for glory. With Murphy in the side, Brian O'Driscoll would have got extra space because opposition defences would have had to be constantly calculating which of Ireland's two big threats was more likely to make the break. Although Geordan has developed the capacity to cut through to score while playing in the rugby equivalent of a sardine tin, the Kildare native was no child prodigy.

'I attended Naas CBS [Christian Brothers School] primary but it wasn't until I began secondary school at Newbridge College that my rugby career took off. I'm the youngest of six and we used to play touch rugby in the back garden. We played games of three versus three. As I watched a lot of rugby as a kid, I also played imaginary games in the back garden where I imitated players like Tony Ward, Ollie Campbell, Hugo MacNeill, Brendan Mullin, Trevor Ringland, Keith Crossan, Serge Blanco, David Campese and the All Black winger John Kirwan as I ran and kicked.

'At Newbridge College, my first coach was Father Canice Murphy. It was difficult for him, because he was presented with a hundred first years and it was hard to know which of us were going to make it at the game. My first-ever game was on the wing for the Under-13 A team. Over the next few years, I was not a regular on the A team but I played at various levels in different positions like winger and fly-half.'

THE KIWI CONNECTION

'I suppose my interest in the game was heightened when we went on a rugby tour to France but a big turning point came in fifth year when I went to Auckland Grammar School in New Zealand for four months, which was something the school arranged for me. It was a big step at the time but it gave me a whole new rugby experience because rugby is the religion in New Zealand. In Ireland, we have Gaelic football, hurling, soccer – and rugby is down the scale; but in New Zealand, it is everything. Everyone you meet there is incredibly well informed about rugby whether it's the guy sitting beside you in class or his grandmother. They will have different opinions on the game but everyone will speak with the most incredible knowledge. The marketing of the All Blacks rugby team has been incredible. Sales of the famous black jersey have soared through the use of imaginative slogans like "All jerseys keep you warm but only one makes you shiver". There is not a boy in New Zealand who doesn't dream of playing for the All Blacks because of all the glamour attached to them.

'I was fortunate enough to be there in 1995 for the World Cup. The big match from their point of view was when they beat England 45–29 in the semi-final and Jonah Lomu played human skittles with the England defenders. He scored four tries and brushed aside his immediate opponent, Tony Underwood, as if he was just a piece of dust. Mind you, as a result of that match, Underwood was given a starring role in a pizza ad! For some reason, the English love using sporting "losers" in pizza ads. The England captain Will Carling described Lomu as "a freak". However, I didn't think of him that way because there were 16 year olds in my class in Auckland who were almost as big as Lomu. Like Jonah, they all came from "the islands".

'The other thing I found different was the way they played the game. Up to then, I had grown up in a culture where everything you did on the pitch was designed to make you look good. In New Zealand, everything was designed to making the team look good. That whole experience brought my rugby on enormously.

'After my Leaving Certificate, I went to Waterford Institute of

Technology to do Legal and Business Studies. I opted to play club rugby with Naas, but I was also playing for Waterpark, so most weekends I was playing two games. The first time I was ever picked to play for Ireland was at Under-19 level. I played at out-half during the Under-19 World Cup in Argentina, with players like Bob Casey and Leo Cullen. That was a great experience.

'Afterwards, Kevin West, who had been my mentor at Newbridge, arranged for Jim Ferris and myself to have a three-week trial at Leicester. It was very intimidating going over to play with one of the biggest clubs in Europe. Most people said to me that it would be a brilliant experience and I went over there just to enjoy it, never expecting anything to come out of it. The 1997 Lions tour to South Africa had just happened and many of the stars of the Lions team like Martin Johnson, Will Greenwood and Eric Miller played for Leicester. There were about 50 in the squad and Jim and myself were thrown into the action pretty much straight away. I was quite overawed, looking around the dressing-room with rugby legends like Dean Richards all around me.'

A FAUX PAS

Murphy cringes at one of his earliest memories from his time in Leicester.

'I had a real Homer Simpson moment standing beside this guy at the club one day. I didn't recognise him from Adam and I asked him if he got a chance to play much rugby at the club. I knew immediately from the way he looked at me that I had said something incredibly stupid. It was the Scottish international Craig Joiner. To complete my shame, when he turned around, I saw on the back of his jersey the word "Joiner"!

'Mind you, since I started playing for Ireland I've regularly found myself the victim of mistaken identity. Justin Bishop [of London Irish] tells me I have a lookalike in London. Even in the Irish squad, people mix up my name with those of Girvan [Dempsey] and Gordon [D'Arcy]. So now and again I find the odd member of the Irish squad addressing me as "Girv . . . Gord . . . Geordan". The best one, though, came after Ireland famously spoilt the world champions England's homecoming party at Twickenham in 2004 when Girvan Dempsey scored that great try. As I was injured, I didn't play in the game, so I was doing some corporate work and after the game I was in my jeans and T-shirt and a man congratulated me on scoring in the corner!

'The legendary Australian coach Bob Dwyer was in charge of Leicester during my trial. In my second week, I was playing in the second team and I had six full internationals in the side with me, including Niall Malone and Dean Richards. It was just jaw-dropping. Bob said he wanted me to stay after the trial. I got a few games with the first team in my first season and played four games in a row after Christmas but shortly after that, Bob got the sack and Dean Richards replaced him. I got on well enough with Dean and he was decent to me. He had a tough job trying to rotate the squad to keep everybody happy. When a new coach like that comes in, the key thing is to find out which buttons to push to make them rate you. If you discover that what they want you to do is kick the ball 50 yards, you kick the ball 50 yards. In my first couple of seasons, most of my appearances were coming on as sub as a utility back.'

With typical modesty, Murphy makes no mention of the fact that Dean Richards christened him 'the George Best of rugby' because of his exquisite skills. He is happier singing other people's praises rather than his own.

'I have been very lucky to play with so many rugby legends at Leicester. As a back, it was an education to play with Joel Stransky. He will always be remembered for scoring the drop-goal that won the World Cup for South Africa but at Leicester he just ran the show superbly on the pitch. However, if I had to pick one legend above all the others, it would have to be Martin Johnson. If you look at him, there are guys who look bigger, stronger and faster but when it comes to rugby, he was just born to play it. He has an aura about him and is an inspirational leader. If he jumped off a cliff, there would be guys willing to follow him.

'With Leicester, there are also great characters and practical jokers. We have a decent spread of them throughout the squad but it comes as no surprise that Austin Healey is the tops in this respect. He is always willing to get a laugh and it is great to have someone like him in the squad, because he keeps morale up. Of course he can rub people up the wrong way and often has done so! He does the craziest things. To give a typical example of an Austin activity, when he was away with the England squad, he was bored and decided to liven things up by playing a game with the English forward Lewis Moody. They sat about ten feet away from each other with their legs apart and the idea was to throw an orange at each other's groin. The problem for Austin was that he wasn't very good but Lewis was the world champion!'

OZ-WORLD

In 'Oz-world', the world according to Healey, pranks sometimes boomerang on him. After he came into the England side in 1997, he put a pair of tracksuit bottoms down the back of his shorts and walked around impersonating Clive Woodward and calling him 'Rhino Bum' in front of everyone in the England squad. Woodward said nothing. Then Healey scored his first international try, against Wales in their next game, and a few days later the girlfriends and wives of all the lads in the squad received in the post a pair of G-string knickers with 'I love Austin' printed on them and a note which read: 'Just wanted to thank you all for your support at the weekend. As you are aware, I scored my first try for England. I think you'll admit it was one of the best tries seen at Twickenham. I know how much you girls admire my play, so I thought I'd send you a pair of these knickers each. Lots of love, Austin. Healey actually knew nothing about it until he was summoned to appear before his furious squadmates. Then he got a phone message from Clive Woodward, who was laughing hysterically, saying, 'Don't ever take the mickey out of me again.'

There was a general perception that, given Murphy's status in English rugby, his place on the Irish team should have been cemented much sooner. Is this a view he shares?

'I'm not sure. I think that perhaps being over here in Leicester was initially detrimental to my international career by virtue of the fact that the selectors didn't see me that often. All I will say is that I was delighted to win my first cap on tour against the USA in June 2000. The previous week, I had played in a friendly against the Barbarians and I'd damaged some ligaments. As a result, I was forced to miss Ireland's trip to Argentina but the then coach Warren Gatland told me they would consider me for the game against the USA if I was fit. I spent most of the next week in an ice bath. I got myself into good enough shape to bluff my way through the fitness test and I played in Boston, which was great because my older brother was living there. To cap it all, I got two tries. I came on as a sub for the injured Justin Bishop on the final game of that tour against Canada but it wasn't such a happy occasion for me. To win your first cap is great, but to play your first game in a home international is also a highlight. My induction was in a friendly against Fiji. Although we won easily, I felt the game did not go as well for me as I would have liked. I probably tried to do too much, to convince people I should be on the team. I suspect, though, there was an element of people looking at me as a little guy and they had doubts about whether I physically had it in me to hack it at the very highest level. As a result, I didn't find myself on the Irish team again for a while. You also have to remember that it takes a while to settle into international rugby, just as it took me time to settle at Leicester.

'Things really came together for me in the Six Nations in 2003. It didn't start off like that. I remember flying over for the first match of the season and I could hear a few lads from Terenure College RFC at the back of the plane having an in-depth discussion on the "Girvan v. Geordan" debate for the full-back position. As they were from Girvan's Alma Mater, you can guess where their biases lay! It was very interesting, though, to hear them going through the pros and cons. When the plane landed and I stood up, I think they were a little embarrassed that I might have heard them but they graciously wished me well. In fact, when Girvan got injured against Italy, I replaced him and held that spot for the rest of the season. Although we lost the Grand Slam decider against England, it was a good season for me and I was really looking forward to taking it one step further at the World Cup, but it wasn't to be.'

BRAVEHEART

In one of the warm-up games against Scotland, Murphy broke his leg. How did he react to this calamity?

'When I woke up in the hospital in Scotland I was devastated. Although I was morphined out, I couldn't believe it. There were a few tears shed. It was very tough to deal with. I can smile and laugh when I think about it now but as I never made it on the plane, I learned the lesson that you should never count your chickens. To be honest, there's still the odd day when I think, "Bugger it, I can't believe I missed out on that opportunity." The specialist carried out the operation in such a way as to ensure that I got back on my feet as quickly as possible. Everything I was asked to do, I did and I played again in under six months which was great. Of course I was a bit rusty in the first few games back but it was great to play some part in Ireland's Triple Crown win. I felt it was a reward for the fact that I had worked so hard to get back to fitness. As the season started so badly for me, I had hoped it would finish well on the tour to South Africa but I picked up a dreadful viral flu in Cape Town and missed out on the Second Test.

'I know I am lucky to play in such a good Irish side. It has been a real pleasure to play with Brian O'Driscoll because he makes loads of space and takes up great positions and the opposition is so terrified of him that they leave gaps for the rest of us. When Gordon D'Arcy burst onto the scene, he was able to do something similar. Of course, there are so many brilliant forwards on the team now, who do great work and give us a supply of good balls. There are some great characters on the team, none more so than Donncha O'Callaghan. He is very funny and is always game for a laugh and above all he can laugh at himself. You could say the same sort of things about Guy Easterby.'

Murphy is emphatic when asked about his favourite position. 'I would play prop forward for Ireland if I was asked to but my favourite position is full-back.'

UNFINISHED BUSINESS

Murphy was selected to tour with the Lions to New Zealand in 2005. With Donncha O'Callaghan, he started more matches on the tour (seven) than anybody else and was rewarded for some fine displays with selection for the final Test. Only a handful of players, like Ryan Jones, Simon Easterby and Shane Horgan, came home with enhanced reputations. It can't have helped Murphy's confidence that a member of the Lions coaching staff is alleged to have made derogatory remarks about his playing abilities. In difficult circumstances, Murphy kept his spirits up. This could be seen two days before the final Test when Murphy was being interviewed and was rudely interrupted by a 'journalist' claiming to be from the *Irish Examiner* – but with an uncanny resemblance to Donncha O'Callaghan – who asked him who his favourite squad member was. Without blinking, Murphy replied in his most deadpan manner, 'Not Donncha O'Callaghan, anyway. His sense of humour isn't to my liking.'

After a nightmare performance against France in the 2006 Six Nations, Murphy rallied to produce three rock-solid games on Ireland's march to the Triple Crown. What remaining ambitions does Geordan have?

'The more success you have, the more selfish you become. When you win one cap, you want to win a second, when you win ten, you want to win twenty and when you win twenty, you want to win forty. I would like to have more success with Leicester and Ireland.'

Murphy has many happy memories from his rugby career.

'One of the funniest is of the warm-up before playing a Heineken Cup final with Leicester. I was throwing the ball around. I tried to do a clever dummy pass and ended up firing the ball into one of my teammates' groin. It made me laugh. It made him cry!'

5

WINGING HIS WAY TO THE TOP

RUGBY IS IN DENIS HICKIE'S BLOOD. FOR YEARS, HIS FATHER, Tony, was one of Ireland's most distinguished full-backs. And like his father, Denis attended the acclaimed rugby nursery St Mary's College in Rathmines, Dublin. He played his first game for the school when he was only eight. He played other sports, like badminton and tennis, and really excelled at athletics. He was also a choirboy with the Dublin Boy Singers but as his rugby career developed, the other commitments had to be sacrificed. His dedication reaped a handsome reward.

'My fondest memory is of winning the Leinster Schools Cup with St Mary's. People who don't understand the magic of Schools rugby will find this hard to believe but anyone who has ever won a Schools cup will know exactly what I mean. At the time, winning it was on a par with winning the World Cup.

'One of the great things we learned in Mary's was the value of humility. Although we won the Leinster Cup for the first time in 25 years, the members of that team were treated no different from everyone else. I'm not sure that was the case in all rugby schools or in schools where successful teams were very important. The emphasis at St Mary's was very much on not blowing your own trumpet, on an individual level or on a school level. You did your best and achieved what you could, and if it was a significant achievement, people would learn about it for themselves without you having to shout it from the rooftops.

'When I was at St Mary's, I had the good fortune to have great coaches like Brian Cotter and Father Flavin. When Father Flavin came into the school, rugby was in a little bit of a lull there. He coached our team and even though we were successful, he never let us lose the balance between rugby and the academic side. I think that was an important lesson for all of us. For that reason, my advice to any young person would be to go to college. The best thing I ever did was going to UCD [University College Dublin] to get a degree in Commerce.'

Hickie is anxious to pay tribute to a number of people who have nurtured his career.

'My dad has been my greatest mentor and to this day continues to be my biggest influence. As he played to a high level, he speaks with authority and I always listen to his advice. Declan Kidney was a big influence on me with the Irish Schools and it's funny the way things come round, because until recently he was coaching me again at Leinster and he gave me very good advice on how to play my game. I am still learning. It is very difficult to compare Eddie O'Sullivan with Matt Williams because Eddie we only see for a few weeks of the year, whereas, as our provincial coach, Matt was with us all the time. Eddie is a top coach but I was constantly under Matt's influence and he helped bring out the best in me.'

EVERY BREATH YOU TAKE

Success for Hickie at St Mary's was followed by success with Ireland, despite the fact that he was diagnosed with exercise-induced asthma. Austin Healey suffers from the more common form of asthma and nearly died from an attack when he was eight years old. He jokes that saying you suffer from exercise-induced asthma is another way of saying you are unfit.

Hickie won the Triple Crown with the Irish Schools side coached by Declan Kidney and again with the Irish Under-21 side coached by Eddie O'Sullivan. In 1997, at the age of 20, he made his Senior debut for Ireland and, with his blistering pace, quickly caught the eye, especially with a number of stunning tries, notably against France in Paris. Then, in 1998, a combination of injury and a perceived below-par performance in a Test match in South Africa saw him fall out of favour for two years.

In 2000, Ireland were humiliated by England at Twickenham. The team needed radical surgery and Hickie found himself back in the fold.

In his second coming on the Irish team, he was an immediate success. Irish rugby fortunes took a dramatic turn for the better, one which climaxed in a stunning win against France in Paris, a match that will always be remembered for Brian O'Driscoll's three tries.

'I was only 20 when I made my debut for Ireland. When I came back into the side, I was 24. By then, I was much wiser. The press had written me off but I was always confident in my own ability. I had a better perspective on life because I had matured as a person.'

The highlight of any player's career is to be selected for the Lions. In 2001, Denis Hickie seemed set to join that elite club. Ireland opened the season brightly but then the foot-and-mouth outbreak intervened. Ireland's international matches were suspended as part of a drive to cut down travel between Ireland and Britain in order to prevent the spread of the disease to Ireland. Irish players were no longer in the shop window. Denis Hickie was controversially omitted from the Lions squad.

'I was very disappointed when I was told that I had been left out. I had really wanted to play for the Lions. I knew that a lot of Irish players would be making the trip and I wanted to be there with them. I think I learned a lot from the experience. At the start of the season, people had spoken of me as a certainty for selection but I didn't make it on the plane. You can't take things for granted.' Thankfully, in 2005, that oversight was corrected and he toured with the Lions in New Zealand.

He is philosophical about his disappointments.

'The best bit of advice I've ever been given relates both to rugby and to life. It was: "It's not the mess you're in but how you deal with it." In other words, no matter what you do, you will have problems in life and the real issue is not the problems themselves but the way you deal with them.'

Despite that disappointment, Hickie feels very fortunate to have played with Leinster and Ireland teams that have been filled with interesting people and great players.

'The Irish team has always had great characters, like Trevor Brennan, Peter Clohessy, Mick Galwey and Keith Wood. Woodie led by example and had a huge influence inside and outside the dressing-room. He took an active role in everything. There are great guys in the Irish side now, like John Hayes, who has a fantastic dry wit to him. Rog [Ronan O'Gara] is another character, as is Guy Easterby. When I first came onto the scene, Gary Halpin always had brilliant stories and most of his stories were against himself, which added to his appeal.

'We are lucky at the moment to have great players such as Brian O'Driscoll. Brian has the two most important assets any player can have: natural ability and natural pace. He also really enjoys the game. The higher the level, the more he enjoys it and the better he plays. He's the sort of player who would like to be playing against the All Blacks every week – that's the standard he wants to compete against. In the past, Irish players didn't always have that kind of attitude.'

HAIR-RAISING

In recent years, Hickie and O'Driscoll have enjoyed a good-natured rivalry as they yo-yoed in the race to be Ireland's record-breaking try-scorer. O'Driscoll grabbed the record off Hickie with his 24th try for Ireland, against Italy in 2004.

An occasion for friendly banter between the two came before the 2003 World Cup when O'Driscoll famously acquired a new blond hairstyle. However, Hickie denies all responsibility for the spate of O'Driscoll blond jokes that swept through the Irish squad during the competition.

Shortly after he arrived in Australia, O'Driscoll was invited to be guest of honour at the Blonds Are Not Stupid Convention. The MC said, 'We are all here today to prove to the world that blonds are not stupid. Can I have a volunteer?' The crowd enthusiastically volunteered the guest from Ireland. The MC asked him, 'What is 15 plus 15?'

After twenty seconds, O'Driscoll replied, '18!'

Obviously, everyone was a little disappointed. The 20,000 blonds started shouting, 'Give him another chance! Give him another chance!'

The MC said, 'OK, mate, as you came all this way I guess we can give you another chance.' So he asked, 'What is five plus five?'

'Twelve.'

The MC let out a dejected sigh. Everyone was disheartened. But then the 20,000 blonds began to yell and wave their hands, shouting, 'Give him another chance! Give him another chance!'

The MC, unsure whether or not he was doing more harm than good, eventually said, 'OK, OK. Just one more chance. What is two plus two?'

'Four?'

Throughout the stadium, pandemonium broke out as all 20,000 blonds jumped to their feet, waved their arms, stomped their feet and screamed . . .

'Give him another chance! Give him another chance!'

After all the excitement, the Irish star just wanted to escape for a quiet night with a few friends but he faced a new problem:

Q: Why did Brian O'Driscoll take 17 Irish players to the cinema?

A: Under-18 not admitted.

THE YOUNG ONES

A serious leg injury cut short Hickie's World Cup in 2003 and meant that he missed out on Ireland's Triple Crown the following year. However, the injury did give him time to think about other things and to get involved in other activities.

Sports personalities get involved with charities for different motives. When David Beckham was appointed a children's ambassador by the United Nations in 2004, the joke went around that he was looking forward to his first Ferrero Rocher, as he had always wanted to drive one. Hickie's approach was radically different.

'I always admired Sister Stanislaus Kennedy and the work she does for the poor, especially the homeless. When I was approached to become a patron of an organisation she set up called the Young Social Innovators, I was delighted to do so. It is a project targeted at Transition Year students in Ireland. Like the Young Scientists, the Young Social Innovators are asked to examine an issue of interest to them and find a solution. They look at instances of social injustice and dream up original ways to solve them. I got the chance to visit their exhibition and see the great work done by students right across the country to help people less fortunate than themselves. I think when young people get involved in this way at an early age, some of that concern stays with them.'

There was considerable controversy in the summer of 2004 when Leinster sacked their coach Gary Ella. In a subsequent article in *Ireland on Sunday*, Ella was very critical of senior players like Brian O'Driscoll, Malcolm O'Kelly and Victor Costello, claiming they did not have sufficient commitment to Leinster. As a result of his injury, Hickie missed out on Gary Ella's reign as Leinster coach. He watched the way events unfolded with dispassion.

'Nobody goes into a job wanting to fail. All I will say is that neither Gary nor the players came out of it looking well.'

Hickie won a career milestone 50th cap in the defeat at the hands of France that ended the much-talked-about possibility of Ireland taking the Grand Slam in the 2005 Six Nations. The combination of injury and the emergence of Andrew Trimble deprived Hickie of his place on the Irish side on its march to a Triple Crown triumph in 2006. Having suffered a number of disappointments in his career, he has one major ambition.

'I would like to be part of an Irish team that can realistically compete in the next World Cup. I would like to think that we could get to the semi-final, and if we were to get that far, anything could happen.'

His Ireland career has left Hickie with many happy memories.

'I have had so many great moments, but three stand out: my first cap against Wales, beating France in Paris in 2000 and beating England in 2001. I have been lucky enough to score over 20 tries for Ireland but my first one is the one that I remember most fondly.'

6

LIFE AT NUMBER 10

CORK CONSTITUTION HAS BEEN HOME TO MANY LEGENDS OF Irish rugby down through the years, including Tom Kiernan and Noel Murphy. A story about these two has entered rugby folklore. The two former famous internationals were on a trip to England and as they passed a shop and saw a notice in the window which read 'Trousers £2 Shirts £1.50', Tom and Noel were thrilled. They resolved to make a killing, buying them cheaply in England and selling them off at a proper price back home in Ireland. They decided to play it cool and speak in English accents. When they went in, they calmly walked up to the counter and said to the manager, 'We'll buy all the trousers and shirts you have.'

The manager looked at them in astonishment. Despite their feigned accents, he asked, 'Excuse me, gentlemen, are you both from Cork?'

Noel and Tom asked in unison, 'How did you know?'

'Oh, call it an inspired guess. You probably didn't notice, but this is actually a dry cleaner's!'

The Cork Con assembly line of rugby talent has produced a new golden boy of Irish rugby in Ronan 'Rog' O'Gara. Never were his ample talents more fully demonstrated than in November 2004 when he gave a man-of-the-match performance, scoring all of Ireland's points, a try, three penalties and a drop-goal, in Ireland's 17–12 victory over the Grand Slam-seeking Springboks. Ronan is not your typical rugby international. Asked on live television immediately after the game about his reaction to the win, O'Gara took the opportunity to say hello to his granny in Sligo.

Initially, rugby was not his only game.

'I grew up in a sport-mad family. We were interested in soccer, rugby and Gaelic games. My mum, Joan, is originally from Mayo and she always had an interest in Gaelic football. It wasn't until I went to Pres that my rugby career took off. I wouldn't say I excelled in school. I did play for Munster at Schools level but I didn't play for Ireland Schools. There is a lot of politics at that level of the game and that is very disheartening.'

There have been a number of formative influences on O'Gara's career.

'The greatest influence on my game was my dad, Fergal. He played a bit for UCG. Even people who have played at the highest levels can sometimes interpret a game you played in a very different way than you would. Sometimes people have said strange things to me after a game but my dad has always been brilliant at analysing my game for me. He has been a great support and encouragement to me. At Cork Con, Ralph Keyes was a great mentor to me. I've had a few good chats with Ollie Campbell about out-half play. Declan Kidney was a huge influence on me at Munster and even earlier with Munster Schools. Alan Gaffney has a great knowledge of the game and did a good job taking over from Declan as coach at Munster. Eddie O'Sullivan is technically a very good coach. I like going into a game with a clear strategy and Eddie always has one laid out for us.'

THE ITALIAN JOB

O'Gara's international debut was delayed.

'I was due to play against England in 2000 but I got injured in the run-up to the game and Eric Elwood's international career was prolonged. With hindsight, it may not have been a bad thing, as Ireland were trounced at Twickenham. Standing to attention as the national anthem was played before starting my first game for Ireland against Scotland at the age of 22 was very exciting.'

With his superb pair of hands and magnificent diagonal kicking, O'Gara really announced his arrival on the international stage when he gained his second cap, against Italy in Ireland's 60–13 win. Ireland led 33–0 at half-time and went into the dressing-room expecting a massive communal pat on the back from coach Warren Gatland. He took the team by surprise when he asked them, 'Are you ruthless enough to put the game out of sight? Have you the guts to put the guys away?' O'Gara did indeed, and gave a superb exhibition of place-kicking, with a magnificent 12 kicks on target from 12 opportunities. In the process, he acquired an Irish record of 36 points in one match, beating the old record by 6 points. O'Gara is characteristically modest when asked about the game.

'The team played well and from a personal point of view, it was a satisfying performance.'

Later that year, he scored a world-record-equalling ten conversions in a Test against Japan. O'Gara's fame spread so rapidly that he was soon starring in an advertising campaign for an oil company. It is not an experience he is particularly keen to talk about!

A BLOODY MESS

One of the defining sporting images of 2001 was the sight of blood streaming from O'Gara's eye. On the Lions tour of that year, Duncan McRae had repeatedly beaten him in the left eye during the match against the New South Wales Waratahs, in an 11-punch attack. O'Gara's popularity with the squad was indicated when after the McRae episode everyone wanted to go and sort out 'Duncan Disorderly'.

Two and a half years later, McRae publicly pronounced his contrition for his actions and his intention to apologise to O'Gara the next time they met. By an amazing coincidence, that admission came two weeks before McRae, as the new Gloucester out-half, was due to play against Munster at Thomond Park. The previous year, Gloucester, who were leading the Zurich Premiership, had lost 33–6 at Thomond Park in the never-to-be-forgotten 'Miracle Match'.

How does O'Gara feel about McRae now?

'I don't have any feelings about him to be honest. There were all kinds of rumours about what freaked him out. It is not for me to comment. What was great, though, was the support I got afterwards, both from within the squad and from back home, and to know that people were thinking of me and wanting things to work out well for me.'

O'Gara had been chosen for the tour ahead of Scotland's Gregor Townsend. While the media focused on the McRae incident, O'Gara himself has more positive memories of the trip.

'Other people seemed to be more affected by the sight of my blood than I was. I look back on that tour with good memories and I found it to be an enriching experience. I learned a lot and have taken a number of things from that trip and incorporated them into my game. It was great to see at first hand the way players like Jonny Wilkinson train. He is so professional and goes about his game with such dedication and attention to detail. Another person I really admired was Rob Howley. He's a great player. Brian O'Driscoll had such a wonderful tournament and that famous try in the First Test will never be forgotten. I get on very well with Brian personally. As the out-half, it is important that you get on well with the backs and the forwards, because you are the link between them.'

Austin Healey, or, as the Aussie press branded him, 'Lippy the Lion', claims that Rog was considered the funniest man on the tour because his sayings became squad sayings. He would answer a question like 'How are you feeling?' with a reply like 'Oh, I'm unnaturally good today.'

He toured with the Lions again in 2005 and, in this world where reputations are edgily tended, his tactical kicking earned him fulsome praise from Clive Woodward. He did get a small measure of reward when he came on as a sub in the final Test.

SNAKES AND LADDERS

In 2003, rumours swept the country that O'Gara had been offered up to $12 million to play American football with the Miami Dolphins. O'Gara has known the slings and arrows of outrageous rugby fortune.

'I have had a lot of great days with Munster but a few bad ones as well. The lowest points were unquestionably the defeats in the two Heineken Cup finals. You have to try and pick yourself up after experiences like that. We probably have a little more work to do on the tactical side of our game. When you look at teams like Wasps and think of the squad they have and the budget we have, you can see that it is very hard to compete with them. I would hope, though, that we could win the Heineken Cup. That is probably my greatest wish.'

Has his rivalry with David 'Humphs' Humphreys for the Irish number 10 jersey been a help or a hindrance?

'It is a bit of everything. Older journalists make a big deal out of it and go on about it being another case of Tony Ward and Ollie Campbell but I don't listen to much of it. What I would say is that for the last few years whichever one of us has been on the team has generally done a good job. The most important thing I have learned is that a week is a very long time in sport. It can also be a long time in terms of the way people write about you in the press. During the build-up to big games, I can't afford to let myself be distracted by talk in the papers. My main job is to stay cool.'

O'Gara's coolness was exemplified by his performance at the Millennium Stadium in Cardiff in 2003. Rog came on as a late sub in the game. Ireland led 22–21 when Stephen Jones drop-kicked Wales ahead. Cometh the hour, cometh the man. From the restart, O'Gara got the ball 40 metres out and calmly dropped a goal to give Ireland a dramatic win. In the autumn international with Argentina in 2004, he replicated this feat with a dramatic drop-goal to snatch the game for Ireland. Earlier in his career, he showed his determination and commitment on a sodden November afternoon at Lansdowne Road in 2002 when he held his nerve and his footing all afternoon and kicked the six penalties required to give Ireland an 18–9 victory over Australia, which led the Irish team to literally squelch around the pitch for a lap of honour.

He pauses for thought when asked about the high point of his career.

'So much has happened in the last few years that there has been very little time for reflection. You don't get the luxury of looking back because you have to be looking forward all the time. You can never sit back and rest on your laurels but must be looking for new goals and challenges. I've never seen a video package of the highlights of my career, so I'm not sure which is my own best game for Ireland. Every game you win with Ireland is a high point. We've had some great wins over France, which were memorable. Beating Australia was a fantastic thrill. It was sweet to beat Argentina in the 2003 World Cup. Probably the match that stands out the most was beating England at Twickenham in 2004. Without wanting to sound arrogant, I knew once we'd won that game that the Triple Crown was on. I would like to think there will be more days like that to come and I had hoped that 2005 would see us winning something again, but it was not to be.'

O'Gara is keenly aware that he needs to keep his life in perspective.

'I switch off by playing golf or the odd time going for a day to the races and I enjoy going out for a cup of coffee with my girlfriend. Holidays are important. I remember in the summer of 2004 going to Croatia for two weeks. I just sat in the sun for two weeks solid. It was perfect after such an intense season, total relaxation for mind and body. Fortunately, the IRFU [Irish Rugby Football Union] recognised how important it is for the players to get some rest away from the game. That meant four weeks off from any sort of training whatsoever, followed by another six-week spell before the squad which toured South Africa started playing again.'

LEGENDS

Fittingly, it was O'Gara's immaculate touch-line conversion against England that sealed Ireland's 2006 Triple Crown victory. Rog is happy to pay homage to players from both the present and the past.

'As a youngster, the player I would have most admired was Andrew Mehrtens. He had such class. Today, my most difficult opponent is Simon Easterby. He is very awkward to play against and keeps annoying me. The player I would most like to have on my team going into battle would be Alan Quinlan. He is a very underrated player and has a great inner steeliness to him. He's dirty in a good way!'

One of the abiding images of O'Gara's early games for Ireland is of the great Mick Galwey putting his arms around Rog and Peter Stringer during the preliminaries to reassure them that they were going to rise to the occasion. It is not surprising to discover that Galwey features prominently in O'Gara's list of great characters.

'Trevor Brennan brought great freshness to the game and he was a real personality. Mick Galwey and Peter Clohessy were old school and are a huge loss to rugby. The spirit they brought to the game and to the Ireland squad was very uplifting. An abiding memory of my days in the Irish squad is of the time the players and management made a presentation to Peter to mark his 50th cap. Peter responded by singing the Frank Sinatra song "My Way". What an appropriate song! He did things his way or no way. That's why I liked him and admired him so much.'

7

DEMPSEY'S DEN

IT WAS SUPPOSED TO BE MISSION: IMPOSSIBLE. GIRVAN DEMPSEY guaranteed himself a place in Irish rugby immortality when he scored the try that beat England in 2004. Against all the odds, Ireland ended England's 22-match winning streak at 'Fortress Twickenham'. They hadn't been beaten there since the 1999 World Cup match against New Zealand. It was England's first Five/Six Nations championship home defeat under Clive Woodward, whose coaching regime began in November 1997. To add the icing to the cake, the English were parading the Webb Ellis Trophy at Twickers for the first time after their World Cup victory in Australia. Dempsey's try immediately entered the pantheon of greatest Irish touchdowns of all time alongside Kevin Flynn's and Ginger McLoughlin's tries, in '72 and '82 respectively, at the same venue and Ken Goodall's celebrated hoof-and-chase try in Ireland's 14–0 win over Wales at Lansdowne Road in 1970. The try came after 51 minutes when Gordon D'Arcy made a classic break through the field, the ball was taken on down the left and then switched back to the right where the pack took up the charge. After the ball was recycled, both D'Arcy and Brian O'Driscoll threw long passes across the field and Tyrone Howe passed to Dempsey who scythed over. Girvan feels that the only people who were not shocked by the turn of events were the Irish team.

'Although nobody gave us a chance, we went into the game with a lot of self-confidence and felt we could take the scalp of the world champions. All week, Eddie O'Sullivan had been asking, "Why can't we beat England?" Training had gone well. Going onto the pitch, the noise from the English fans was incredible. They got a try from Matt Dawson early on. Brian O'Driscoll called us together and said, "Right, lads. This is a big game. Let's buckle down." I know it's a cliché, but the try was straight off the training ground. We had worked that move again and again when the squad was training in Naas and everyone played their part perfectly.'

Many Irish fans were very annoyed by the rash lunge Ben Cohen made at Dempsey as he scored the try.

'I know some people were very unhappy about it but I bear no ill will towards him. You have to do everything you can to stop a try. The problem was that I had to go off with a damaged right knee because of the incident. While I wasn't angry with him, I was livid that I had to leave the pitch on what was to be one of the greatest days in the history of Irish rugby.'

The defeat immediately spawned a rash of jokes. One was in the shape of a small ad:

> For sale: one chariot (low-swinging, sweet type), in urgent need of repair (wheels have come off again). One careless owner. Details from Clive. Tel: Twickenham 19–13.

Another came in the form of a death notice:

> In memoriam Slam, G. Passed away 6 March 2004, sorely missed by Clive and the boys.

After beating the English, the Irish team still had unfinished business.

'It was great then to go on and win the Triple Crown against Scotland at Lansdowne Road. Down through the years, Scotland had given us many a beating in the Six Nations, even on days when we were expected to win. They had performed poorly in the competition up to that game but with Matt Williams in charge of them and with his intimate knowledge of so many of our players, we knew they would raise their game. It was such a fantastic feeling once the final whistle went. Nobody wanted to leave afterwards. We felt it was a tangible reward for all the hard work we had put in down the years. The previous year, losing the Grand Slam decider against England had been such a massive disappointment. We felt the distance between us was nowhere near as great as the scoreboard suggested. Jonny Wilkinson produced the greatest display of rugby I have ever seen that day and the margin of their victory flattered them, so it was doubly nice to win the Triple Crown at Lansdowne Road 12 months later. Once Gordon got the try, we just knew it was going to be one of those great days.'

THE FIRST CAP IS THE SWEETEST

However, neither scoring the try that beat the World Cup champions nor winning the Triple Crown was the high point of Dempsey's career. For him, a bigger moment was his first call-up to the Irish Senior squad, having played for the Ireland Under-21s, for the game against Georgia in November 1998. He started on the bench that day but won his first cap when he replaced Conor O'Shea.

'During the second half, I was warming up with Ciaran Scally. I hadn't really thought I was going to be brought on but then Donal Lenihan, who was the manager at the time, turned to me and said, "Get your kit off. You're going on." When you're a kid, you dream of winning your first cap. At that moment, my dream was coming true, which was an unbelievable thrill. My parents were in the crowd and I knew how proud they would be. To add to the occasion, I scored two tries.'

Three former Ireland internationals made a huge impact on the young Dempsey.

'When I was going to school, Ciaran Clarke was a big influence, particularly as he was a former Terenure College pupil himself and, like me, he was a full-back. I trained with him and I learned a lot from him. He was a great left-footed kicker and he was also a fantastic runner. When I broke into the Irish squad, myself and Ciaran Scally were the two new kids on the block. Conor O'Shea was the Irish full-back at the time and as he too had gone to Terenure, he went out of his way to look after me and show me the ropes. The other former Terenure boy who was around at the time was Niall Hogan, who of course captained Ireland; all of us had huge respect for him because of that.'

Into every rugby career some rain must fall and Dempsey has had his share of disappointments.

'My lowest point was when I broke my collar bone playing for Leinster against Connacht at the stage when I was establishing myself on the Irish team. I knew immediately I had broken a bone. It came just before the 1999 World Cup and I realised I had no hope of playing in the tournament. I suppose, though, it made my involvement in the 2003

World Cup all the sweeter. It was an amazing experience and very emotional at the end because of Keith Wood's retirement. It was a real roller-coaster for us, with the massive pressure of the Argentinian game, nearly beating Australia and then being disappointed with our performance against France.'

RIVALS

In recent years, Dempsey has found himself competing for the Ireland full-back position with Geordan Murphy.

'There has been a lot of talk in the media about the contest between Rog and Humphs for the number 10 shirt and of course they all compare it to the Ward–Campbell debate back in the '80s. There has been less media comment about my duel with Geordan for the number 15 shirt. This is possibly because a lot of the time one of us seems to be injured when the other is not or one of us has been needed to fill in on the wing, as I was during the 2005 Six Nations, with the injuries to Shane [Horgan] and Gordon [D'Arcy].

'We have roomed together a few times and I get on very well with Geordan. I look forward to playing with him because he has such silky skills. He did get a lot of slagging from the lads after he was described as "the George Best of rugby". We started calling him "Bestie". The reality is, though, that both he and Brian O'Driscoll would have been brilliant soccer players. Sometimes before we start a training session we bring out a soccer ball and the skills the two of them have are amazing.

'It was such a shame Geordan got injured before the 2003 World Cup, as he was on fire all that year and was set to become one of the biggest names in world rugby. I think the competition for places is a good thing. It brings out the best in players and I relish the challenge. I just want to be part of a successful Irish team. With Geordan and the current squad of players, I know we have the potential to achieve great things, even though it was obviously a big disappointment not to win the Grand Slam in 2005.' However, Dempsey came off the bench to play his part in Ireland's Triple Crown decider against England the following year.

IN THE EYE OF A MEDIA STORM

After Ireland's defeat in Paris in 2004, Dempsey found his performance lacerated in the media, his abilities questioned and even derided. As the journalist Billy Keane colourfully put it, he 'got more stick than a lazy donkey during the turf-cutting season'.

'I never considered myself the same sort of flair player as Denis Hickie, Geordan Murphy, Gordon D'Arcy or Brian O'Driscoll; my game is based on doing the bread and butter stuff well. In a Heineken Cup game for Leinster and in the France match, I made a couple of mistakes I normally wouldn't make and as a result, some of the comments about me in the press were at the very least not constructive and some were nasty. Dealing with the press is part of the job of being a professional rugby player today. It thickens the skin and makes you try harder when they write you off. The problem is that when they write nasty things about you, it is very difficult for your family to read it and they find it very upsetting. My parents have been at all the games I have played in over the last few years and they have given me great support, so they take it badly when they see destructive comments about me. That said, the best way to answer your critics is to let your performances do the talking.'

Ironically, to spend an hour in Dempsey's company is to see that his keen rugby intelligence marks him out as a pundit in the making and that some media involvement will certainly beckon for him. But has he given any thought to life after rugby?

'I studied Business in college but I think those of us who have been involved in professional rugby will struggle with the routine of a nine to five job and I suspect most of us will end up self-employed. I suppose we are always thinking of things we might do. When he came to coach at Leinster, Declan Kidney made a lot of players more conscious of the fact that our rugby careers are finite and that we need to boost our CVs by doing courses or whatever.'

BEHIND THE SCENES

Dempsey has come under the stewardship of a number of top coaches. Each in his own way made his impression.

'I started out at school at Terenure College under John McClean who is now director of rugby at UCD. He was ahead of his time. He would go to watch our opponents play and analyse their strengths and weaknesses before we played them. He had an excellent approach and we won Leinster Schools Cups under him in fourth and fifth year. More than anything else, though, I am grateful for the fact that he brought on my basic skills.

'At Leinster, Matt Williams was a big influence. He initially came as an assistant to Mike Ruddock, who is now the Welsh coach. When he became coach after Mike left, Matt brought a lot of the Australian style to us and made us very professional in our training and in our diet and in everything we did. He left no stone unturned in his preparation for games.'

How does he react to the rumours which surfaced after Williams left Leinster to become Scotland coach that some of the so-called 'fringe players' in the squad were disaffected with the Australian's reign?

'There were certain players who were not getting a game under Matt. You don't train hard in rugby just to be a sub, so I suppose it's only natural that guys who weren't in the team were a bit fed up. They would have the wrong attitude if they were content to be perennial subs.'

Dempsey is quite understandably wary when asked about Gary Ella's reign.

'It's a tricky area. Gary has given his side of the story to the media, and his criticisms of senior players like Brian [O'Driscoll], Mal [O'Kelly] and Victor [Costello] have been widely reported. He had a tough year in so far as the internationals were away a lot and there were a lot of injured players in the squad. To be fair to him, he brought on young players like Shane Jennings and Gary Brown and they probably have a lot to thank him for. I think the internationals found his laid-back attitude a bit strange. We were so used to Matt's authoritarian style and to him telling us what to do all the time. Gary was inclined to leave it to us and maybe we needed a bit more direction. I think it is fair to say we were all delighted to see Declan Kidney coming in as the new coach, given his record with Munster and the fact that so many of us knew him from his involvement with Ireland. So many of the Leinster players have been around a long time, craving success, that we wanted someone like Declan to progress us further.'

Dempsey goes on to discuss his experiences with Ireland coaches.

'Warren Gatland gave me my first cap. He is an excellent coach, as he has proved since with Wasps. He instilled a lot of toughness in us, though I think he was never fully forgiven for losing against Argentina in Lens in 1999.

'Eddie O'Sullivan is a superb coach. He is meticulous and spends every waking moment thinking of ways to improve us. His analysis is so thorough that sometimes we can see our opponents' moves before they can. He is also very innovative and uses imaginative ways to motivate us. A speech just before, during or straight after a game rarely means anything. It's what's done in the weeks leading up to it that wins a match for you. During the run-up to the World Cup in 2003, Eddie brought in two very different guest speakers to talk to us at the Citywest Hotel. They were the explorer Sir Ranulph Fiennes and the former champion boxer Marvin Hagler. They both struck a chord with a number of players in the squad. Sir Ranulph talked about the preparation that is needed for a major expedition and the steps you need to take to achieve what you want to achieve. Marvin spoke about the importance of self-confidence. They both really touched me and many of us found them inspirational; they were just the right choices to get us psyched up for the World Cup.'

POWER TO ALL OUR FRIENDS

Dempsey enjoys the congeniality of the rugby community.

'Mick Galwey and Peter Clohessy were great fun. They were always joking and messing at the back of the bus but once the game started, they were immense on the pitch. I was always in awe of the Claw's work rate. He used to get a lot of slagging from the Munster lads because he would come up with the most skilful of touches. I will never forget the way he set up Kevin Maggs with the most deft of passes at Lansdowne Road. Gallimh was a man whose career was written off many times but he just kept coming back again and again, and the effect he had on those around him was incalculable.

'Trevor Brennan is one of the great rugby characters. He is larger than life and has made a massive impact since he moved to play rugby in France. I was talking to some of the French players at the dinner after our Six Nations match in Paris in 2004 and they were all singing Trevor's praises. He's even opened a pub over there now.

'Trevor was responsible for my funniest moment in rugby. It was one of my first starts for Leinster and we were playing Treviso on a pre-season tour in Italy. After we flew into the airport and collected our bags, our manager at the time, Jim Glennon, told us there would be a delay because there was a difficulty with Dean Oswald's passport and that the problem was compounded by the fact that there was a language problem. Trevor immediately piped up, "I'll sort it out for you. I know the lingo." We were all stunned because Trevor was not known for his linguistic skills. When we turned to him and asked him when he learned to speak Italian, he coolly replied, "I worked in Luigi's Chip Shop one summer."'

8

MILLER'S CROSSING

IN 1997, ERIC MILLER SEEMED SET TO BECOME ONE OF THE biggest names in world rugby. His career, however, has had more twists than a Hitchcock thriller. Miller first made his mark in another sport.

'As a kid in Dublin I played soccer and Gaelic football. I went on to win a Minor and an Under-21 championship at Gaelic with Ballyboden St Enda's GAA Club and if I've got a half-alive body when I retire from rugby, I'd love to go back to Gaelic football.

'I only began rugby when I went to secondary school at Wesley College and after I left school I went to play with Leicester. My family had friends at the club and I wanted to play for them, especially as they had a great side then. At the time, I planned to be a PE teacher, so I also attended Loughborough University which was nearby. I started playing for Leicester's second team. Most of the English teams had very strong squads, so the standard in the Seconds League back then would be comparable with Celtic League standard today. Bob Dwyer came to Leicester as head coach with a new approach and he brought me onto the first team. Dwyer had coached Australia to the World Cup in 1991.

'Within a fairly short time, towards the end of Murray Kidd's reign, I was invited to a training camp with the Irish squad in the Algarve. It rained for the week! Out of the blue, I was picked for Ireland for the Italy game at the start of 1997. It happened so fast and I played for most of the Five Nations, although we didn't have the back line we have now and we didn't do as well as we have done recently.'

Soon after, Miller found himself making headlines throughout the rugby world.

'To everyone's surprise, I was selected for the Lions that year, the first tour to South Africa after the end of apartheid. The Springboks had won the 1995 World Cup and this was the first Lions tour of the professional era. I was only 21. I was the baby of the group by a few years. Alan Tait, later one of the assistant coaches in Scotland, really took me under his wing. He wore the number 11 shirt in the Tests. I got on very well with him. Things didn't work out for me as I would have liked. I got picked for the First Test but I got badly sick and they ruled me out the day after the side was announced. I was gutted. It is a day I will never forget. When you're that young, you think you'll get chances like that again but as you get older, you realise that kind of opportunity doesn't come around too often and you become aware of just how much you missed out on. Tim Rodber got my place and they were never going to change a winning team. I played really well between the First and Second Test and got a place on the bench. I did get a run in the Second Test, but I ended up playing in the backs because there were so many injuries. Jeremy Guscott had just got his famous drop-goal and we were three points up with five or ten minutes to go. There was a lot of injury time and it was backs-to-the-wall stuff. I made a few tackles but never really got my hands to the ball. I damaged my quad muscle but I only discovered it when the euphoria of winning the match and the series died down. There were a few injuries before the Third Test and I would have been playing had I not been injured myself. It was a run of bad luck.

'It wasn't all bad. Ian McGeechan was a great coach. He made a great effort to reach out to all the nationalities and that was very noticeable on that tour. He wasn't swayed by personalities. He was fair and unbiased. He picked you if you were on form and for no other reason. On the players side, there were three dominant personalities: Martin Johnson, Lawrence Dallaglio and Keith Wood. The spirit in the squad was phenomenal.'

There were other personalities who shone for different reasons.

'John Bentley was the life and soul of the party and always telling jokes at the top of the bus. It was a serious tour and I think they got the balance exactly right between work and play, unlike what seems to have happened in 2001. There was no partying until after we won the Second Test.

'Austin Healey was another character. He loves attention. The more you slag him off the more annoying he becomes. You have to take him with a pinch of salt. Sometimes his mouth runs away with him. He probably should have held his fire during the 2001 Lions tour and voiced his criticisms when he came home.'

Like most players, Miller has a number of Healey stories. As a kid, Healey was known as 'Melon Head' because of his big forehead. He has unusual tastes: at Neil Back's stag party Healey decided that 'Backy' should snog a pig's head for 30 seconds. Humour in rugby crops up in the most unlikely situations; Saturday, 13 February 1999 was an unlucky date for London Irish's Kevin Putt when he was stamped on by Austin Healey. Putt's face was left a bloody mess and he required six stitches. A contrite Healey apologised: 'Sorry, mate, I couldn't put my foot anywhere else.

Putt magnanimously replied, 'I'm not surprised considering the size of my nose.'

CATCH A FALLING STAR

Like Andy Dufresne in *The Shawshank Redemption*, Miller has weathered troubled times and learned the virtues of patience, hope and determination. There is a view that the Lions tour was more of a hindrance than a help to Miller's career in the long term.

'People have said that it happened too soon. My attitude was "better too soon than not at all". It was a learning curve. Most people going on tour have baggage but I had none. I was there as a free spirit and that was great.

'It was a comedown afterwards and there was a lot I had to deal with in subsequent years, such as the '99 World Cup when I wasn't first choice and various injuries I had to get to grips with. I had played a lot of games on the Lions tour. I played when I was battered and bruised, and that did take its toll. I had a difficult season after that. In the second half of the season, Bob Dwyer stopped picking me for Leicester. I returned to Ireland to play with Leinster because I felt I didn't have any balance in my life. The provincial structure was getting better here and I missed my friends and family. I always wonder if things had been going well in Leicester would I have stayed – or should I have stayed?

'My lowest point was probably the 2003 World Cup. I was not getting a start for the big games even though I was after playing really well. I scored two tries against Namibia and felt really strong. I was prepared not to be picked against Australia but it was a real low time, because I felt I deserved to be selected. I also missed out on the Triple Crown in 2004 with a shoulder injury, which was very disappointing as I had been playing well before the injury.'

COACHING MANUALS

Miller has worked with a number of different Irish coaches. He is circumspect in his analysis of their respective strengths.

'They all had their own strengths and each was very different with his own philosophy and approach. It is very hard to compare them because they all operated with different squads. Murray Kidd I never got to know. I was only there for one game before he was gone. Brian Ashton let players do the talking a lot. He wanted to play a very expansive game. He was probably in the right place at the wrong time. We didn't have the talented players to play the game he wanted. Of all the coaches, his vision of the type of game he liked to see played was probably closest to my vision. Warren Gatland got better and better as he went on. He was a very shy guy. The timing of his demise was strange as we were starting to show some serious potential and play well. Eddie O'Sullivan is very astute tactically and very professional. He expects a lot from his players. He's got the results he has because he demands 100 per cent and has got the best out of his players. All we need now is consistently to challenge the top three. The team is still very young, especially the backs.'

In January 2006, Miller dropped a bombshell by announcing his immediate retirement from international rugby, at the age of 30. The injury-plagued star stated his intention to hang up his boots completely at the end of the 2005–06 season, bringing down the curtain on a career which saw him winning 48 caps for Ireland.

He is not a player who pines for a media career. This may be because he has not always had the best press.

'I haven't let the coverage get to me. As my dad says, if you believe the good stuff they write about you, you have got to believe the bad stuff as well. I don't like the way the press attack players personally, although thankfully that hasn't happened to me. Players don't think too much about it, because they know journalists have their own opinions and agendas.'

An unexamined life is not worth living and Miller is well able to offer a mature assessment of his career to date.

'There have been times when I became disillusioned and didn't want it badly enough and didn't work as hard as I should have. Generally, though, I always give 100 per cent. In fact, that was maybe part of the problem. There were times when I didn't do myself any favours by playing with injuries.'

Miller feels he owes a particular debt to one man.

'Matt Williams instilled a lot of confidence in me. When things went wrong, he told me he still believed in me. He was very good to me personally. Because of him, I believe I'm as good as anybody in the world in my position.'

Miller has a nuanced view of Williams' successor Gary Ella's time in charge.

'Gary had a tough year with a lot of injuries in the squad. His head was probably on the block from the start of 2004. We as players didn't take enough on ourselves. We'd been spoon-fed by Matt Williams. Before Matt came here, Leinster were in the doldrums but he made us a good team. Gary was very laid back. The players didn't react to him as quickly as we should have – he wanted the senior players to take on a lot. To be fair, he wasn't helped by us but, equally, he didn't have the experience or whatever to get the best out of us.'

Miller is a big admirer of Ella's successor, Declan Kidney.

'Declan has a very good philosophy. He worries about the players in their personal lives. He wants to make sure that every player is OK in his private life because he knows that if there are problems there, they can't do their best on the park. Players want to play for him because he's so interested in their welfare, and that's good for the team.'

Who are Miller's favourite players and characters?

'My favourite player was [All Blacks great] Zinzan Brooke. I think [Australian fly-half] Stephen Larkham at his best is one of the greatest players in the world.

'In the Ireland squad, Guy Easterby is a really funny guy. He's always grabbing the microphone on the bus and cracking jokes. I admire him because, although he hasn't had many opportunities with Ireland, he always puts on a brave face. He contributes a lot to the spirit of the squad when others in that situation wouldn't be so chirpy.'

ALL CREATURES GREAT AND SMALL

It has to be said that there are some Irish players who would consider Eric himself something of a character. After he roomed with Miller,

Malcolm O'Kelly recalled waking up and only being able to see a silhouette of a bloke not moving and not saying anything. Big Mal found the silence the scariest thing until he discovered that Miller was relaxing by doing transcendental meditation. Eric too has witnessed some strange sights with the Irish team.

'As the tour of South Africa in 2004 was coming to an end, we organised John Hayes' stag party. We dressed John up in a gymslip. The sight of a 20-st. man in a gymslip is one that I never want to see again! Someone arranged for two strippers to come along but they weren't the stars of the show because Colin Farrell was filming there at the time and he came to join us for the party. He was a very sound guy and certainly knew how to have a good time! We gathered around in a circle with John in the middle and everyone got to ask Colin a question. Everything was going to plan until Donncha O'Callaghan, as only Donncha can, asked, "What was it like to be the star of *Titanic*?" The whole place cracked up and we nearly fell off our seats laughing.'

It's not surprising that Donncha's adventures from that tour spawned another story. In this account, Donncha stayed on afterwards to go on a safari holiday. While there, he came upon an elephant, in great pain, with a giant thorn in its foot. Donncha very carefully approached the elephant and gingerly removed the thorn from its foot. The elephant began to walk away, then turned and stared at Donncha for a full minute, locking eyes with him. The elephant then continued on its way. 'I wonder, if I ever saw that elephant again, would it remember me?' Donncha mused to himself.

The following Christmas, Donncha was back in Munster at a circus. He noticed that one of the elephants kept looking at him, almost like it knew him. Donncha wondered, 'Could this be that elephant I helped so long ago?' He decided to get a closer look. With the elephant still giving him the stare down, Donncha moved in closer, getting right up in front of the elephant. They locked eyes. A knowing look seemed to cross the elephant's face. It reached down, carefully picked Donncha up with its trunk, lifted him high in the air and then threw him crashing to the ground and stomped him to near death.

Turns out it wasn't that elephant.

9

BAND OF BROTHERS

FEW SCORES HAVE EVER BEEN GREETED AS ENTHUSIASTICALLY AS
David Wallace's try against Scotland in 2004. The match was supposed
to be a mere formality which would allow Ireland to win their first
Triple Crown in 19 years. However, the Scots had not read the script
and had the cheek to draw level eight minutes into the second half. Irish
fans started to get anxious. Wallace steadied their nerves when he used
his extraordinary power to pivot out of a tackle and dash for the line,
allowing all of Ireland to relax. As he left the Scottish defence in his
wake, a great roar shook the Lansdowne Road stadium. Wallace has
always been quick off the mark. In August 2003, he came on as a sub
against Wales in a World Cup warm-up game and scored a try after just
38 seconds.

O BROTHER, WHERE ART THOU?
Wallace is part of a unique rugby family. Two of his brothers have
played both for Ireland and the Lions.

'Dad had a huge interest in rugby and we all got involved from an
early age. At the school sports day my mother won the mothers' race,
so I think we all got a bit of speed from Mum.'

Richard Wallace won the first of his 29 caps on the Irish wing
against Namibia in 1991 and his last against England in 1998. Like his
brother Paul, he scored five tries in Test games for Ireland. Paul won
the first of 45 caps in the Irish front row against Japan in 1995 and the
last against Georgia in 2002. Though injury forced him to retire

prematurely from the game, he has found a new niche in the rugby world as an intelligent and perceptive media analyst.

'Richard went out on the Lions tour as a replacement in '93. I was only 16 at the time and it was an incredible thrill for us as a family to see him playing with and against the legends of world rugby. I would have to say that it was also a fantastic experience to see my eldest brother, Henry, and Richard play for the Irish Colleges team together. To think of Richard playing for the Lions was inspirational for me, particularly as he was relatively new to international rugby. I learned a lot from him about the training and the physical preparation that is required for rugby at the highest level. When Paul was selected to replace Peter Clohessy before the Lions tour to South Africa in '97 actually began, he was at the airport when he saw the Claw coming towards him on the way home. It was awkward for him. But the fact that he made it onto the Test team and was considered one of the stars of the tour was great for the family.'

THE NEW KID ON THE BLOCK

1997 was also a significant year for David Wallace's emerging rugby career.

'I played in all the games on the Irish development tour to New Zealand that year but I lost my way a bit after that in the new professional environment. I was probably in a bit of a comfort zone. The following February, I won my first Ireland A cap coming on as a replacement for Alan Quinlan against Scotland. One of my happiest memories of that year is of being part of the Under-21 team that won the Triple Crown. That summer, I was called to the Senior squad for the summer tour to South Africa. I had been recovering from injury and I wasn't at my best, and although I played in three games, I probably didn't do myself any favours. I wasn't firing on all cylinders after that so it took me two years to win my first cap, against Argentina on Ireland's summer tour. It wasn't the fairy-tale debut I dreamed of and we lost, which was very disappointing. I do remember that I felt a little bit nervous before the game began, as we togged out, and that the crowd was very intense. I've never seen a video of the game. A week later, I won my second cap against the United States. We beat them well in the hottest temperatures I have ever played in.'

HISTORY MAKER

2001 would prove to be a big year for Wallace.

'I played against Italy and France in the Six Nations but the foot-and-mouth outbreak interrupted the championship. I had been in the preliminary squad for the Lions tour but, like other players on the Irish team, I was out of the shop window at a crucial time because of the foot-and-mouth scare. I was kind of disappointed not to make the original touring party but knew that I might still make the trip because I was on standby. I won my fifth cap in a friendly against Romania but as the Lions tour was progressing, I was starting to worry that I wouldn't get the call. I was going off to a summer training camp in Poland with the Ireland team and was halfway there on a stopoff at Copenhagen Airport when I got a phone call from Ronan O'Gara telling me that there was an injury and that I was going to be called up. I got a flight back to Heathrow and then another one on to Australia. I had 45 hours of airports and planes before I eventually got there. I then had to learn about 101 squad calls very quickly because almost immediately I had to play against New South Wales.

'It was pretty unbelievable to find myself playing for the Lions and to discover that I had made history by becoming the third member of the one family to play for the Lions, which had never been done before. I discovered pretty early on, though, that there was a negative vibe within the camp. Players like Austin Healey and Matt Dawson were unhappy not to be playing in the Test side. You can understand why they might be unhappy but then they vented their grievances with the management in their newspaper columns, which obviously did nothing to improve morale within the squad and added to the media circus.'

What was at the heart of the problems within the squad?

'I would attribute the difficulties to two factors: the training regime and poor communication. Some of the players found that the training was excessive and did not allow enough time for rest. Any time you have disharmony within a group like that you can be certain that there are failures of communication.

'For my own part, I seemed to gel quite well with everybody. The squad was pretty much divided between the Test side and the mid-week side, and the players on each team tended to mix largely with the rest of "their team" rather than the entire squad. As a result, the only one of the English players I really got to know was Ben Cohen. Before the Second Test, Scott Quinnell picked up an injury. There was major doubt about whether he would be able to take his place on the bench for the game and I was in line to replace him. He passed his fitness test the day of the game, so I missed out on having any involvement on the Lions Test team which was a bit of a disappointment, as you would expect.

'I was a regular in the Irish side for the Six Nations the following season but I got a bad shoulder injury which required surgery and I missed out on all the Six Nations matches in 2003. I did travel on the summer tour to Australia that year but I was still bothered by my shoulder and wasn't playing well, which in turn affected my confidence. It had been a big goal of mine to play in the World Cup but unfortunately I wasn't selected for the squad. I was sitting at home watching the Argentina game when Alan Quinlan got that bad injury and I had an hour or two to throw my stuff into a bag. It was not the way to get there I had dreamed of and while it was good to experience the tournament, it was disappointing to be at the World Cup and not be part of the action on the pitch.

'Some of my earliest childhood memories are of Ireland's two Triple Crowns in the 1980s. It was great to play a part in Ireland's Triple Crown win in 2004. It was particularly sweet for me to score a try against Scotland in the decisive match.'

For the next 18 months, it seemed that Eddie O'Sullivan had forgotten Wallace, but Ireland's poor performances in the 2005 autumn internationals led to his restoration to the Irish back row for his second taste of Triple Crown glory in 2006. His highs and lows with Ireland have been replicated with Munster.

'I've had so many great days with Munster, especially some incredible wins against the odds on French soil. On the other hand, losing two Heineken Cup finals was very hard to take. The one that hurt the most was losing the final to Northampton. The game was ours for the taking that day but we left it behind us.'

LEGENDS OF MUNSTER RUGBY

Wallace enjoys the joking between his playing colleagues. A case in point was after Rob Henderson required 15 stiches in his lip following a 'clash' in a Celtic League match in autumn 2004. Noticing Hendo's concern about his appearance, his ever helpful teammates started calling him 'Bubba' after the 'aesthetically challenged' character in *Forrest Gump*.

Wallace had the pleasure of playing with Peter Clohessy for many years and looks forward to a new generation of Clohessys making as big an impact on Irish rugby as their father did. One of the stories that illustrates the Claw's passion for the game dates from the first time he saw his son Luke play a game. Clohessy senior was voicing strong opinions about the referee from the sidelines. After one of the Claw's many vocal contributions, the coach called Luke over to the sidelines and said to him, 'Do you understand what "cooperation" is? What "team" is?'

Luke nodded in the affirmative.

'Do you understand that what matters is whether we win together as a team?'

The little boy nodded yes.

'So,' the coach continued, 'when a penalty is awarded, you don't argue or curse or attack the ref. Do you understand all that?'

Again Luke nodded.

'Good,' said the coach. 'Now go over there and explain it to your father.'

10

THE STAR OF DAVID

THE OUT-HALF REQUIRES A COOL HEAD. HE IS SOMETIMES called 'the general' in rugby jargon, as he is the link between the backs and the forwards. It can be the glamour position but, conversely, if things go wrong, it is the place not to be! Ireland's most capped out-half David Humphreys has seen both sides of the coin. On the way, he has amassed a number of records, becoming Ireland's top point-scorer and most prolific drop-goal-scorer. In the 2004 autumn international against the USA, he became the first Irish player to have scored more than 500 points in international rugby. His running game has not always got the credit it deserves – take the way he skinned Aaron Persico for pace before scoring a try in Ireland's 37–13 win over Italy in Rome in 2003. He was Irish Schools captain in 1990 and in 1996 he won his first full cap against France. He is keen to acknowledge the role of a number of formative influences on his career.

'The biggest influence on my game has been my dad, George. He played rugby to a fairly high level and has a great passion for it. I learned a great deal about the game from spending a lot of time with him in the back garden over the first 20 years of my life.'

The Humphreys are a very talented family.

'Sport was a huge part of our upbringing whether it be hockey, football or rugby. My sister Karen has won many more caps than I have for Ireland. However, because she won hers in hockey, she has got none of the financial or other rewards that I have. I have huge admiration for the sacrifices amateur sportspeople like her make in terms of having to take time off work and so on.'

Early on in his career, Humphreys had the benefit of the wisdom of one of the legends of Irish rugby.

'After I qualified as a solicitor, I was taken on by a firm where the senior partner was Mike Gibson. He gave me a lot of good advice about how I could balance my legal career with my rugby in terms of my training schedule.'

THE STREETS OF LONDON

The great Gareth Edwards once claimed, 'Rugby football is really a simple game; it's only the coaches who make it complicated.' This remark should be treated with caution because such was Edwards' talent that he could make things look easy which other mortals would have found impossible. Although it may have more than a grain of truth, the reality is that coaches exert a huge influence in the modern game. Humphreys is quick to pay homage to two of his earliest coaches.

'Shortly after qualifying, I moved to London Irish, where I was coached by Clive Woodward, who was excellent. It is very difficult to pinpoint what made him so good; in terms of pure technical ability, he probably wasn't the best but his man-management skills were excellent. His greatest achievement was to get the best out of all of us. Willie Anderson later became coach at London Irish. Willie has been a big influence on my career there and at different stages with Irish teams, and he was a huge factor in my decision to come home and play for Dungannon and Ulster. He is a wonderful coach because of his enormous technical ability, but above all for the strength of his passion for the game.'

ULSTER SAYS YES

The highlight of Humphreys' career came in January 1999 when he captained Ulster to victory in the Heineken Cup.

'We didn't have a very good team but we got on a roll. There were just a few hundred people at our first match but our success struck a chord, initially across the province and then throughout the whole of Ireland. When we were driving down to Dublin for the final in Lansdowne Road, all the flags of support for us really inspired us.

'All of Ireland got behind us, as we were bidding to become the first Irish side to win the competition. I suppose it was all the sweeter for me, as I was captain. Mark McCall was captain for the opening match but he got injured and the captaincy fell on my shoulders by default. The whole day was an incredible experience.'

It is often said that a week is a long time in politics but Humphreys was to learn the hard way that seven days can be a long time in rugby. Exactly seven days after the zenith of his career came the nadir.

'Unquestionably, the low point of my days in the Ireland shirt came in the 1999 Five Nations against France at Lansdowne Road. I had a chance to win the game with a penalty very close to the end but I missed it. It was just such a horrible feeling when the final whistle went. To go from top of the world to being the villain was a very sobering experience and I suppose it highlighted just how cruel sport can be.'

One of the most memorable moments of the Euro '96 football championship came when Stuart 'Psycho' Pearce bravely stepped forward to take a penalty in a shoot-out, having famously missed in the World Cup semi-final in 1990. He held his nerve and scored. A year after missing the penalty against France, Humphreys was faced with the chance to redeem himself with another penalty which was to give Ireland its first victory in Paris in 28 years.

'It wasn't like it was the last kick of the game, so the pressure wasn't weighing as heavily on me as it had been the year before. There were still a few minutes to go, so if I missed, there was another chance. It was for situations like those that I spent hours and hours practising so that I would be able to slot the ball between the posts, and that helped me to relax as I faced up to the kick.'

From a personal point of view, another highlight for Humphreys came in 2002 when he scored a record 37 points for Ulster (including a try and four drop-goals) in a Heineken Cup tie against Wasps, a 42–16 victory.

TWO INTO ONE WON'T GO

In the early '80s, there was a massive rivalry between Tony Ward and Ollie Campbell for the out-half position on the Irish team. In the late '80s, there were very strong views in the media about whether Ralph Keyes or Brian Smith should wear the number 10 shirt. Smith had played for Australia against Ireland in the '87 World Cup and could have ended up playing for Ireland against Australia in the World Cup in 1991 if he had hung around a bit longer. In the early years of the third millennium, there has been much discussion about whether Humphreys or Ronan O'Gara should be the Irish fly-half.

'The rivalry was a huge challenge for both of us. As a player, all you can ask is that you are given a chance to earn your place. I can't complain. I was given plenty of chances to cement my place – mind you, I didn't always take them! At different times, I have benefited from injuries to Ronan and vice versa. I think, though, the competition between us left no room for a comfort zone and raised the bar for both of us.'

Humphreys does not hesitate for a second when asked about his most difficult opponent.

'Brian O'Driscoll is the best performer I played with or against. I remember the first time he came into the Irish squad when he was still in his teens and I knew from day one that this was a phenomenal talent – the kind that doesn't come along very often. Jonny Wilkinson when he is on his game is also a very special player but different players bring different challenges. When you play a game at international level or in the Heineken Cup there will always be someone who will make life difficult for you.'

BY GEORGE

Humphreys is one of the most amiable and articulate people in rugby. Yet at the mention of one name he is uncharacteristically reticent. After a series of uncomplimentary comments about him on RTÉ television from panellist George Hook, Humphreys allegedly refused to be interviewed by RTÉ. What, then, is his attitude to 'the Right Hook'?

'The one subject I have never spoken about on the record is George Hook. I have no plans to change that policy.'

Humphreys has had more positive exposure in the media – including one brief interlude as a celebrity chef. Is that where he sees his future now that his retirement from international rugby is on the horizon?

'I have no ambitions to be the new Jamie Oliver! When you are a professional sportsman and are getting paid to do the job every kid dreams about, you are always scared of the day coming when you will have to say goodbye to the game and go back to the real world. I've always known that if I got injured, I had my training as a solicitor to fall back on and that's what my future has in store for me. My wife Jayne and I have three young kids, Katie, James and Lucy, and they are going to take up a lot of my spare time.'

One of Humphreys' opponents at Munster is believed to be responsible for the story that surfaced about the end of Jayne's third pregnancy when David rang the operator.

Operator: 999. What's the nature of your emergency?

Humphreys: My wife is pregnant and her contractions are only two minutes apart.

Operator: Is this her first child?

Humphreys: No, you idiot. This is her husband.

TIME TO SAY GOODBYE

Early in 2005, speculation was rife that Clive Woodward, a self-confessed admirer of the Ulster out-half, would select Humphreys for the Lions tour to New Zealand. In the event, he was not selected. Instead, he had the consolation of journeying to the 'land of the cherry blossoms' and captaining Ireland to a two-Test series win over Japan. During the 2006 Six Nations campaign, there was much controversy about when Humphreys would annouce his retirement from international rugby. He watched Ireland claim another Triple Crown from the subs' benches.

As he prepares to leave the international stage, Humphreys will take away a lot of happy memories from his time in rugby.

'I have met a lot of great characters like Alan Quinlan. All the Munster guys in the Irish side are a laugh. While they are serious about rugby they are all very funny in different ways. Trevor Brennan is another great character. You could probably write a book of the stories that are told about him.'

One goes back to the time when Brennan was a little boy and answered the phone.

A man asked, 'Hello, is your dad around?'

Trevor whispered, 'Yes.'

The man then asked if he could talk to him.

'He's busy at the moment,' Brennan whispered.

'Then is your Mum there?'

'Yes,' the boy whispered.

'Can I talk to her?'

'No, she's busy,' Trevor whispered.

'Is there anyone else there?'

'Yes,' whispered little Trevor.

'Who?'

'A policeman,' came the whispered reply.

'Well, can I talk to him?'

'He's busy too,' Trevor whispered.

Annoyed, the man asked what they were all doing.

'Looking for me,' Brennan whispered.

Closer to home, there were other incidents which would be imprinted forever on Humphreys' brain.

'Probably my favourite rugby story is from 2003, just before the World Cup. The international players were away with the Irish squad and Johnny Bell was made captain of Ulster for a Celtic League match. Just before the game, Johnny gathered all the players around him, brought them into a huddle and said, "Right, lads, there's just two things I want from you in this game." He paused dramatically. You could have heard a pin drop as the lads were hanging on his every word. You could almost cut the tension with a knife as he said, "Honesty, commitment and work rate." The lads almost fell on the floor laughing at his gaffe. Ulster lost badly and Johnny's career as a captain came to an abrupt and undistinguished end!'

11

THE WIZARD OF OZ

MY FIRST MEETING WITH ROB HENDERSON WAS MEMORABLE. ON
the eve of a Munster–Leinster Celtic League match, Henderson invited
me up to his hotel room. When I knocked at the door, he ushered me in.
I was more than a little taken aback to discover that all he was 'wearing'
was a bath towel! Despite many hours of expensive therapy, I have
never been able to erase that disturbing image from the dark corners of
my subconscious.

His accent immediately reveals that he was not born and bred on
Irish soil. 'I am one of the lucky ones that can play for Ireland with Irish
parentage. My mother is a native of Wexford. My parents split when I
was a young fella and I was living with my mum. Even though she
wasn't throwing her Irishness at me, I picked it up from her, although
my brother and sister didn't. As soon as I started playing rugby, I
wanted to progress to playing for the Irish Under-21 side and ultimately
to win my first full cap for Ireland. I'm always happy to put on the
green shirt.'

SIR CLIVE
During his playing days with London Irish, Henderson came under the
stewardship of Clive Woodward. Apart from developing a working
relationship, they got to know each other socially.

'I've spent some time with him. I've even had Christmas dinner with
him. I invited myself! We had a delightful Christmas. He's a lovely fella
and he's very smart. He was as good at business as he was at organising

the England team. The guy is focused to the nth degree. I expected that he would do a great job coaching the Lions. I told that to everyone I could think of who knew him before the tour in the hope he might pick me! He got the results he did with England because he got the best out of people. He did that by giving everything he had himself to it. He doesn't do anything unless he does it wholeheartedly.

'I played golf with him one day. I'd started playing two or three months beforehand but I'd got all the gear from a sponsor. We came to the first tee and I hit one down the middle, which was a miracle. I was really keyed up but by the time I got to the eighth hole I had lost all the balls in my bag and about 14 of Clive's. He loves his golf and when I hit another ball into the woods he just looked at me sadly and said, "I think we'd better go in now."

'I gave him the green jersey I wore when I won my first cap for Ireland. I presented it in a grand manner as befits Clive – in a Tesco bag. He wasn't there when I dropped it into his home, so he wrote to me and said when I eventually grew up he would return it to me!'

HIGHS AND LOWS

Henderson takes me by surprise when I suggest that the high point of his career must have been the Lions tour of 2001.

'No. Without question, the high point for me was when we beat France 27–25 in the Stade de France in 2000, the first time we'd won in Paris in 28 years. It was an unbelievable atmosphere. It obviously helped that the fella next to me scored three tries. That was a day that I will never forget. Obviously, the Lions tour was also a real highlight. To make the trip in the first place was fantastic, but to play in all of the three Tests was wonderful.'

Hendo's awesome power was the perfect foil for Brian O'Driscoll's sublime skills, and the two of them provided the coach, Graham Henry, with the perfect midfield combination of strength and flair. Henderson's teammates were not so appreciative of his off-the-field activities. Rooming with Henderson was the ultimate nightmare: according to Austin Healey, he smokes like a chimney and snores like a blocked-up chimney, sarcastic is his middle name and he could turn any sentence into a jail term.

2001 was a significant year for Henderson because he signed for Munster. However, a serious knee injury sustained on the Lions tour meant Hendo only began playing competitively in December 2001.

'That April, it was announced that I would leave Wasps after five seasons there to join Munster. The following week, I travelled with hordes of Munster supporters on the Waterloo to Lille train to watch Stade Français versus Munster in the Heineken Cup semi-final. The Lions squad was to be announced three days later and, to my horror, Donal Lenihan walked straight past me in the ground. Poor Donal hadn't even noticed me in the crowds of supporters but I was convinced that the fact that he didn't acknowledge me was some sort of sign that I wasn't picked for the tour to Oz. Thankfully that wasn't the case and he rang me three days later to inform me of my selection.'

THE FIRST CAP IS NOT THE SWEETEST

For most players their first cap is an unbelievable thrill. Henderson is an exception.

'My first cap was against Samoa in November 1996. I'd been playing well that season. I'd played in the Peace International against the Barbarians that April and scored a try. Against Samoa, I didn't play particularly well and we got thrashed. As a result, the team got slagged to the high heavens and I didn't get capped for another year, against the All Blacks.

'Another bad time was the New Zealand development tour in 1997. Oh my God, was that a low point. Terrible. We played eight games on that tour, lost seven and won one. I played in seven games and each of those we lost. The side we beat, when I wasn't playing, was New Zealand's equivalent of Ballybunion rugby.

'Being dropped for the World Cup in '99 was another low point. Ever since that day, I've been trying to drive myself forward and push my career on. I've been blighted with injuries recently. Every single one of them was a low point. Just ask my wife. Fortunately, rugby has provided me with a lot of opportunities to meet people and to travel to interesting places.'

Every cloud has a silver lining and Henderson's injuries opened a new door for him. BBC television asked him to present a number of features for *Grandstand*.

'I would be interested in working in the media after my rugby days are over, be it television or newspapers. I want to work somewhere where I would be meeting people and wouldn't be tied to a desk.'

RUCK AND ROLLERS

2005–06 was a frustrating season for Henderson, as he was largely ignored by the Munster selectors. However, it did see one of the highlights of his life, the birth of his daughter, Mia.

Henderson has made many friends and met some interesting people through rugby.

'One of the greats is Jason Leonard. He played, like myself, in the amateur days and switched over to professionalism. His record speaks for itself; he was the cornerstone of every team he played on, whether it was England or the Lions. What most appeals to me about him, though, is that he is very down to earth. You'd meet him down the pub having a pint, he's amiable to everybody. He's a lovely fella.

'Another great guy is Simon Mitchell, the best man at my wedding. He's a lunatic but he's pulled me through many a scrape.

'The Irish team are all great. If Malcolm O'Kelly was any more laid back his head would be touching the ground.

'Another character is Patrick O'Reilly. He played hooker for Terenure and is now the kit-man for the Ireland team. Everybody knows him as "Rala". He got the nickname because when he was in Irish class at school, he was brought up to the blackboard and told to write his name. After he wrote "Rala", he couldn't remember the Irish version of the rest of his surname, so all the kids called him Rala and the name stuck for the rest of his life. If you ever need advice or shoelaces, or you're in a scrape or need help, he's the "go-to man", as they would say in the NFL. If he can't do it, he will find someone who can. The only problem is that he delegates his work to everybody else. He may have 15 bags but he'll have 16 people who want to help him carry them! He's a guy who I will never forget.

'He tells a great story of playing against Garryowen when his opposite number was the former Ireland hooker, and later manager, Pat Whelan. It was a windy day with a howling gale. A call came in from the second row but Rala couldn't hear it. One of the second rows stepped forward and said to Rala, "Low and hard at number two." Rala shrugged his shoulders and stepped back. He then threw the ball very hard at Pat Whelan! Rala spent the next 45 minutes both apologising to and running away from Whelan.'

Rob's most loyal fan, his wife, Angie, offers a revealing insight into the legendary status of one player in the Irish set-up.

'Peter Clohessy left more than just a hole in Irish rugby when he retired in 2002 – he left his seat at the back of the bus vacant too! I was amused to find that, like a school bus, the team coach had the naughty big boys who always sat on the back seat. The "usual suspects" included the Claw, Woodie, "Axel" [Anthony] Foley and Rob. In 2003, after joining the team on their coach to travel the short journey across town for a celebratory dinner, I found a spare seat that just happened to be next to the man I married. The conversation unfolded as follows:

Me: Oh, that's nice, darling, you saved me a seat.

Rob: That's Claw's seat.

Me: But, Rob, Claw's not here, he didn't play, he's retired.

Rob: Yeah . . . but it's still his seat.

Hendo has his fair share share of rugby stories but his favourites deal with the exploits of one particular former Ireland international.

'Ken O'Connell's nickname is "the Legend" but you would have to know him to understand why. He gained his legendary status in a different way to Brian O'Driscoll! He's now gone off to India or Thailand to find himself. We played together with London Irish. At one stage, we were playing in the European Conference. We were all getting ready to travel to Bordeaux. We were getting kitted out and were all there with our kitbags as if we were heading to Monaco – we looked a million dollars. Just as we were ready to leave, someone shouted, "Where's Ken?" Half an hour later, he shows up with Malcolm O'Kelly. For once, miraculously, Mal had all his gear and luggage. Somebody must have dressed him! Ken turned up wearing a T-shirt and shorts. His T-shirt had a picture of a fella wearing shorts and a T-shirt but with his "manhood" sticking out. His only luggage was a kitbag which was the size of a big ice-cream tub. I said, "Ken, what are you carrying, mate?"

He replied, "I've got all I need. I've got my boots, my gumshield and my heart." With that, he was off to get the plane. That's Ken boy. That's why he's a legend.

'I will never forget my first introduction to Ken. Before he played his first game for London Irish, he wandered into the changing-room with his togs around his ankles. He looked down at his private parts and said to me, "I bet you thought St Patrick chased all the snakes out of Ireland."'

12

VICTOR BRAVO

WITH THE WELSH WINGER NIGEL WALKER, VICTOR COSTELLO IS one of an elite club who have competed in athletics in the Olympics and then gone on to play international rugby. The biggest formative influence on Costello's career was his late father, Paddy.

'My first cap gave me great satisfaction. I will always remember ringing my dad from Atlanta to tell him I had been selected and him running down the corridor to tell my mum and then running back to tell me her reaction. It is a special family moment and is very personal to me. My mother and my sister, Suzanne, have always been a great support to me.

'My father played once for Ireland, in 1960 against France in Paris. I reminded him when I won my second cap that I had played twice as many times for Ireland as him!'

Victor also followed in his father's footsteps by excelling at athletics.

'My dad had been a national champion in the shotput. I put a huge amount of pressure on myself to get to the Olympics. I grew up on athletics. I was good at it but I was never going to be a world champion. I didn't like the loneliness of life as a shotputter. I didn't fancy spending all my time in a gym with just a German coach. I gave what I had to give to go to the Barcelona Olympics in 1992 and after that I didn't care. Even back then, if you'd asked me to name the top shotputters in the world, I wouldn't have been able to do so. That probably says it all about my attitude to athletics. I saw some fabulous athletes who gave everything to the sport but got nothing out of it in terms of recognition compared to what I would get in just one year in rugby. I became good friends with people like Gary O'Toole and I know how much they gave for so little in the way of rewards.

'Drugs in athletics were rampant at the time. I never saw them being administered because I wasn't hanging around in the right places but I certainly saw their effects. I was just a skinny little kid from Ireland compared to the guys I was competing against.

'I liked the team aspect of rugby and the extra responsibility that brings. When I went out and competed for Ireland in athletics, if I did badly, I let myself down. When I put on the green shirt for Ireland, if I played badly, I let Paul O'Connell and Ronan O'Gara down and I couldn't allow that to happen.'

ROCK ON

When he was a schoolboy, Costello's rugby talents shone like a beacon in Blackrock College.

'Things were relatively easy. I was big and I was playing in the top team in the school. In Blackrock, you can get a high opinion of yourself. I saw this after I left and I still see it today, and I probably was a bit arrogant as well. At the time, Senior rugby was nowhere near as professional as it is now but Schools rugby then was probably as professional as it ever will be. I came out of this disciplined scene in school where rugby is a huge part of your daily life to go to the club scene where you only train twice a week. It was very difficult to make that transition smoothly and, like most people, I probably went a little wayward for a while. I had athletics as an excuse. Because I was competing in shotput at the same time, I probably got away with being less focused than I might have been.

'The year after I finished athletics, I was brought into the Irish squad. I went on the tour to Australia in 1994. I tore ligaments in my shoulder in the opening game in Perth. I probably came back onto the team too soon but that's what you do when you're young and keen. As a result, I didn't have a good tour.

'In 1996, I went to Atlanta with the Irish squad for warm-weather training to get us ready for the Five Nations. It was ironic that it poured with rain while we were there and it took us 36 hours to get home because we were caught in a snowstorm and had to return via Copenhagen and Manchester. At the end of the week, we played the USA at Lansdowne Road on a rain-sodden pitch. I won my first cap and played reasonably well but I missed a tackle and they scored from it. My defence was questioned at the time. More than now, players got labelled back then. It is interesting that in 1994 Keith Wood was the undisputed star of the Irish team on the tour to Australia. Yet the following year he was not the Ireland hooker because people said he was "too loose a player". Nowadays, there are specialist coaches to improve skills that are lacking but in those days that wasn't the case. I always think of Niall Woods, who was a brilliant attacking winger but everyone doubted his defensive skills even though I've seen him putting in many a big tackle.

'When I missed the tackle against the USA, I knew it was going to work against me. I was dropped for the next game but after they unexpectedly lost to Scotland, I was brought back for the France match. At the time, whenever we travelled to Paris, it was to get our arses kicked – and we did! There were a few good performances in the green shirt, though, like that of David Humphreys, and I played well. I hung in there for the next few internationals.'

He had the disappointment of missing out on the development tour to New Zealand in '97 and his run in the Irish squad under Warren Gatland came to an abrupt end after Ireland's tour to Australia in 1999.

'Unfortunately for me, competition for places in the back row is such that I had to play up to 85 per cent of my ability if I was to hold on to my place. I played badly against England in '99, I just wasn't streetwise enough and that dented my confidence. Then on the Australian tour I was dropped. Of course when you lose your place you're devastated but back then about 5 per cent of me was relieved. Warren Gatland was under tremendous pressure because the team wasn't playing well and he responded by picking essentially a Munster pack. They traditionally have very strong forwards and he wanted people who were used to working together. I knew I had to change as a player. I never had a problem with Warren Gatland. Nothing ever happened between us. He wasn't a good man-manager. That was his deficiency but I had lots of deficiencies as a player so I'm not blaming him. I had to reinvent myself and he reinvented himself when he went to Wasps.

'If I hadn't made it back onto the Irish team in 2002, I probably would have a lot of regrets about my career. Matt Williams coming into Leinster shook things up a bit. He gave us all belief individually. For some people it didn't work but for me it definitely did.'

THE COMEBACK KID

Eddie O'Sullivan's appointment as Ireland coach was to result in the resurrection of Costello's international career.

'I approached Eddie in the summer of 2002 at our training camp in Poland. I was on the fringes of the squad but not actually in it and I asked him what I had to do to get back in. We sat through a couple of videos and he said, "Well, this is what you have to do." I went out and did it, and he, true to his word, brought me back into the squad. I kind of pride myself on the fact that I listen to people I respect like Eddie O'Sullivan and Declan Kidney and when they ask me to do something, I do my damnedest to get it done. That's why I was delighted to get back into the squad. At least I was back on the radar, despite those who were writing me off because of my age or for other reasons. Playing out of position and beating Australia in autumn of 2002 was a real highlight for me, especially because there were a number of people who said I should never have been picked there in the first place. Running out onto the pitch at Lansdowne Road is always a great feeling but it was particularly sweet that day. After competing in the Olympics, I was really keen to play in the World Cup in 2003 because they are the greatest stages of all, so when I got my chance to be selected for the team I took it.'

CARELESS WHISPERS

Throughout his career, Costello has been the subject of a number of rumours. One of the earliest murmurs to emerge was that he left his first club, Blackrock, for St Mary's in slightly acrimonious circumstances.

'I'm very proud of my time in school at Blackrock. When you play Schools rugby with Blackrock, it is natural that you go on to play your club rugby there. In some ways, a lot is expected of you because of the reputation you have in the school. Yet there are always guys within the club who are willing to knock you for some aspect of your rugby. Eddie O'Sullivan was the coach and Dean Oswald was coming in to play at 8; I had been playing there semi-regularly but that was obviously going to change with Dean's arrival. Eddie suggested that I move to the second row but I didn't want to play there. At the time, I was friendly with a lot of the players from St Mary's and Mary's were very successful at the time. Any time I was going out after a match, it was always with the Mary's lads. I found them very welcoming and at one with each other, and that's what I wanted. Back then, it wasn't the done thing to move clubs. I told Eddie that I was moving and he wished me well. People said to me at the time, "Eddie O'Sullivan is going to be Ireland coach and he won't like you for leaving." The ironic thing is that it was Eddie who revived my international career. That tells you everything you need to know about the man.

'When I went back to play against Rock I always wanted to beat them. In fact, I never once lost against them! I got to know Dean Oswald well. I ended up playing at 8 for Leinster and he was 7. When he was returing to New Zealand, Blackrock had a function for him and I attended. I think people liked that I turned up as a St Mary's player to honour the guy who took my place at Blackrock.'

The next story to circulate was about the manner of his departure from London Irish.

'I moved to London to advance my career. It was a case of the grass is always greener. It was universally believed at the time that there was a higher standard of rugby in England. I chose London Irish rather than a club like Saracens because I wanted a bit of "home". I didn't settle in and it wasn't a good move for me. My career was on a slippery slope and I called it early and came back to Ireland.'

There has been a lot of speculation that he had an unhappy relationship with Clive Woodward during his sojourn in London.

'Everybody thinks I had a problem with him but I didn't. He was trying to do things with us that we weren't able to do. It was like when Brian Ashton was Irish coach. Brian couldn't communicate with the Irish team and what he did try to teach us was way beyond what we were up to. Clive was a very hard worker and very ambitious but didn't have the players. He recognised things weren't going to work out and went to Bath. There never was any bust-up or row between us. The money was good but I was on a downward curve and got back home quickly.

'That was the lowest point of my career. It was tough to call it quits and get out. To people back home, it probably looked as if I couldn't hack it outside my comfort zone. I was coming back to Ireland with my tail between my legs. When you do something like that, you feel that your peers have less esteem for you; you've got to start from scratch and do it all over again. At that time, in '97, my father had just died and unfortunately I was only climbing out of the bad patch when he passed away. I only had six caps when he died. Then again, I mightn't have been able to win any more caps without his help up there. It would be very easy to say that neither Clive Woodward nor Warren Gatland fancied me as a player but that would be too easy. I had to improve as a player.'

The most high-profile controversy which Costello was unwittingly embroiled in came in 2004 when Gary Ella publicly questioned his commitment to Leinster.

'I was over in the States on holiday and I heard about his comments when I was on a boat in Long Island. His Leinster career ended in the summer of 2004 but there were 38 careers going backwards under his reign. Gary Ella was a bad time for Leinster. When you look at the respect Leinster players had later for Declan Kidney, there was a striking contrast.

'In that interview, he said that I had come up to him and apologised for playing badly because I had other things on my mind. When I play badly, I hold my hands up and admit it. I don't make excuses.

'I felt enormous pride each time I pulled on the number 8 jersey for Leinster and I was very conscious of the huge responsibility it brings. I remember when I was young getting Hugo MacNeill's autograph and it meant an awful lot to me because I looked up to him so much and I still do. I was very aware of the obligation I had to the young kids watching when I pulled on that jersey and there's no way I would be casual about lining out for Leinster. I heard that Gary Ella later claimed he was misquoted. The furore happened in the middle of the summer break and really everybody was sick of rugby then. I laughed it off because I thought it was more of a reflection on him than it was on me.'

Such is Costello's friendly disposition that he is much happier when he is praising people rather than criticising them. Equally indicative of his generosity is his tendency to applaud people who are not generally in the spotlight.

'Johnny O'Hagan is the "bagman" for Leinster. He is probably the glue that keeps everything together for us. He's the type of guy that has a smile on his face every day. You could be Brian O'Driscoll or the lowest member of the squad and he'll treat you just the same. If you think you're up there, he'll bring you down a peg but if you're down there, he'll bring you up. He's a phenomenal character.'

FAST FOOD

2005 saw Victor's retirement after winning 39 caps but it also marked the beginning of a new career emerging for him as a media pundit on

RTÉ radio. Looking back on his first cap all that time ago, he recalls that while it was the highlight of his career, it also left him with an enduring legacy.

'The tradition is that when you win your first cap everybody buys you a drink. When I won mine, I took a knock on the head and had to go to bed for a while but I met up with the lads later on in the night. When I got back to the hotel I was starving. The problem was that it was three in the morning. I asked the receptionist how I might get some food. She told me that I could ring out for pizza but that it was very slow. Just after I dialled in my order, though, a guy walked in with a pizza. I was rooming with Neil Francis at the time and I quickly realised the pizza was for him. I pretended it was for me, though, and I brought it to the tearoom and scoffed it all down. When I went up to our room, "Franno" was watching television. I was absolutely stuffed but I pretended to be starving and asked him how I could get some food. He told me that I could phone for pizza but he told me not to bother because it was so slow that he had rung for a pizza over an hour earlier and it still hadn't arrived. I was very sympathetic and I asked him if he would mind waking me up and giving me a slice when his pizza finally arrived. He generously agreed.

'The only problem was that the next morning he found the pizza box in the tearoom and he discovered it was me that ate it. He actually was really annoyed and to this day he has never forgiven me! In fact, whenever he writes about me in his column he will never call me "Victor" – he insists on referring to me as "the pizza robber".'

13

TOUCH WOOD

TONY O'REILLY TELLS A GREAT STORY ABOUT BRENDAN BEHAN.
Behan turned up on a chat show on Canadian television totally drunk.
The presenter was very unimpressed and asked him why he was so
drunk. Behan replied, 'Well, a few weeks ago I was sitting in a pub in
Dublin and I saw a beer mat which said "Drink Canada Dry". So when
I came over here, I said I'd give it a go!' O'Reilly deftly uses that
incident to speak of the need to have the kind of positive attitude that
says, 'I'll give it a go.' That was the kind of upbeat mentality Keith
Gerard Mallinson Wood played with.

Among the Irish players chosen for the Lions tour in 1959 was the
late Gordon Wood. He was capped 29 times for Ireland between 1954
and 1961 at loose-head prop, scoring one international try and forming
a formidable front row in the late '50s and early '60s with Syd Millar
and Ronnie Dawson. As those four great philosophers Abba famously
suggested when they won Eurovision in 1974, the history book on the
shelf is always repeating itself. Thirty-five years after the 1959 Lions
tour, Ireland's tour to Australia would see the emergence of a new star
– Gordon's son Keith earned rave reviews for his performances as
hooker. In fact, Wood was singled out by Bob Dwyer as a potential
great on his Ireland debut against Australia in 1994. As early as the first
match, the potential was there.

Such adulation brings its own problems. From the young players'
point of view, it can delude them into fostering unrealistic ideas about
their own importance, encouraging them to imagine they are better than

they are, only to leave them embittered when their careers fail to deliver what they appeared to promise. Far more damaging than anything opponents can do to them is the burden of unrealistic expectations. Yet Wood went on to realise and even surpass those expectations with a series of dazzling performances for Ireland and the Lions (in South Africa in 1997 and Australia in 2001, playing in five of the six Tests) which saw him selected as IRB Player of the Year in 2001. In the process, he won 58 caps and became Ireland's most capped hooker, surpassing the great Ken Kennedy. Wood, though, was no ordinary hooker. He kicked like a fly-half, linked like a centre, jinked like a winger and was always inspired by his father's words: 'Never be ashamed at being proud of what you are good at.'

FLOWER POWER

Despite numerous serious injuries, his attitude was right. The late Bill Shankly is remembered almost as much for his famous words as for his achievements with Liverpool: "Some people believe football is a matter of life and death . . . it is much more important than that." It sounds like a cliché but rugby would become Wood's life. Everything else was an intrusion that tended to be pushed to one side as much as was practicable as he immersed himself in what really mattered: rugby.

Even in his most sublime moments, he played with a competitiveness that was as essential to him as breathing. He brought a no-nonsense approach to the game, believing that if something is worth doing, it is worth doing well, with everybody mucking in. Some players take a casual approach. In this category was a former England international who, as captain of the London Counties side, asked his players to do a team whistle as their entire training session. Keith Wood, though, was a stickler for preparing properly. This sometimes created problems during the run-up to his marriage. His wife-to-be was telling him about her dreams for their wedding. Keith, however, had his mind on one of Ireland's upcoming internationals and was not listening properly. His fiancée noticed this and decided to test him on how much he had taken in: 'So, what's my favourite flower?'

Woodie thought deeply: 'Self-raising?'

UNCLE FESTER

The bald wonder first made his name with Garryowen, but in 1996 he crossed the channel and joined Harlequins. The following year, he became the club's captain and then remained with them until his retirement, except for the 1999–2000 season when he returned to play with Munster, leading them to the narrowest of defeats in the Heineken Cup final. He first captained Ireland against Australia in November 1996 and immediately established himself as an inspirational leader. His motivational qualities were evident in one of the most tangible legacies of the 1997 Lions tour, England's John 'Bentos' Bentley's critically acclaimed video diary of the trip, *Living with Lions*, with which he made as big a name for himself off the pitch as he did on it. Woodie's passionate outbursts before games were one of the most striking features of the film. It was as if his tactics were to try and equalise before the other side scored.

Mind you, the attention would have been focused less on Wood had not one part of Bentley's recording been sabotaged. One of the unexpected developments on the video was that Austin Healey became known as 'Mr X the Invisible Wanker'. Having been on tour for eight weeks, Healey was experiencing sexual frustration and decided to retreat to the bathroom to give himself some pleasure. He was doing so with the bathroom door locked when all of a sudden it sprung open, as Bentos had picked the lock and before Healey knew what was happening, he had a camera filming him. Bentley went straight down to lunch and announced to the rest of the squad that there would be a special screening. Meanwhile, Healey broke into Bentley's room, turned the place upside down, found the video camera and erased the offending footage. Shortly afterwards, Bentley got the whole squad together. Bentley started the video. The players saw Bentley sneaking into Healey's room whispering, 'I know the bastard's in here somewhere, I'm going to catch him out.' They saw Bentos pick the lock but just as the door swung open, the screen went black. Healey wet himself laughing. Bentley's cinematic coup had vanished.

However, Woodie's one blemish was also to emerge on the trip. Bentley had the misfortune to be rooming with him. As a result of his shoulder problems, Keith could only sleep in one position. He propped two pillows under his shoulders and as soon as he began to sleep, he started snoring loudly. After seven sleepless nights, Bentley could take no more and sought medical advice. On the eighth night, as soon as Woodie started sleeping, Bentley kissed him on the cheek. For the next three nights, Woodie lay awake in case Bentley made further advances towards him.

Another story about Woodie goes back to the 2001 Lions tour. Graham Henry was surprised to see Wood hanging up a horseshoe on the wall. Henry said with a nervous laugh, 'Surely you don't believe that horseshoe will bring you good luck, do you, Keith?'

Wood chuckled, 'I believe no such thing, coach. Not at all. I am scarcely likely to believe in such foolish nonsense. However, I am told that a horseshoe will bring you good luck whether you believe in it or not!'

HOOKERS AND LOOSE . . .

Classically, hookers were players who won their own ball in the scrum, down whatever channel was nominated and who could throw the ball accurately into the lineout. Woodie rewrote the manual for hookers with his play anywhere style and willingness to kick. Indeed, there were times when he seemed to play more like a full-back, apparently believing that to win without risk was to triumph without glory. Almost every time he got the ball in his hands and took off on a bullocking run, he could bring the Lansdowne Road crowd to its feet with his sharp turn of pace for such a powerful figure and his joy at running at opponents or into space. He will forever be remembered for his pivotal role in depriving England of a Grand Slam in 2001, when the Ireland v. England game was held over due to foot-and-mouth disease. He scored the crucial try with a peel move from the lineout. Yet when a combative approach was needed, he could mix the bash with the flash.

From the outset of his career, he was recognised as not just one of the great rugby players but as one of the great characters in world rugby. His irreverent wit endeared him to everyone – apart from one of his Harlequins teammates who Keith claimed was dyslexic because he went to a toga party dressed as a goat!

There were some low moments, though. In 1999, he was embroiled in a ruck with the IRFU over a row about his image rights. Woodie was prepared to waive his international match fees rather than have the most distinctive face and head in rugby, apart from Jonah Lomu's, 'owned' and exploited by the IRFU sponsors. The row saw him forfeit his captaincy and his place on the Irish team.

2002, though, was his *annus horribilis*. He played in only one of Ireland's Six Nations games and then aggravated a neck injury in the World Cup qualifier against Russia. These problems paled into insignificance compared with the personal tragedies that affected him.

His brother Gordon died of a heart attack at the tender age of 41, two days before Keith was due to captain Ireland against Romania, and he missed the birth of his first child, Alexander, after being delayed on his return from the funeral. Then, two months later, his mother, Pauline, died on the morning of Ireland's international against Argentina.

One of the defining moments of the 2003 World Cup came when Ireland's campaign ended literally in tears when Wood poignantly cried after Ireland lost to France in the quarter-final. Within moments, he announced his retirement from rugby. His body just could not take any more, having endured 15 major operations since 1995.

In conversation with this scribe, the Irish coach Eddie O'Sullivan observed, 'I think we have lost a legend from the game of rugby and someone that will be known well after he is gone. He was written off by everybody when a disc in his neck leaked and then he wrecked his shoulder. The measure of the man is that he came back and the World Cup was his goal; nobody put more into the last World Cup than Keith Wood. From a rugby point of view, I think I described him once as the identikit of the professional rugby player – if you were to put together the perfect player, it would be him. The man pursued his profession as assiduously as he could, every minute of the day, to become the best player that he could be at any time. We've seen the retirement of a legend and I don't think he can be replaced.'

Woodie's name will live long in rugby folklore because there are so many stories told about him.

FORLORN IN THE USA

According to legend, Woodie went to Dallas after the 2003 World Cup for a well-deserved vacation. He checked into a downtown hotel but when he got to his room, he immediately called the front desk. Keith said, 'This here bed could sleep the whole Munster team! I only wanted a regular-sized bed.'

The clerk responded, 'That is a regular-sized bed, sir. You have to remember that everything's big in Texas.'

Woodie went to the hotel's bar and ordered a draught beer. When he was served, he said to the bartender, 'This is as big as Peter Clohessy. I only asked for a glass of beer.'

The bartender answered, 'That is a glass of beer, sir. You have to remember that everything's big in Texas!'

When the waiter in the hotel's dining room brought out the steak

Keith had ordered for dinner, Woodie exclaimed, 'That steak's as big as John Hayes' thigh and the baked potato is bigger than Reggie Corrigan's head. Where'd this come from?'

The waiter replied, 'It's all local, sir. You have to remember that everything's big in Texas!'

When the waiter asked Woodie if he wanted to see the dessert menu, Keith said that he might be able to squeeze something in but that after consuming all that food and drink he needed to use the restroom first. The waiter directed him to go down the hall to the first door on the right.

By this time, Wood was quite inebriated and mistakenly went through the first door on the left. He walked across the tiled floor and fell into the swimming pool. When the rugby legend came spluttering to the surface, he yelled out, 'For f⋯k's sake, please don't flush!'

14

THE CLAW

Prop forwards don't get Valentine cards for religious reasons –
God made them ugly!

Tony O'Reilly

THE ENGLISH LANGUAGE HAS YET TO INVENT A WORD THAT adequately sums up Peter Clohessy. 'Legend' and 'character' give hints at his essence but no more than that. He is one of a kind. It was Mae West who famously observed, 'A hard man is good to find.' In Irish rugby, we found one in Peter Clohessy. He knew how to mix it. He believed that a good prop forward should be so mean that if he owned the Atlantic Ocean, he wouldn't give you a wave.

It was evident from an early age that the Claw was going to be the strong silent type. According to folklore, when he was four he went to the dentist. The dentist tried to strike up a conversation with the future rugby legend. 'How old are you?'

No response.

The dentist then asked, 'Don't you know how old you are?'

Immediately, four fingers went up.

'OK,' the dentist then asked, 'and do you know how old that is?'

Four little fingers went up once again.

Continuing the effort to get a response, the dentist asked him, 'Can you talk?'

The young Clohessy looked at him menacingly and asked, 'Can you count?'

AFFAIRS OF THE HEART

In the Shannonside city, sport is a communal obsession, as is evident in the astonishing breadth and depth of knowledge on all major sports and the highly polished and refined sense of the sporting aesthetic. The Claw could not have chosen a better or more nurturing environment to begin his career. Between 1988 and 2002, he would both feed off and fuel the fires of passion in one of rugby's greatest shrines in a career that saw him capped 54 times for Ireland. The passion for rugby in Limerick is the envy of nearly every touring side in the world and Clohessy is quick to acknowledge the debt of gratitude owed to this most benevolent of patrons. He also had the right type of temperament and physicality to endear himself to the Limerick faithful. There were very occasional blips.

'One Tuesday evening after a particularly galling loss to Shannon, I was heading onto the field for training with Young Munster and there was this old lady, I'd say she was 85 if she was a day, and she called me over to the wire. I knew I was in for an earful straight away. She shouted at me, "What the hell was wrong with you on Saturday? You were hoisted so high in the scrum, I was going to send you a parachute!"'

The home of Limerick rugby, Thomond Park, is famous for the 20-foot wall which surrounds it but which is insufficient to prevent the ball from leaving the ground from time to time. When balls were lost, the crowd were wont to shout, 'Never mind the ball, get on with the game.'

Yet Clohessy also had a sophisticated rugby intelligence. There was a lot more to his game than 'Hump it, bump it, whack it'. This approach might be, for those of a certain disposition, a recipe for a good sex life but it won't win you 54 caps and a Lions selection.

Clohessy's keen brain was to the fore in one of the bonding exercises before the Lions tour in 1997. As is common practice with rugby teams, they were taken to a military base for exercises. At one point, they were given an instruction in unarmed self-defence. After their instructor presented a number of different situations in which they might find themselves, he asked Clohessy, 'What steps would you take if someone were coming at you with a large, sharp knife?'

The Claw replied, 'Big ones.'

Clohessy is said to be the only man in Limerick who can leave his car unlocked. His love of the city is immediately apparent when he is asked about the highlights of his career.

'I suppose my first highlight was winning the All-Ireland League with Young Munster in 1993. After that, the others were my first cap for Ireland, beating England at Twickenham in 1994 and France in Paris in 2000.'

The Limerick bias is also evident when he is asked who are the great characters of rugby: 'Mick Galwey, Philip Danaher, Keith Wood and Anthony Foley' – all players associated with Limerick clubs.

Another passion is Munster.

'The low points in my career were losing two Heineken Cup finals with Munster. To be so close twice and to lose on both occasions was very tough. We just seemed to be always the bridesmaids.'

The manner of the defeat in the 2002 Heineken Cup final – Neil Back's infamous 'backhander' – left a bitter taste. One Munster fan was heard to remark, 'The Leicester Tigers should be renamed the Leicester Cheetahs.'

They also told a story about Back himself. In this account, Back went on a skiing trip but was knocked unconscious by the chairlift. He called his insurance company from the hospital but it refused to cover his injury.

'Why is this injury not covered?' he asked.

'You got hit in the head by a chairlift,' the insurance rep said. 'That makes you an idiot and we consider that a pre-existing condition.'

The Claw has happier memories of another English World Cup hero.

'I always got on well with Jason Leonard. When we played England, there was always a bit of banter between us because we'd been playing against each other so long. With about 20 minutes to go of our trouncing at Twickenham in 2002, Justin took me by surprise when he said, "Peter, I believe you're away to a wedding straight after the game?"

'I am not sure how he knew that but I was indeed off to a friend's wedding in Cork immediately after the match. I replied, "The quicker I get out of this place the f**king better."'

MISFORTUNE AFFLICTS THE BRAVE

The Claw did have a few setbacks. In 1997, he was chosen among an elite group of players – Martin Johnson, Neil Jenkins, Tim Stimpson, Nick Beal, John Bentley, Ieuan Evans, Tony Underwood, Allan Bateman, Scott Gibbs, Will Greenwood, Jeremy Guscott, Alan Tait, Paul Grayson, Gregor Townsend, Matt Dawson, Austin Healey, Rob

Howley, Jason Leonard, Graham Rowntree, Tom Smith, David Young, Mark Regan, Barrie Williams, Keith Wood, Jeremy Davidson, Simon Shaw, Doddie Weir, Neil Back, Lawrence Dallaglio, Richard Hill, Eric Miller, Scott Quinnell, Tim Rodber and Rob Wainwright – to tour with the Lions to South Africa but although he made the trip to London to meet up with the squad, he was forced to return home with an injury.

Before the 2002 Heineken Cup semi-final, he faced a more serious injury when he was badly burned in a domestic accident. This prompted his wife to remark, 'I always knew you'd go out in a blaze of glory but I didn't think you'd do it literally.' The small matter of multiple burns was not enough to deter Clohessy from playing in the game. In solidarity with the Claw, Munster fans wore T-shirts to the game saying 'Bitten and Burnt, but Not Beaten'.

A much happier event had come earlier that year when Clohessy's son, Luke, accompanied him as he led the Irish team out against Wales in the Six Nations to celebrate his fiftieth cap. To add to the occasion, he was followed closely onto the Lansdowne Road turf by his great friend Mick Galwey, captaining his country for the first time on the famous sod. Clohessy played like a man possessed in Ireland's demolition job of the Welsh, even setting up a try for Geordan Murphy with a masterful reverse pass. When he was substituted near the end, he received a massive standing ovation.

It was not always thus. One man's meat is another's poison. Clohessy unexpectedly found himself cast as the *bête noire* of Irish rugby in 1996. During a Five Nations match in Paris, he 'misplaced his boot' on Olivier Roumat's head during a ruck. The 6 ft 6 in., 242-lb lock was himself no angel. He was once so incensed by the loud snoring of his roommate Abdel Benazzi on the eve of a Test that he ran over to his bed and punched the mighty Moroccan-born forward.

Clohessy's character was unfairly traduced after the affair, and the amount of intimidation and provocation he was subjected to was ignored. He was quoted after one match against French opposition as saying, 'It's a bit much to have some French f**ker gouging you in the eyes without him grabbing you by the bollocks as well.'

The six-month ban that ensued and the trial by media almost caused him to walk away from the game, but one maid in shining armour came to his rescue.

'The biggest influence on my career has been my wife, Anna. After all the bashing I got in the media after the stamping incident, I was very tempted to pack in rugby but she persuaded me to stick with it. She really got me through what was a difficult period for me. While I was suspended from rugby here, I went to play in Brisbane, Australia. That was my introduction to playing rugby at professional level and an experience I really enjoyed.'

Some birds are not meant to be caged; their feathers are just too bright. A series of top-notch performances for Munster and Ireland quickly earned Clohessy any redemption that might have been necessary in the eyes of rugby fans, to the extent that he became a father-figure of Irish rugby, especially for young players. He adhered to the motto 'Say little but say it well'. He earned the nickname 'Judge Dredd' in the dressing-room because his word was law.

DON'T FORGET TO REMEMBER ME

How would he like to be remembered by Irish rugby fans?

'I'd just like them to think of me as someone who always played in the green jersey, or any jersey, with passion.'

History has already decreed that this is an incontestable fact. The Claw himself has many happy memories of his time in rugby.

'I think the nice thing is that when I look back now at my career, what I remember most is all the good times we had on and off the pitch. Although we trained hard, we had a lot of fun. My fondest memory is of before we played Scotland one time. The night before the match, Mick Galwey discovered his togs were missing. There was a minor panic because nobody else had any to spare. Eventually, someone got him some togs. Ireland were sponsored by Nike at the time. The problem was that Mick's togs didn't have the Nike name or swoosh so someone gave him a black marker and he wrote the name Nike on the togs. Later that night, I crept into his room and changed the word "Nike" to "Mike" and wrote "Mike loves Joan". The next day, we were changing in the dressing-room before the match when I saw Mick putting on his togs. He didn't notice the change but noticed I was laughing at him. He asked, "OK, what have you done to me?" When I told him, he had a great laugh. It was just an hour before a big international but it was a great way of breaking the tension for us.'

15

GALLIMH

THE RICH HISTORY OF THE GAELIC ATHLETIC ASSOCIATION HAS been greatly enhanced by its cross-fertilisation with Irish rugby. Dick Spring has an impressive GAA pedigree. His father, Dan Spring of the Kerins O'Rahilly's club, captained Kerry to All-Ireland football victory in 1940. His maternal uncles, the Laide brothers of Crotta O'Neill's, are considered among Kerry's finest hurlers. Dick himself played both hurling and football for Kerry and might well have gone on to emulate his father's and uncles' achievements had not rugby beckoned.

At times, though, claims about the GAA's connections with rugby have been exaggerated. Former Ireland out-half Mick Quinn's father was not a sporting man but he was very proud that his son played for Ireland. He seldom drank but when he did, he really knew how to enjoy himself. Once, he was having a few drinks with John Joe Whyte of the *Irish Times*. He told John Joe that Mick had acquired his ability from him and that he himself played for Monaghan in the 1928 All-Ireland Gaelic football final – not even knowing at this stage if Monaghan had played in the final that year! The next day, this story appeared verbatim in the *Times*. John Joe had not realised he was being wound up and didn't bother to check out the facts.

The intertwining of Gaelic football and rugby is particularly evident in Kerry. Their 1981 All-Ireland-winning captain Jimmy Deenihan also played rugby for Tralee. Mick Galwey could have been one of the Kerry greats but chose the road less travelled in his native county and opted for rugby as his main game. His decision was vindicated with 41 caps for Ireland (Galwey captaining his country in four of those games), over 130 appearances for Munster, a place on the Lions tour in 1993 and the award of an honorary Doctor in Laws degree from Trinity College in 2002 for his services to rugby.

THE GENTLE GIANT

It is only when you meet someone like Mick Galwey, or ''Gallimh, that you really understand the phrase 'larger than life'. Although he was the epitome of lionheartedness when under the fiercest pressure during a match, he is modest and unassuming off the field. Time passes quickly in his company.

When he was a boy, his hero was Mick O'Connell.

'I came from a football area – Currow, near Castleisland – the same area as Moss Keane came from. I played for my parish side every year from when I was 9 until I was 32, when contractual obligations prohibited me. Football was my first love, before rugby came along. After I left school, my interest in football increased when I started working as a baker with Charlie Nelligan, who was a star with the great Kerry team. I got Minor trials with the Kerry team and played at midfield for them in the Munster Minor final in the centenary year when we lost to a very strong Tipperary team. Three years later, we beat them at Under-21 level only to lose the All-Ireland final to a first-class Donegal side.'

History casts a long shadow in the area of Kerry where Mick grew up. Memories of the civil war lasted a very long time. This was most tellingly revealed in a conversation between supporters of Éamon de Valera and Michael Collins in the 1960s.

The Dev fan said, 'De Valera was as straight as Christ and as spiritually strong.'

The Collins fan replied, 'Wasn't it a great pity the hoor wasn't crucified as young?'

Galwey joined Kerry in the wake of their infamous 'Only Bendix Could Whitewash This Lot' advertisement. The morning of the All-Ireland final in 1985, two Sunday newspapers carried full-page ads which showed several Kerry players in a state of undress as they posed around a washing machine. The internal strife caused by the advert – the players went on strike over the manner in which they were to be compensated for their venture into modelling – was to Galwey's advantage.

'Some of the players were on strike and the club were looking for 15 lads to go to Tourmakeady in Mayo so I was brought into the Senior team because I had played Under-21 the previous year. It was a weekend away and I'll never forget it, especially because we all got Aran jumpers after the match, which was great. Then I was called into the regular squad for training.

'I was 19 at the time and it was a great experience for me to be rubbing shoulders with all these great players and Mick O'Dwyer, the coach, who were not just very talented but totally committed as well. I was very impressed by their professional approach and what I learned from them probably stood to me in my rugby career and gave me an edge. Every game with them was very competitive, which is not a bad thing.

'It was very intimidating going in to train with such fantastic players. Mick O'Dwyer was a great man to push the young fellas especially. The training back then was like the way we train in rugby now: short and sharp. Sometimes lads would get sick in training but he never managed to make me sick! Afterwards, it was a case of us going down to the Imperial Hotel in Tralee and we used to have steaks and chips with onions and a pint of milk. Now it's different and you're not advised to eat like that but it didn't do that Kerry team any harm.

'Mick O'Dwyer had a great way of making us play in a very competitive way and of getting the best out of his players. He would get old lads sprinting against young lads on a one-to-one basis. Wire to wire, it was called. Then we'd play backs against forwards, which was awesome. Some of the tackling was ferocious and you'd never see anything like that in a proper match. It was kind of like the law of the jungle but it really prepared fellas for Championship football.

'In fairness to O'Dwyer, he really knew when to push and when to rest players. I remember in 1986 up to the Munster final he hadn't really pushed the players too hard and after the match he announced that the team were to have a few days off but that six people would have to return early for extra training. Everyone's ears pricked up straight away. Paídí O'Sé, Eoin "the Bomber" Liston and Seanie Walsh were three of the names. They were all exceptional players but for different reasons probably needed a bit extra training. In the autumn of my career, I reached that stage myself – where you have to train twice as hard just to keep up with the young fellas. I was brought in with them because I wasn't sharp enough and I needed extra training. The six of us were given extra laps, and push-ups and sit-ups. It was hard work but it had to be done.

'It wasn't all criticism, though. O'Dwyer would pull you aside from time to time and say you were going well or whatever. At the time, Jack O'Shea and Ambrose O'Donovan held the midfield places, and Dermot Hanafin and I were challenging for them. We were never going to get ahead of them but we kept them honest. I can remember Seanie Walsh saying one time that the contests between the four of us in the midfield were very good.'

Galwey could hardly have chosen a more auspicious occasion for his Championship debut.

'That summer, I came on as a sub for the Bomber in the final ten minutes of the All-Ireland semi-final when he went off with a hamstring injury. It was thrilling to come on at Croke Park against Meath, who were a "coming" side while Kerry were on the way down. It was a baptism of fire because I went in on Mick Lyons! Mick, obviously, was a great footballer but I wasn't two minutes on the pitch before he gave me a dig in the ribs. I was still very nervous, so I swung back at him but I didn't connect. I have to tell you, he didn't waste any time in letting me know he was still the main man! Some young fella wasn't going to steal his glory. I played a few times on him after that and he turned out to be a grand fella but my first introduction to Mick Lyons wasn't the nicest!'

The encounter with Mick Lyons was the second-biggest fright of Galwey's life. According to legend, the biggest came one night in his courting days when he took a short cut through a graveyard and he heard a tapping sound. As he walked, the tapping got louder and his fright grew into terror. Suddenly, he came across a man crouched down chiselling at a gravestone.

'Oh, thank goodness,' Gallimh said with great relief. 'You frightened me. I didn't know what that noise was. What are you doing?'

The other man turned his face into the moonlight as he said to the rugby star, 'They spelt my name wrong.'

The Meath match was the summit of Galwey's Gaelic career.

'I touched the ball once in that semi-final. I caught it and I'll always remember passing it on to Ger Power, who in turn gave it on to Mike Sheehy, but the goalie made one of the saves of the year. I really felt that I was part of the set-up because I had actually played a game.

'Coming up to the All-Ireland against Tyrone, I injured my ankle but

I was lucky in that Mick O'Dwyer kept it quiet and carried me along for the final. Having got a taste of Croke Park in the semi-final, it was a step up again to be there for the final. It looked bad for us when Kevin McCabe stepped up to take the penalty but after we drove the ball over the bar, we got into our flow. I remember Timmy O'Dowd coming on as a sub and playing a stormer, as did Pat Spillane. That was the great thing about that Kerry team, there was always someone who could turn the game for you.

'Earlier that year, I had won a Munster Senior Cup medal with Shannon RFC. Shortly before the Tyrone final, we played the football League champions Laois in a benefit for the charity GOAL. After the match, we were going into O'Donoghue's pub, which is a real Kerry haunt, and Denis "Oige" Moran turned around to me and said, "Jesus, Mick, you could be the only man to win a Senior Cup medal in rugby and an All-Ireland medal in football in the one year." I remember thinking that would be a wonderful achievement if it came to pass.

'The following year, on foot of vintage performances from Larry Tompkins and Shay Fahy, Cork beat us in the Munster final. It was the end of the road for that great Kerry team. A lot of players retired after that, so it was the end of an era. I played for Kerry for a few years after that, mostly as a sub. My main commitment was to rugby, which probably didn't go down too well at Kerry at the time. I do regret not being able to play more for Kerry but overall I wouldn't change anything about my career.'

Galwey had the good fortune to play in a team full of characters.

'Paídí O'Sé was a great personality. He stood out because he was so committed and enthusiastic. Even back then, you knew he'd be the one to keep going and make his mark in management. Football was his life then. Tommy Doyle was actually very funny. Publicly he kept to himself but with the lads he was great fun. Charlie Nelligan was also a great character. The young fellas had to show a bit of respect to those guys.

'Dermot Hanafin was a gas man and was always in great form. Dermot and I had the distinction of playing together at midfield for Kerry in an Under-21 match which we lost to Clare. No disrespect to them, but at the time it was the worst thing in the world that could happen, to lose to Clare. Dermot brought a breath of fresh air to everything. He was a great mimic and was always going into Micheál O'Muircheartaigh mode but he was also great taking off O'Dwyer.

Micko would be wondering why the lads would be collapsing with laughter, not realising he was being "done". O'Dwyer was always very keen to keep an eye on all the balls at training so that he had the same number at the finish as he did at the start, but there were always fellas trying to steal them on him which did nothing for his blood pressure!

'The best fun, though, came after training as soon as O'Dwyer left the dressing-room! If somebody got a bit of a bollocking from O'Dwyer the whole squad would take the mickey out of him.

'That's one thing that rugby has in common with Gaelic football: there are so many characters, like Keith Wood. Like the Bomber, Woodie was one player who could turn a game. He played hurling and Gaelic football in Clare and that didn't do him any harm. Woodie was the world's number-one hooker but he was still one of the lads. He was one of the "Limerick Under-14s", as we called ourselves, with myself and Peter Clohessy. Of course Clohessy is one of the great personalities of Irish sport. I remember once playing in France with Munster when Peter got a bad knock on the knee and had to be carried off. It was the strangest sight I ever saw in a match, because the guys who brought on the stretcher for him were wearing wellingtons! I said to the Claw, "Don't worry, the fire brigade are coming."'

How does Gallimh react to the criticism that Mick O'Dwyer held on to his team too long and didn't do enough to introduce new players at Kerry?

'There's probably something in that but, to be fair to O'Dwyer, it was hard to change such a successful side. I don't think that he ever left better players on the sideline. Anyway, O'Dwyer's record speaks for itself.'

YOU CAN BE MY HERO

Galwey missed out on the rebuilding programme which followed O'Dwyer's departure because he had opted to devote his energy to rugby. At the root of his interest in the oval ball was another noted Gaelic player.

'As Moss Keane was from Currow, he was my hero. There was massive interest from people in the area when he started to play for Ireland. The first time I saw him play, though, was in a Gaelic match in Currow. He was their full-forward and target man and he did the job well, though I think rugby robbed him of his athleticism. You need bulk and brute force for rugby rather than the finesse that makes a great football player. Then there was the whole Moss legend, which added to the glamour of rugby.'

A line about a Lions reunion dinner – 'Moss Keane and Willie Duggan read that alcohol was bad for you, so they gave up reading' – gives a clue as to one part of the myth that was Moss. On the Ireland team Moss linked up with another former distinguished footballer from Kerry, Dick Spring. After a match at Twickenham, Spring and Keane returned home and had a very-late-night session in St Mary's rugby club. They stayed in Moss's 'high-class' flat in Rathmines. They woke up the next day at midday very much the worse for wear and went to 'Joe's Steakhouse' for some food. Moss ordered a mixed grill. Spring's tastes were more modest and he just asked for plaice and chips. When the food arrived Moss looked a bit queasy. He looked up and said, 'Springer, would you ever mind swapping? Spring duly obliged. That day has entered legend because it is said to be the only time in his life Moss turned his back on a big meal!

Another time, Moss and Spring were together for a match in London. They were both starving on the Saturday night. The two of them crept into the kitchen of their hotel and sought out some food. Suddenly, they were caught in the act by the porter. They expected to have the face eaten off them. After a dramatic pause, he said, 'Ye know, ye're lucky lads. There's now three Kerry men in the room.' The two lads got the meal of their lives.

There were other formative influences, too, on the young Galwey.

'Castleisland had a great tradition of rugby as well and John Browne, the coach at Castleisland RFC then, had a huge influence on my development as a rugby player. I think back to playing for Ireland against Western Australia in Perth at the Subiaco Oval in front of the Prendiville stand which was called after a fella from Castleisland.'

Notwithstanding his commitment to rugby, Galwey retains a keen interest in the fortunes of his native county's favourite game. Which of the great Kerry team did he admire most?

'They all impressed me. The Bomber stood out. He was exceptional but he was probably the player that had to work the hardest on his game and, a bit like myself, if he didn't stay away from the table, he put on the pounds. He was one of the players that could change the direction of a game for you. The likes of Pat Spillane, Mike Sheehy and Jack O'Shea probably got more of the limelight, but to me the Bomber was the key to Kerry's success.

'I remember playing an Under-14 club match once and the opposition had this 11 year old at corner-forward who could do things with the ball that nobody else could. It was Maurice Fitzgerald and you just knew he was going to be a real star. I was very young then and not a great judge of a player but I remember saying, "Jaysus, that guy's amazing."

'Dublin had a lot of great players at the time, even though we never liked the Dubs! Kevin Moran was the one who caught the eye, especially because he made it in both codes. Roscommon gave Kerry some of their toughest matches and you'd have to mention Dermot Earley who was an exceptional player, maybe the best in my time not to have won an All-Ireland medal. When Kerry were beating Cork every year in the Munster final the Leesiders had some great players like Dinny Allen. Kevin Kehilly was probably the only player who could ever have held the Bomber. Offaly's Matt Connor was a class act and scored freely against a great Kerry back line which said a lot about his talent.'

In Kerry, you are considered to have an inferiority complex if you only consider yourself as good as anybody else, so it comes as little surprise to discover that Gallimh's dream team is the Kerry team of the '70s and '80s. He feels that most of that team could also have been great rugby players.

'Jack O'Shea was a natural athlete and a powerful player who would have made a great number 8 or flank-forward. The Bomber would have been a good second row. You could slot all the great Kerry players into positions on the rugby pitch. Mike Sheehy would have been a natural out-half. Paídí O'Sé would have been the perfect prop forward – in the Peter Clohessy mould!'

THE KERRY CONNECTION

Gallimh feels that his training as a Gaelic footballer was a big help to his rugby career, primarily in terms of having an eye for the ball. However, he feels that the primary benefit of his association with Kerry was not to his abilities on the playing field. Former Ireland rugby coach the late Mick Doyle's first love was the GAA, though when he began his secondary education as a boarder in Newbridge College, rugby exploded into his life. 'Doyler' aired his trenchant views about the state of Irish rugby through his weekly column in the *Sunday Independent*. His criticism was such that Moss Keane once said to him, 'Thanks be to Jaysus I don't play any more. Otherwise I'd be afraid to open the paper on Sunday because of what you'd say about me!' Gallimh never incurred Doyler's wrath.

'The best help my Kerry roots have been to my rugby reputation was that Mick Doyle never wrote anything critical about me – unlike other second-row forwards that people could think of! In Kerry, it's a bit like the Mafia: come hell or high water we always stick together!'

Doyle was sometimes far from generous with his praise for the Ireland team, so when he described an Irish victory as an '80-minute orgasm', you knew he was talking about one hell of a match. The match which elicited this enthusiastic response in 1993 was a 17–3 win over England. It was Gallimh's finest hour in the green jersey.

In a team performance in which all the boys in green were heroes, it is difficult to single out one player for special attention, but Galwey particularly deserves recognition. Six weeks before that match, he lay in a Dublin hospital with his neck in a brace, his rugby future shrouded in uncertainty. At one point, he was even told that his playing career was history. A shadow on his X-ray cast an ominous cloud on his prospects. For four fear-filled days, he waited for the all-clear. Then it was out of hospital and onto the training field. A week later, he played for Ireland against France – a game which offered the prospect of redemption for the Irish side after embarrassment at Murrayfield. The next match saw Ireland (with Eric Elwood making a hugely impressive debut) overcome the Welsh in Cardiff. The win over England was sealed when Galwey scored a fine try, helping him to become (with Nick Popplewell) one of only two Irishmen to secure a place on the Lions tour to New Zealand.

One of Galwey's biggest rivals for a place in the Irish second row was Paddy Johns. Johns was a dentist by profession. Galwey once joked that Paddy's motto was 'We can floss that bridge when we come to it.'

THE AULD ENEMY

Mick is one of rugby's great diplomats. He is loath to criticise anybody. As with many Kerry people, you have to read between the lines to figure out what he is saying. When asked his opinion about Brian Ashton's tenure as Irish coach, he kicks for touch. Galwey denies that towards the ignominious end of Ashton's reign, one of the Irish squad asked him, 'Tell me, how long have you been with us not counting tomorrow?' It was rumoured that a prominent Irish official said to

Ashton, 'Today, I'm going to mix business and pleasure: you're fired!'

In 2004, a new chapter in Gallimh's life began when he was appointed coach of Shannon, having enjoyed great success with the club as a player. It is a difficult appointment, particularly given the fierce competition between Shannon and local Limerick rivals Young Munster and Garryowen. In 2003, immediately after England won the World Cup, BBC Five Live were getting the responses of ecstatic English fans at the match when they stumbled across a sad-looking Shannon supporter. He was asked if he was happy with the result.

Fan: Not at all, I'm Irish, I'm from Limerick.

Reporter: But would you not support England when Ireland are no longer in the competition?

Fan: No way.

Reporter: Why not?

Fan: 800 years of oppression.

Reporter: Is there ever any time you would support England?

Fan: If they were playing Young Munster or Garryowen.

16

SUBLIME SIMON

THE ULTIMATE TEST OF A PLAYER IN ANY SPORT IS WHETHER THEY have the power to make the pulse skip a beat when they are in full flight. Once a great player gets the ball, a buzz of expectancy goes around the ground. Before Brian O'Driscoll came on the scene, the one player who consistently had this effect was Simon Geoghegan. Unlike O'Driscoll, Geoghegan did not have the good fortune to play with a strong Irish team. Indeed, sadly, he seemed to spend much of his international career waiting for a pass. It is surprising that he never got the nickname 'Cinderella', because it often seemed nobody wanted to take him to the ball. However, at his best he lit up the stage like a flash of forked lightning, brilliant, thrilling and, from the opposition's point of view, frightening. He scored 11 tries in his 37 caps for Ireland. Geoghegan was born and bred in England, so why did he play rugby for Ireland?

'My father is from Killimor, County Galway, a great hurling area, and growing up I spent most of my summer holidays there, so I got a great love for places like Ballinasloe and all the Galway area. Because of that, I always had a sense of being Irish.'

EVERY BREATH YOU TAKE

Despite the young Geoghegan's talent and speed, there was a cloud on the horizon which could have threatened his rugby career.

'When I was 15 or 16, I discovered I had a condition known as exercise-induced asthma. It is different from conventional asthma in that, as its name suggests, it is brought on by strenuous activity. With medication, though, I can cope, and it doesn't inhibit me at all, really. My only problem, if you want to call it that, is that I don't have a great lung capacity.'

As a teenager, he smoked 20 cigarettes a day. Did that contribute to his breathing difficulties?

'I was surprised to discover that it was not a significant factor. It's really all down to the asthma. Willie Duggan used to run on with a packet of fags in his pocket and cadge a light from somebody in the crowd and it didn't seem to do him any harm!'

Did he have a misspent youth? He laughs but his tone quickly changes to that of a man who knows exactly where he is going in life.

'Well, at boarding school I was doing a lot of things I shouldn't have been doing and while I was doing OK on the rugby field, I wasn't doing as well as I could have been. I decided it was going to be all or nothing, so the cigarettes went and the serious drinking went and I started to make my mark with London Irish. In 1991, I won my first cap for Ireland and, fortunately, I think I developed a good rapport with the crowd at Lansdowne Road.'

One man familiar with Geoghegan's condition is Ireland coach Eddie O'Sullivan.

As a player, O'Sullivan was a star for many years with Garryowen. However, his success on the field was a triumph over the odds.

'It was Tony Ward who first brought me onto the Garryowen team. When I started playing with them, I discovered that I was having major problems with breathlessness. It was very traumatic. I was told I had exercise-induced asthma. When I was coaching with Connacht, I came into contact with Simon Geoghegan, who was one of the greatest Irish players of his generation. He too had the condition, which will surprise most people, because he had such incredible speed. He was one of that rare group of players who could electrify the crowd with his thrilling runs. Every time he got the ball in his hands, the crowd at Lansdowne would be almost on its feet. Anyone fortunate enough to have seen him zooming down the wing will never forget it. He is a legend of Irish rugby. He probably was in the right place at the wrong time. Had he been in an Irish side with more class players like him, such as Brian O'Driscoll, he would have got the success his great talent deserved.'

DESTINED FOR GREATNESS

Great tries in 1991 against Wales and England established Geoghegan as the rising star of Irish rugby. However, the following season, as Ireland lost every game, he got no chance to impress. Things went from bad to worse the next season, when he had hoped to make the Lions tour to New Zealand. His ability as a defender was not just questioned, it was derided – particularly after the way Derek Stark scored a try "on" him in Murrayfield.

'Yes, 1993 was a bad season for me. My club form was poor and that probably affected my confidence when playing for Ireland.'

His problems at the time were not just on the field. He was temporarily suspended from the Irish squad. What prompted this exclusion?

'I'm not the most diplomatic person in the world. When I give my opinion, I tend not to mince my words. I was unhappy with the way the team was playing and the fact that I was getting so few opportunities, and I made my views known in a public way. But that's all water under the bridge now.'

A prominent rugby journalist openly questioned his commitment to the Irish team because of an incident in which he threw his Ireland jersey on the ground. Did this type of criticism hurt him?

'Not in the least. Anybody who knew me knew of my commitment to Ireland and judged me by what I did when I was wearing my green jersey on the pitch, not by what I did with it in the dressing-room.'

It was no coincidence that Ireland's best performances in the early '90s coincided with those of the flying winger, notably Ireland's 17–3 victory over England in 1993. The tragedy was that the eye-catching appearance came too late for him to claim a place on the Lions tour. When injury struck, it was his partner on the wing, Richard Wallace, and not the golden boy of Irish rugby that got the call to go south as a replacement.

Still basking in the glory of their win over the All Blacks, the English expected to extract retribution in 1994 at Twickenham but a splendid try from Geoghegan helped Ireland to secure another shock win, this time on a score of 13–12. Geoghegan recalls the game with undisguised affection.

'We performed excellently for 80 minutes. It was probably the first pass I received all season with a bit of space in front of me.'

TO BATH AND BACK

The same year saw Geoghegan departing from his club, London Irish, for the spa town of Bath. The area around Gloucester, Bath and Bristol is a hotbed of English rugby. Bath's status in English rugby during the 1990s is comparable to that of the great Kerry team of the 1970s and early 1980s in Gaelic football. Joining Bath was a move Geoghegan made with his eyes open.

'I knew I was taking a risk. There was no guarantee that I would get my place on the team. Reputations meant nothing at Bath. You either performed to the highest level or you were off the team. That was not a problem for me. In fact it was the reverse. I knew that if I joined Bath, I would be playing at a consistently higher standard. Basically, I had the confidence in my own ability to believe I could hold my own at the highest level. But believe me, the work ethic was very strong in the club.'

Bath were the team of all the talents. They even tried to sign David 'Campo' Campese but even their resources could not stretch to Campo's salary demands. The joke at the time was that Campese was either going to France to play for the Cannes Openers or to China for the Peking Toms.

Geoghegan enjoyed the folklore about the giants of Bath rugby. After their summer break, Simon was talking to the England fly-half Stuart Barnes about his trip to Switzerland. In particular, he asked Barnes if he had enjoyed the beautiful scenery.

'Not really,' Barnes replied, 'I couldn't see much because of all the mountains in the way.'

Another concerned Jeremy Guscott. Guscott was walking through the centre of Bath one day when an old man stopped him and held out paper and pen. Jeremy gave him his best smile and assumed it was an autograph hunter. His ego took a bit of a blow when the old man said, 'Can you address this postcard for me? My arthritis is acting up and I can't even hold a pen.'

'Certainly, sir.' said Guscott. He wrote out the address and also agreed to write a short message and sign the card for the man. Finally he asked, 'Now, is there anything else I can do for you?'

The old man said, 'Yes, at the end could you just add, "PS Please excuse the sloppy handwriting"?'

The most distinctive face on the Bath team was Gareth Chilcott. He was a very effective prop forward but no Tom Cruise. His wife was complaining about her husband spending so much time in the club bar, so one night he took her along with him. 'What'll you have?' he asked.

'Oh, I don't know. The same as you, I suppose,' she replied. So Chilcott ordered a couple of Jack Daniels and threw his down in one.

His wife watched him, then took a sip from her glass and immediately spat it out. 'Yuck, that's terrible!' she spluttered. 'I don't know how you can drink this stuff.'

'Well, there you go,' cried Chilcott. 'And you think I'm out enjoying myself every night.'

NEIL DOWN

Tragically, injury brought Geoghegan's career to a premature end, and Irish, as well as world, rugby was deprived of one of its most thrilling wingers. They may have been brilliant, but Geoghegan's performances have not always been enhanced by his Irish teammates. He was rooming with Neil Francis the night before the Fiji game in November 1995. Francis got thirsty during the night and disposed of a glass of water he found in the bathroom. The next morning when Geoghegan went to retrieve his contact lenses, he discovered that Francis had unwittingly drunk them with the glass of water.

17

WHERE WE SPORTED AND PLAYED

DONAL LENIHAN WAS BORN INTO A GAA-MAD FAMILY. HIS KERRY-born father, Gerald, played with the hurling immortals Jack Lynch and Christy Ring but still found time to become an international heavyweight boxer. Although Lenihan was destined for a glittering career with Ireland and the Lions, his heroes were not rugby players but the stars of the 1973 All-Ireland-winning Cork Gaelic football side, like Jimmy Barry-Murphy and Billy Morgan. As is so often the case, his rugby career owes a huge amount to his school, CBC, and to the influence of one man, Brother Philip O'Reilly, who has been responsible for the early development of a string of internationals.

THE KEANE EDGE

After captaining his school to Munster Junior and Senior Schools titles, Lenihan was capped for Irish Schools and would later follow this up with caps at Under-23, B and Senior level, joining a select group to have been honoured in this way, including Jimmy Bowen, Moss Finn, Harry Harbison, Brian McCall, Jim McCoy and Donal Spring.

'My first full cap, against Australia in 1981, was really a natural progression from all that went before. Trevor Ringland also made his debut that day. There's always a special friendship between players who won their first caps on the same day. But I usually roomed with Moss Keane. He was coming to the end of his career at that stage. Our room was like an alternative medicine centre, with pollen, garlic tablets and a half-dozen eggs. The mornings of internationals, I'd wake up to see Moss eating three raw eggs. It's not the sort of sight that you want to wake up to! Having said that, Moss was an enormous help to me in the early days. I especially appreciated that he let me make the decisions about the lineout.'

Lenihan was a key member of the Triple Crown-winning sides of 1982 and 1985. He has fond memories of many of the players who soldiered with him in various triumphs.

'We had great players like Nigel Carr. I've never met anyone who could match Nigel for fitness and commitment. He used to do 1,000 sit-ups while watching *Top of the Pops* and 1,000 press-ups while watching some other programme.

'The best Irish forward I ever played with was Willie Duggan. He was the Scarlet Pimpernel of Irish rugby because he was so hard to find for training! Having said that he wouldn't have survived in international rugby so long without training. Willie's captaincy manual was from a different world. His speeches were not comparable with anything I've ever heard before or since.

'One of my clearest memories of Willie's captaincy is of the morning after the Scotland game in 1984. The papers all had a picture of Duggan with his arm around Tony Ward, speaking to him. It was just before Wardy was to take a penalty. It appeared that Willie was acting the real father-figure but knowing him as I do, my guess was he was saying, "If you miss this penalty, I'll kick you all the way to Kilkenny!"

'Another of the great characters was Ginger McLoughlin. In 1983, I was chosen to tour with the Lions to New Zealand but because of injury, I was unable to make the start of it. Later on, both Ginger and I were called out as replacements. Ginger hadn't trained in about two months. We had to travel to London, Los Angeles, Auckland and Christchurch. Both of us were very concerned to get there in the best shape possible and were not drinking at all. There was a lot of supporters on the plane and they were in high spirits. We hit an air pocket and a few of the fans spilled their drinks all over us. We smelt like a brewery. Willie John McBride was at the airport to meet us and was not impressed.

'Moss Finn was another great character. The morning of his international debut, the team were staying in the Shelbourne Hotel and Moss was telling the players how good he was feeling. It was his first trip to Dublin and he went on to say that he had been out for a lovely walk in front of the hotel to see the ducks in the Phoenix Park. He had really been to Stephens' Green but he genuinely thought that was the Phoenix Park!'

Given his loyalty to Cork, it is not surprising that Lenihan is a keen admirer of Tommy Kiernan, the former Cork Constitution star who coached the Irish team to the Triple Crown in '82. Kiernan had a great brain. He once succeeded in getting the best out of England international Andy Ripley in a competition, which was a unique distinction. It was after a game for touring side the Irish Wolfhounds and they were all on the drink. Somewhere along the line, Tom had bet that he could mix a drink that would finish Andy. Andy said that he couldn't, so the game was on. Tommy produced a vile, green, evil-looking mixture from behind the bar and Andy was to drink it. Andy was built like a Greek god, so his optimism seemed justified and he knocked back the drink with no effect. Kiernan conceded defeat. A short while later, there was a loud crash: Ripley had fallen over and had to be carried out feet first. Kiernan was laughing like a schoolboy.

CAPTAIN'S LOG
When the Ciaran 'Fitzie' Fitzgerald era ended in 1987, Lenihan stepped into the breach and took on the mantle of captaincy.

'I struggled a bit during my first term as captain but was much more comfortable in the role second time around.'

He led Ireland to the inaugural World Cup in 1987. It was not a happy experience for him as he saw his side struggle to make any impression. Ireland's slide accelerated the following season, when Jimmy Davidson succeeded Mick Doyle as coach, culminating in a humiliating defeat at Twickenham. Lenihan attributes the decline, at least in part, to non-playing factors.

'Jimmy Davidson was a very good coach with excellent ideas, who never got the recognition he deserved. The problem was that there was a breakdown in communication between him and some of the players. I don't think he really understood the difference between the personalities of the Munster players and the lads from Ulster.

'I welcomed the news of Fitzie's appointment as coach but I don't think the IRFU did him any favours by appointing him so early in his career. The World Cup in 1987 changed rugby. We were certainly not ready for that change. In 1991, we let a golden opportunity slip through our fingers. Our preparation for that competition was pretty abysmal.'

For a long time, it seemed that Lenihan himself would not participate in the tournament.

'Earlier that year, following a serious injury, I was told my rugby career was over by the surgeon who operated on me. I missed most of the build-up matches. The team were due to tour Namibia in the summer of 1991. I went for a physical assessment at Thomond Park, and Fitzie and the team management were amazed at how fit I was but I had missed out on too many matches and was ruled out of the trip to Namibia. There is a lot of nonsense talked by players who are dropped about how badly they want their team to win. In my heart of hearts, I wanted Ireland to do badly because it was the only chance I had of getting back into the team.

'One Sunday, I was bringing my son to the Tall Ships Race in Cork. I heard on the car radio that the Ireland management were trying frantically to contact me. Brian Rigney had damaged his knee and they wanted me to fly out immediately. I had to get so many connecting flights I didn't know where I was – London, Frankfurt, Johannesburg and then a four-seater to the middle of the desert. Ciaran Fitzgerald asked me if I would be fit to play the following day. I said I would. The one consolation I had was that the match was scheduled for the evening, which would give me a chance to get rid of the jet lag. To my horror, the match was rescheduled for the afternoon because they were concerned about the state of the floodlights. Before the match, I told Terry Kingston, who was captain, not to worry about me if I didn't participate in the warm-up. I sat in the toilet conserving energy while the others got ready for the game.'

Lenihan acquitted himself well in the game and in the Second Test and found himself back on the side for the World Cup campaign. From an Irish point of view, the tournament was a let-down.

'The Australian match was the greatest disappointment of my career. We had the match won but we lost it. I remember our bus got stuck in a traffic jam on the way to the match, which meant that we literally ran in off the bus, got togged out and ran onto the pitch. It was a tremendous performance. I think the game was lost when we failed to find touch after the kick-off following Gordon Hamilton's try.

'I genuinely believe we would have had a 50:50 chance of beating New Zealand in the semi-final in front of our home fans. Our form had been poor up to that match and nobody expected us to do well. Had we won that game, I think it would have generated a whole new level of interest in rugby throughout the country. It could have been like the mass hysteria which the Irish soccer team generated during the 1990 World Cup in Italy.

'It's funny the things that go through players' minds. I was speaking to Australia's Tim Horan after the match. After the Hamilton try, he thought it was all over for them and they would be on the plane home the following morning. He had put a lot of his clothes in the laundry that morning and his big fear was that the clothes wouldn't be dry for the following day! Then Michael Lynagh intervened and got them out of jail with his try.'

HOME AND AWAY

Lenihan toured down under with the Lions in 1989. There he came close to two of the great figures of international rugby, David Campese and Murray Mexted. Campo's status in the game is probably best illustrated by the following conversation:

Bill McLaren: How do you coach David Campese?

Bob Dwyer: Well, I make it a point never to interfere with bloody genius.

Murray Mexted was for nine years the All Blacks number 8. Like George Best, he has an interesting personal life. He married Miss Universe. The conventional wisdom is that those who can do, while those who can't talk about it. Mexted is the exception to the rule. Since his retirement from the game, he has become one of the best-known rugby commentators down under, though more for his idiosyncratic use of language than for his insights into the game. Describing a helicopter drying a ground in New Zealand, he said, 'It's just like a giant blowjob.' His analysis of a ball kicked on a wet ground was 'My father used to call it a "testicles kick" because you actually ended with your balls up.' His most famous comment about an Irish player concerned Keith Wood tackling like a man possessed: 'You don't like to see hookers going down on players like that.'

On the tour, Lenihan was left to muse on the historical unfairness of Ireland's relationship with Australia. We gave them thousands of our emigrants which helped to make their country great. What did they give us in return? *Neighbours* and *Home and Away*.

Injuries forced Lenihan to depart from the international stage slightly ahead of schedule, having captained Ireland 17 times. 'I knew it was time to retire when the bits and pieces started falling off my body.'

Gone too soon: the late John McCall holds the Ulster Schools trophy aloft.

The strife of Brian: for once, Brian O'Driscoll suffers from having wide-open space in front of him.

Rallying to the cause (left to right): Brian O'Driscoll, former snooker champion Ken Doherty, Reggie Corrigan, Victor Costello and Shane Horgan get ready to motor.

So this is Christmas: Paul O'Connell gets in the Christmas spirit.

A nun's story: Denis Hickie with Sister Stanislaus Kennedy
and young friends.

Inside out: after the disappointment of losing the Third Test on the 2001 Lions tour, David Wallace, Rob Henderson and Brian O'Driscoll try to lighten the mood in John Eales's bar in Sydney by turning their jackets inside out and dancing accordingly, i.e. crazy.

The young Lion: Eric Miller breaks for the Lions in 1997.

The fab four: Malcolm O'Kelly, Eric Miller and
Girvan Dempsey tee off with Eric's father, Gareth.

Having a ball (left to right): Ollie Campbell, Mike Gibson, Suzanne
O'Connell, Ken Ging, Jack Kyle and Johnny Moloney at a charity event
for Outreach Moldova.

Take me higher: Rob Henderson gives Mick Galwey a lift.

Drink up: Rob Henderson is joined by (left to right): Paddy 'Rala' O'Reilly, Angie Henderson, Peter Winterbottom, Dixie O'Reilly and Lawrence Dallaglio.

Get to the point: Ciaran Fitzgerald points the way forward.

My ball: Jim Glennon wins a lineout for Ireland against Scotland in 1980.

A defensive fortress: Fergus Slattery, Mick Quinn, Dick Milliken and Wallace McMaster (on the ground) thwart an English attack.

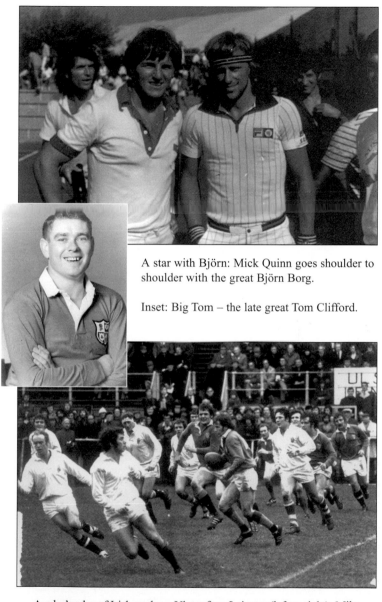

A star with Björn: Mick Quinn goes shoulder to shoulder with the great Björn Borg.

Inset: Big Tom – the late great Tom Clifford.

A who's who of Irish rugby – Ulster face Leinster (left to right): Mike Gibson, Roger Clegg, Dick Milliken, Stewart McKinney, Willie John McBride, Jimmy Davidson, Kevin Mays, Mick Quinn, John Moloney (head), Sean Lynch and Jim Flynn.

Three of the best: perhaps Ireland's greatest ever back row (left to right): Bill McKay, Des O'Brien and Jim McCarthy.

Gone but not forgotten: the late, much missed Tom Rooney.

He cut his teeth as Ireland team manager but resigned to concentrate on his job with the 2001 Lions. The former England coach Jack Rowell was once asked what it was like to be in charge of a top team. He replied, 'You have fifteen players in a team. Seven hate your guts and the other eight are making up their minds.' Lenihan was to find out what he meant. His stewardship of the Lions was made more difficult by damning claims about the preparation and training methods of the squad made in the press by two Lions players, Matt Dawson and Austin Healey, during the tour. That controversy and the fact that the Lions lost the series did take some of the shine off what should have been the crowning glory of Lenihan's career. It was a case of what might have been. A friend of Donal's put the scale of the disappointment well: 'It was like thinking you've gone to bed with Liz Hurley only to wake up to the terrible realisation that you've slept with Red Hurley.'

18

SUPERMAC

CAPPED 37 TIMES FOR IRELAND, HUGO MACNEILL SCORED 8 international tries, a record for a full-back, making him perhaps Ireland's greatest attacking full-back of all time. A schoolboy wonder, he captained the Leinster and Ireland Schools sides. Having won his first full cap against France in 1981, he was one of only six players to play in all six matches of the 1982 and 1985 Triple Crown victories, and he won three Test caps on the 1983 Lions tour of New Zealand.

In 1982, Ireland's 20–12 victory in the opening Five Nations game against Wales raised hopes of a Triple Crown. The away fixture against England was going to be crucial to achieving this ambition. The match is best remembered for a moment from Gerry 'Ginger' McLoughlin, the carrot-haired Shannon prop, who scored a try after he was driven over the line by the sheer weight of Irish players who were up in support. Ginger claimed that he pulled the other players over with him. However, what is often forgotten is that Ireland's second try that day in their 16–15 win was scored by Hugo MacNeill, his third for his country. On 20 February, Ireland scored 21 points against Scotland's 12 to secure a historic victory, thanks to 6 penalty goals and a drop-goal from Ollie Campbell. The Irish team on that auspicious occasion was: Hugo MacNeill, Moss Finn, Michael Kiernan, Paul Dean, Keith Crossan, Ollie Campbell, Robbie McGrath, Phil Orr, Ciaran Fitzgerald (capt.), Gerry McLoughlin, Donal Lenihan, Moss Keane, Fergus Slattery, Willie Duggan, John O'Driscoll.

TREAD SOFTLY, BECAUSE YOU TREAD ON MY DREAMS

In the early years, MacNeill had a unique way of releasing the tension before home matches.

'I was studying Anglo-Irish literature at Trinity College at the time. On the Thursdays before international matches, we gathered together in the Shelbourne Hotel. We always had some time off on the Friday morning. I would take a break from the build-up by popping down to Trinity and sitting in on Brendan Kennelly's class on Yeats, which I really enjoyed.'

After his sojourn at Trinity, MacNeill won two Oxford Blues, captaining them in the Varsity match.

Having been a virtual novice in 1982, MacNeill was one of the more senior players when Ireland regained the Triple Crown in 1985.

'In 1985, grey clouds hung over the entire country. To those back home in Dublin in the 1980s, I was one of the rats that had deserted the sinking ship. I was studying at Oxford at the time, a world away from the recession and depression at home. I was working on a thesis: how do you reduce the Irish unemployment problem? It wasn't easy. There was almost 20 per cent unemployment and I always think that's why our triumph in '85 was so important, because it lifted a nation at a time when it desperately needed lifting. It wasn't just that we won the Triple Crown; it was the style we played when winning. Much of the credit for this has to go to our coach, Mick Doyle. He best summed up his philosophy when he said, "I want you to run and if it doesn't work out, I want you to run again." On a personal level, I feel eternally grateful to Doyler because he kept faith with me even when the media were clamouring for me to be dropped. Mick said to me in training, "Hugo, I want you in this side, OK?" We had a good chat and he made me feel confident again. He had a great gift for man-management.

'Doyler had a wicked sense of humour. He was taking us for a Sunday-morning training session. His prop forward, Jim McCoy, was not moving as swiftly as Doyler would have liked. Big Jim was an RUC officer and brought up in the Protestant tradition. Doyler shouted at him, "Hurry up, McCoy, or you'll be late for Mass!"

'There was a great bond between the team. It was probably most evident at Cardiff Arms Park when we beat Wales 21–9. We hadn't won there for nearly 20 years. I will never forget that we linked arms before kick-off. It wasn't planned. It just happened naturally. It showed how united we were.'

However, this was not the highlight of Hugo's season. That came at Murrayfield.

'The Scots had beaten us 32–9 at Lansdowne Road the previous March and we were going into their back yard with a young team. We were whitewashed in 1984 and so many experienced players retired that year. Ollie Campbell, Moss Keane, Fergus Slattery, Willie Duggan and John O'Driscoll had all moved on. Mick Doyle asked us, "What are we afraid of?" The answer most people would have given him was the wooden spoon. But literally from the first minute, I sensed that something special was about to happen to us all. Deano [Paul Dean] moved it wide, Keith Crossan split the line, Brenny [Brendan Mullin] passed to me and the ball squirted forward as I was tackled over the line. If I'd had the ball in my other hand, we'd have scored a breathtaking try with our first attack. Our confidence was instantly lifted. We thought, "Wow, did we really do that?"

'The Scots got on top of us slowly and it looked like it was going to end badly but then we produced a little piece of magic. The back row created a position on the far side, the ball went wide and through the hands of nearly every back on the team before Trevor Ringland scored in the corner. We won 18–15.

'It was an extraordinary day, made all the more special by the scenes in the dressing-room afterwards. I played 37 times for Ireland as well as for the Lions and if you ask me to single out one moment from all those years that will live with me forever, then it is the Murrayfield dressing-room on the late afternoon of 2 February 1985. There was an ecstatic air about the place. Nobody could sit down. It was almost childlike. We had all played hundreds of championship matches as children in our back gardens but this was the real thing. It was the most amazing feeling I ever had in my career.

'That year, there was great uncertainty and apprehension before the Scotland game. We had no recognised place-kicker and were such a young side. After our win, there was so much excitement and freshness that no one could sit down. I had come through the schools and universities with these guys, and I really enjoyed the buzz.'

A DOWNWARD SPIRAL

What caused Ireland's star to wane so dramatically the following season?

'We won the Triple Crown playing good rugby but I think we got complacent the next season. If you look back at our matches in 1985, we could have lost all of those matches. We had a lot of good fortune. In 1986, we were not going to surprise people playing more of the same. We needed to advance our game but we didn't.'

Ireland's form in the post-Mick Doyle era slumped dramatically. The lowest point was a 35–3 defeat away to England in 1988. At least the match generated one of the most celebrated stories in recent Irish rugby folklore. MacNeill went AWOL during the game. Although Ireland went in with a 3–0 lead at half-time, they were slaughtered in the second half. When the second half started, Hugo was not there and nobody knew where he was. The joke after the game was that he went in to make a phone call. By the time he came back onto the pitch England had run in for two tries. MacNeill was involved in a similar situation in a match against France. What was the explanation for these incidents?

'It's the usual story of a mountain being made out of a molehill. What happened in both cases was that I picked up head injuries in the first half and had to go off with Mick Molloy, the team doctor, for treatment. In the French match, I returned with my head strapped, so I could never understand the mystery.'

Now based in London, Hugo still retains an interest in Irish rugby. With Trevor Ringland, he was the brains behind the Peace International between Ireland and the Barbarians in the wake of the Canary Wharf bombing and the breakdown of the IRA ceasefire in 1996.

MacNeill is a good friend and huge admirer of Ollie Campbell but he enjoys stories which show his illustrious teammate in a poor light. Typical of this kind is the one where Campbell goes on a fishing holiday with Willie Duggan. They rented a boat and fished in a lake every day. After six days, they still had caught nothing but on the seventh day they caught thirty fish. Ollie said to Willie, 'Mark this spot so that we can come back here again tomorrow.'

The next day when they were driving to rent the boat, Campbell asked Duggan, 'Did you mark that spot?'

Willie replied, 'Yeah, I put a big X on the bottom of the boat.'

Ollie said, 'You stupid fool! What if we don't get that same boat today?'

He is also well able to tell stories against himself.

'I was down in Cork with Moss Finn, Donal Lenihan and Michael Kiernan, and we were having lunch with five or six rugby fans. In any other place in Ireland, sports fans would have passed the time by picking their greatest ever Irish team. Not so in Cork. They picked the worst ever Irish team! I kept my head down as they discussed the merits of three of my predecessors for the position expecting to have my name mentioned at any minute. After they made their choice for full-back, I remarked with relief, "I suppose I can relax now." Quick as a flash, someone said, "Hang on, boy, we haven't picked the subs yet!"'

19

OUR WILLIE IS BIGGER THAN YOUR CONDOM

IN SPORTING TERMS, HE IS ONE OF A KIND. HE IS FAMOUS IN THE rugby world for playing the bagpipes. Whatever that indefinable quality called charisma is, this guy has it in buckets. He has a keen appreciation of the black humour of life, an easily discernible kindness and sensitivity, particularly for those down on their luck, and his smile signals a warm affection for friend and stranger alike. He lacks one thing – a capacity to dissemble. Despite his 27 caps for Ireland, his then record of 78 caps for Ulster, his achievements as a coach at home and abroad, Willie Anderson will probably always be remembered as the player who precipitated an international diplomatic incident. He was on a tour of Argentina with the Penguins in 1980 when he took a shine to the Argentinian flag and decided to claim it as his own.

'Myself and another player were walking home to the hotel around midnight. The Argentinian flag was hanging outside. I liked the look of the flag and its colours, so I took it back to my room. Shortly after that, six guys came through the door with machine guns. They said, "Someone in here has an Argentinian flag." I immediately handed it back and said I was sorry. I was quickly told that saying sorry was not good enough in this situation. As I was brought down to the jail, two Irish internationals, David Irwin and Frank Wilson, volunteered to come with me for moral support. For their consideration they were both thrown in jail with me for three weeks!

'I was strip searched and had 30 sets of fingerprints taken. I was literally in the interrogation chair for a day. Anyone who has seen the film *Midnight Express* will have an idea of the naked terror you can experience when you're in prison and there's a gun to your head. Things got worse before they got better. I was put into this box which is the most frightening place in the world before being taken to my cell. The cell was six foot by four and had nothing but a cement bed in the centre. The people who had been there before me had left their excrement behind. It was pretty revolting. The only blessing was that I wasn't put in the "open" cell with a crowd of prisoners, because I would have never survived.

'The next day, I was taken out in handcuffs, which is the ultimate in degradation. I was taken up the stairs and was stunned to discover that there were about 60 or 70 reporters and journalists waiting for me. For three or four days, I was not just front-page news in Argentina, I was the first three pages. To me, the press were not much better than terrorists. As I had a British passport, they tried to whip up a nationalistic frenzy and portray me as an imperialist. They didn't print the truth. Some said I had urinated on the flag. Others said I had burned it. Yet more said I had done both. My lawyer got death threats.

'It was much more serious than anybody realised here at the time. I know for a fact that two or three army generals wanted to have me executed. Others wanted to make sure that I served at least ten years' hard labour. The whole episode cost my parents £10,000 in legal fees and so on but you can't put a price on the mental anguish that they had to endure. I remember one letter I sent them home that I would hate to have to read again because I had struck rock bottom.

'The two lads and I were taken back to a cell where we came into contact with two South Koreans. They had tried to smuggle some Walkmans into the country. Dave Irwin taught me how to play chess and we had the World Chess Championships: South Korea v. Northern Ireland.

'One of the guards was a ringer for Sergeant Bilko. At one stage, he was marching us around the yard and Frank roared out, "Bilko!" I said, "For Christ's sake, Frank, just keep your mouth shut." Thankfully the guard didn't know who Bilko was. I think things could have been much worse had the warden not wanted to learn English. His colleagues would have been happy to throw away the key to our cell. In that country, we were guilty until proved innocent.

'After three weeks, Frank and David were sent home. It was the loneliest day of my life. I had to wait a further two months before my trial and release. Someone arranged a hotel room for me. I wouldn't wish what happened to me on my worst enemy. Many rugby players contributed via the clubs to a fund to pay for the legal expenses. The people of Dungannon rallied around and raised a lot of money also. I owe them a lot. I wrote to my then girlfriend, now wife, Heather, every day. The following year we got married. I think the Argentinian experience consolidated our relationship. I also learned a lot about myself. In the beginning of that experience, I prayed intensely but I gradually realised that I could not leave things to God. I had to take control of things myself. I ran every day and made a great effort to learn something about the culture and the political system. Bad and all as things were for me, it was a real culture shock to visit the town square and see all the women who were frantically looking for their sons. It was part of the way of life there that people disappeared and were lost forever. If you were seen as any kind of threat to the state, you were eliminated.

'In rugby terms, I was to pay a heavy price for my indiscretion. I was perceived as a rebel and was quietly told later, by a prominent personality in Irish rugby, that my first cap was delayed because of the incident. In fact, I was 29 when I first played for Ireland. I met Denis Thatcher some years later and told him that I could have told his wife the Argentinians were scrapping for a war.'

A LATE STARTER

Anderson made his international debut with Philip Matthews, now a celebrated analyst with the BBC, against Australia in 1984. That day was to prove the most significant in Matthews' life because at the post-match reception he met Lisa Flynn, daughter of former great Kevin Flynn – the woman who would become his wife. Love stories begin in Irish rugby! Matthews cringes at the memory, as he was in a bit of a drunken haze at the time. He remembers he was also introduced to Kevin that night and doubts if his future father-in-law was very impressed. He is pretty sure that Flynn didn't want his daughter falling for a drunken yob! Matthews asked Lisa to be his guest at the dinner after their next home international against England. He almost forgot about it but the rest of the lads reminded him and told him that as Kevin Flynn was a former chairman of the Irish selectors, it would not be a good idea for Matthews' international future to let his daughter down!

As a player, Willie Anderson had many highs and lows, the highs being the 1985 Triple Crown and the night he captained a scratch Irish side to a famous victory over France at Auch in 1988 – Ireland's only victory over France on their territory in almost 20 years. His appearances against France were memorable for his epic struggles with the French lock, Jean Condom. Hence the banner that appeared in the crowd at Lansdowne Road at the Ireland–France match in 1985: 'Our Willie is bigger than your Condom'. Playing for Ireland was the fulfilment of a childhood dream for Anderson.

'I have a clear memory of watching Ireland play the All Blacks in 1972 and waiting to play for my country after that. The players I most admired were Ken Goodall and Mervyn Davies. I even grew a moustache to look like Mervyn! I was fortunate in that my brother Oliver represented Ireland at both the discus and the shot. I was very impressed with his Ireland tracksuit and this spurred me on even more.

'Nowadays, players are getting paid a lot of money to represent Ireland. If those terms had been around in my day, I would have earned a fortune. After I was chosen for my first cap, my father gave me an old 50-punt note. Every time I took out the note to buy a drink, nobody would let me split it, so I never had to pay for any drink. At least my first cap saved me a lot of money!

'I can still feel that tingle that went down my spine when I first heard the national anthem as an Irish player. People couldn't understand how an Ulster Protestant could feel this way. It was the ultimate honour to be chosen as captain.'

RUBBING THEIR NOSES IN IT

As Irish captain, he was also famous for a piece of sporting theatre before Ireland played the All Blacks in 1989 when he led the Irish team literally up to the noses of the New Zealanders in an effort to intimidate them. Whose idea was this ploy?

'It was a joint effort between myself and our coach Jimmy Davidson. After the match, Wayne Shelford was asked if he was scared. He answered that he was absolutely petrified. When asked why, he answered, "I was terrified that Willie Anderson would kiss me!" In fact, I once got a kiss on the top of my head in an international from Donal Lenihan after I made a try-saving tackle.

'More seriously, a few days before that famous match against the All Blacks a good friend of mine was killed as part of the Troubles. He died just because he was a builder. At my after-dinner speech, I spoke about the importance of keeping perspective. While you want to win at rugby there is more to life. Not everybody appreciated my comments but a number of All Blacks spoke to me afterwards about how impressed they were by the sentiments.

'Jimmy Davidson had been coach at my province, Ulster, before he took the Ireland job. Jimmy was ten years ahead of his time. He had a crucial role in my development as a player. It was he who pointed out what was wrong with my game. The feeling we had when we ran out to play for Ulster you could have cut with a knife. We had great players like Nigel Carr. I've never met anyone who could match Nigel for fitness and commitment.'

HOME THOUGHTS FROM ABROAD

Anderson is grateful for all the opportunities rugby has provided for him, particularly in relation to touring. Despite the apparent glamour of travelling abroad, it can be a very isolated existence, wherein the only thing you see of the country is a hotel room, a few bars and many rugby grounds – though in which precise order varies greatly depending on the team.

'Rugby has been my passport to travel the world. Most of the time, it has been very pleasurable. When we toured Romania with Ulster, though, it was horrifying to see the scale of the poverty. I have one clear image of that trip. We passed by what must have been a 1,000-acre field and there were lines of women with hoes working away. They all looked about 100 but they were probably no more than 30.

'Even when things are at their blackest from a rugby point of view on tour, there are moments of comedy. After we lost to Australia in the World Cup in 1987, Donal Lenihan rang home. As a result of the time difference, the match was shown live on Irish television at 6 a.m. His mother had seen the match and knew the result already. Instead of offering him sympathy, she said, "Anyone stupid enough to play rugby at 6 o'clock in the morning deserves to lose!"

'Once when I played in the Hong Kong Sevens, I had the most terrifying moment in my rugby life. There were 100,000 people watching when we played Australia. At one point, there were twelve players in a small corner of the field and what seemed about thirty-five acres with just two players – David Campese and me. I was petrified about having to try and tackle Campo when he had so much space, so I screamed my head off for some cover.'

Like Campo, Anderson believes in having an upbeat attitude to rugby and life, which is typified in the story of the man at his 103rd birthday party who was asked if he planned to be around for his 104th.

'I certainly do,' he replied. 'Statistics show that very few people die between the ages of 103 and 104.'

THE WILL TO WIN

Anderson played against some of the greatest players of all time but mention of one name in particular brings a broad smile to his face: Will Carling.

Some of his critics portray Carling as a bit tight with money. When Anderson is asked if this is a fair perception, he recalls that one wag suggested that Will's idea of a Christmas treat for his children was to take them to Santa's grave!

One of Anderson's favourite stories about the former English captain is from early in his marriage to Julia, when, after being away a long time on tour, he thought it would be good to bring her a little gift.

'How about some perfume?' he asked the girl in the cosmetics department. She showed him a bottle costing £100.

'That's too much,' he said.

The girl then said, 'We do have this smaller bottle for £50.'

'That's still too much,' he said. The girl brought out a tiny £20 bottle, but even that was too costly for him. 'What I mean is,' he said, 'I'd like to see something really cheap.'

The assistant handed him a mirror.

20

DEANO

WITH THE RETIREMENT OF OLLIE CAMPBELL IN 1984, THE POPULAR opinion among rugby fans was that the stage was set for Tony Ward to return to the Irish team. Not for the first time, the selectors had a surprise in store. When the St Mary's club partnership of Ward and Johnny Moloney had been the half-back pairing for Ireland, St Mary's College supplied the half-back partnership on the Irish Schools international team in Paul Dean and Philip McDonnell. In fact, Dean had the distinction of being a Schools international in both fifth and sixth year.

An injury sustained by Ward while playing for Mary's against Monkstown at Sydney Parade on a dark autumn afternoon in 1984 opened the way for Dean to become Ireland's out-half. Ward had been due to travel to Cork the next day to play for an Irish selection against Highfield in an exhibition. Ward's difficulty was Dean's opportunity and he played out-half to Mick Bradley. The rest of the back line comprised Brendan Mullin and Michael Kiernan in the centre, Trevor Ringland and Keith Crossan on the wings and Hugo MacNeill at full-back. They went to town against Highfield, inspired by the brilliance of Dean. That back line would subsequently help to win the 1985 Triple Crown and win it in style.

When it came to a running, 15-man game, Deano was peerless. His genius was in the way he diverted attention from his centres, in his back-line alignment and in his speed of delivery. Few Irish players have been better able to straighten a back line. He could run incredibly straight and was also a beautifully balanced runner with an outstanding hip movement which he used to great effect in beating the opposition and creating space for those around him. He had magnificent hands. He was rarely, if ever, seen dropping a pass. He was also an exceptionally good tackler. Although he was the linchpin of the Triple Crown-winning side in 1985 at out-half, he initially made his mark in the green jersey as first centre.

WE'RE ALL GOING ON A SUMMER HOLIDAY

Ireland's summer tour to South Africa in 1981 marked Dean's initiation into the Irish set-up. It was to prove an education in every sense of the term.

'I am still learning what happened on that tour. There were three young lads in the squad: Michael Kiernan, John Hewitt and myself. We were going to bed very early at night, getting up early to go training, and we couldn't understand why the older players were so tired in the mornings. We were on different clocks. They had a different agenda.

'The three of us were so naive and innocent. To give you an example, I roomed with one very senior player, who shall remain nameless, for four nights, but I never saw him at night-time and I was so naive I thought he didn't want to room with me because he was afraid I'd be snoring!

'My most vivid memory of the tour is of one night when one of the "small lads" was annoying the "big lads" so they grabbed him and dangled him by the legs outside the hotel window – 17 storeys up. They were going to drop him into the swimming pool below but nobody was sure which was the deep end and which was the shallow end, and that was the only reason they didn't throw him in the pool. When you're just 20 years old and watching the biggest names in Irish rugby, guys you've idolised all your life, up close and personal and seeing them behave like that, it comes as a shock.'

The next year, Dean found himself at the centre of Ireland's first Triple Crown victory in 33 years. He is surprisingly downbeat about it.

'1982 was a great year for Irish rugby but not a great year for me. I was only a small cog in a very big machine. Of course, I know I was lucky to be there. I played very averagely. Ollie Campbell played fantastically behind a very efficient pack. I was doing a lot of chasing and tackling. It was workmanlike stuff rather than being creative. You don't realise at that age how fantastic it was until afterwards. Yet I wasn't playing the type of game I wanted. I was fulfilling other people's dreams but not my own.'

If '82 was not a high point for him, '84 was a low point.

'I was out of favour and I lost my place on the Irish team. I was disillusioned playing the centre because I was an average centre and I wanted to play out-half. It was reflected in my game and I was dropped. After that, I declared my intention to play out-half which caused trouble at St Mary's because Tony Ward was there and he had the number 10 shirt. I told them, "I don't care if you play me in the seconds, I want to play at out-half".'

THE SECOND COMING

Mick Doyle's appointment as Irish coach transformed Dean's career.

'I was fortunate to play with three different Irish coaches and when you look back and recall the amount of time and effort they put into it in an amateur era, you would have to admire all of them. I was never as fit as when I was training under Tommy Kiernan. He would run the socks off you. Jimmy Davidson was very intense and a great academic coach. He would sit and talk to you for hours about your game, which was very helpful. The problem was that he wasn't versatile enough to talk to different players in different modes, whereas Doyler was very streetwise and would talk to no two players in exactly the same way, because he knew you had to do that to push the right buttons.

'Doyler had been a fan of mine since I played my first game for Leinster on tour in Romania. He was the coach and before the match I jokingly said to him, "The first ball I get I will score." The problem was that the first ball I got was on the halfway line. But I did score. He liked the way I ran with the ball and played the game.

'The Scottish game in '85 was the high point of my career. It wasn't just that we won the Triple Crown but the way we played that season. Doyler had the guts to let us play the game we wanted to play. We felt we could have taken on the world. I was 25 and at the peak of my career.'

What should have been the crowning glory of Dean's career became the nadir.

'My goal was to play for all the teams I could possibly play for: Ireland, the Barbarians and the Lions. I succeeded but the pity for me was that my Lions adventure in 1989 only lasted eight minutes. It was so frustrating, because I was going to be playing alongside the best back line in the world, with the likes of Rory Underwood, Ieuan Evans and Gavin Hastings. In training, I continually reiterated that I was always going to pass the ball and that if somebody was going to kick the ball, it wasn't going to be me.

'Before the Lions team was announced, we all knew that there were three candidates for the two out-half spots: Craig Chalmers, Rob Andrew and myself. When we were playing in the Five Nations, Rob Andrew was very confident he was going to get selected and in fairness to him, he was playing quite well. The rumour was that he had planned to bring his girlfriend with him and had even bought an Apex ticket for her. When the squad was announced and he wasn't selected, I rang him and said, "I'll look after your girlfriend while she's out here and you're not!" When I got injured, he was brought out as a replacement, so he had the last laugh.

'I was 29 years old and had had almost ten years of international rugby, and my body was shaky. It was a simple injury. I was putting too much pressure on my knee on an uneven part of the pitch and my cruciate snapped. I was in tremendous pain. It was like a knife had cut through my knee, I was almost in tears. I knew immediately I was going home and it nearly killed me to miss out on the opportunity of playing with such great sportsmen. We had the benefit of a fantastic coach in Ian McGeechan, who was someone you would willingly work hard for. He was superb, a wonderful tactician and had great man-management skills. He was a lovely fella and I couldn't say enough about him.

'Shortly after I came home, I got married and then I took over the Umbro business in Ireland. It was the start of a new business career and there was no looking back. I was terribly, terribly tired and in a way I was kind of relieved to get out of rugby.'

HOT DOGS AND ENGLISHMEN

One of the other regrets Dean has about his career is that in one respect he was in the right place at the wrong time.

'I was around at the same time as Campbell and Ward. I got 32 caps, Ollie Campbell got 22 and Tony Ward got 19. If we could have spaced out our careers, we'd all have way, way more. Mind you, having Ollie and Wardy rivalling me for the one spot made me very competitive and that tends to lead to better performances.

'It was a different era but I enjoyed it. We had great fun. When I look at Brian O'Driscoll, I see someone with rock-star status. We never had anything like that – but then none of us were as good as Brian! Ireland is very lucky at the moment to have extremely special players in the centre: Brian and Gordon D'Arcy. When I think back, though, my diet was very different to what I'd imagine Brian O'Driscoll's is today. I was living in a flat and all I was eating was sandwiches, hot dogs and hamburgers.

'In 1985, we were due to play England but the match was called off because of snow. As soon as we heard the news, we all went down to O'Donoghue's and got completely drunk. That kind of thing wouldn't happen today.

'There was an unwritten code about fair play back then, too. I saw this over two years in internationals between England and Ireland. After we played England at home, we had the post-match dinner, except for the first time, women were allowed to attend. That was the end of rugby for me! We were on strict instructions from our girlfriends to get to the function in a "decent state", otherwise we'd be in trouble. Before the dinner, a lot of drink had been consumed and one of my Irish teammates was tired and emotional, and had to go to bed. When his girlfriend came down from her room, there was an English player in the lift with her. He thought she fancied him, so he grabbed her and groped her. She was terribly embarrassed. Her boyfriend didn't get to hear about it until the following day. The next year when Ireland played the return fixture, a lineout took place and the call was made to the Irish forward in question. He was marking the English player responsible. The English guy jumped and the Irish player planted him and put his nose to the other side of his face. The English player huddled up his forwards and told them that the next time they got a lineout they were to throw the ball to him and he would plant his opponent in turn. The English players knew about the incident the previous year and told him he deserved it. That night, the English player came to the Irish lad and apologised. The basic rule was "What goes around comes around." Nowadays if you struck a player like that, especially with the media coverage and video evidence, you would be sued for GBH.'

Two French players top Dean's list of most-admired players.

'I was only interested in backs. Forwards were only there to get me the ball. Mind you, the forwards would say the backs are there to lose that ball. The two players that impressed me the most were Philippe Sella and Serge Blanco. Although Sella is no longer the most capped international player of all time, very few of his caps were won from the subs bench, unlike a lot of other players we could think of. The one player I always hated seeing getting the ball in his hands was Serge Blanco. You knew immediately you were going to be in trouble if he got on a run. He could do magic on the ball.'

One player who was Keane by name but not by nature tops Dean's list of rugby characters.

'Moss Keane always hated me getting the ball because he knew I'd pass it and that meant, in his eyes, that the backs were going to lose it and he'd have to chase it and win it back again. A common instruction from him was, "Jaysus, now, don't let the little fellas have it." Like Willie Duggan, he hated having to run around the pitch.

'The young players looked up to Moss as if he was God. New players from the North found his thick Kerry accent particularly difficult to decipher. The senior players devised a little ritual for those new players. When Trevor Ringland was brought onto the team for the first time, they put him beside Moss for dinner and Trevor was in awe of him. They primed Moss to speak for two minutes in fast-forward mode. He was talking pure gibberish. Then he turned to Trevor and asked him what he thought of that. Trevor answered lamely, "I think you're right", not having a clue what Moss had said. Then Moss launched into it again, only faster. The panic on Trevor's face was a sight to behold. He was going green. All the senior players were killing themselves trying to keep a straight face until Trevor found out he was being wound up.

'Another great guy was the Scottish international John Jeffrey. He became a good friend of mine. The night before we played Scotland in 1985, we went to the cinema, as was the tradition back then. All I remember of the film was that it starred Eddie Murphy and his catchphrase was "Get the f**k out of here." As soon as the film was over, the lights came on and when we stood up we saw that the Scottish team were sitting three rows behind us. We had a popcorn fight with them, which was great fun and they started shouting at us, "Get the f**k out of here." Almost as soon as the match started the next day, John Jeffrey tackled me very late. He knew exactly what he was doing. It was too early in the game for him to be penalised. As he pinned me down on the ground, he whispered in my ear, "Get the f**k out of here." The nice thing was that we did get the f**k out of there – but with a victory.'

Dean enjoys the story told about the young John Jeffrey and his first girlfriend. They were sitting on a low stone wall, holding hands and gazing out over the loch. For several minutes they sat silently, then finally the lassie looked at the future Scottish legend and said, 'A penny for your thoughts, John.'

'Well, uh, I was thinkin' . . . perhaps it's aboot time for a wee kiss.'

The girl blushed, then leaned over and kissed him lightly on the cheek. Then he blushed.

Then the two turned once again to gaze out over the loch. After a while, the girl spoke again. 'Another penny for your thoughts, John.'

The young Jeffrey knit his brow. 'Well, now,' he said, 'my thoughts are a bit more serious this time.'

'Really?' said the girl in a whisper, filled with anticipation.

'Aye,' said Jeffrey. 'Dinnae ye think it's aboot time ye paid me that first penny.'

WITH A LITTLE HELP FROM MY FRIENDS

There is one former teammate whose name elicits a very animated response from Dean.

'When I started with Ireland, I loved playing with Michael Kiernan because he was so fast. However, as he got older, he put on weight and started to lose his speed! My job was to make our talented back line look good. The problem was that I made Michael look much, much better than he actually was.'

Many rugby fans felt Michael Kiernan left the Irish team prematurely. For the first time, Deano can exclusively reveal the real reason for Kiernan's early retirement. 'He left because of illness. The truth is, everyone was sick of him!'

He very reluctantly denies, though, that he christened Kiernan 'Pepper' because he always got up your nose. Not surprisingly, Kiernan features in Deano's personal favourite rugby story.

'Michael Kiernan was always a terribly bad influence on me! After we lost badly at home to England one year, we went to the post-match dinner at the Shelbourne. Will Carling was the young, up-and-coming captain of England. It was one of his first games as captain. There were 300 people there, all men. It was black tie only and a bit stuffy. At the Shelbourne, there were waiters going around with double gin and tonics on silver trays at the reception before the dinner. Will Carling arrived in a white dinner jacket with his hair gelled back. Everybody else was wearing a black suit. Michael and I steered Will into a corner and grabbed a silver tray full of G and Ts and toasted Will, many times, on England's success. We had been drinking before the reception and were getting pretty sloshed. Will's mistake was to think that because we were senior players, he was safe with us. The English manager, Roger Uttley, was looking for Will and he grabbed him and took him away, saying forcefully to him, "You're captain of England. You have to be careful. You have responsibilities. You have to give a speech." The players sat down for the dinner around circular tables. I was completely dwarfed sitting between Paul Ackford and Wade Dooley. It was a very stuffy environment and so before the dinner we entertained ourselves with drinking games. The problem was that we were terrible drinkers. Roger Uttley was minding Carling for the meal but during it Will slipped away from him, came down from the top table to us and sat down between Paul Ackford and myself. The English players, being very prim and proper, were not too happy with Will, especially as he was wearing a white dinner jacket. We pushed him under the table and closed in our seats. It was a big table and Will was under the middle of it shouting, "Lads, let me out." His voice couldn't be heard in the noisy room, though. Roger Uttley was looking frantically for him because it was coming up for the speeches. Will started kicking us to get out. We couldn't see him so we started kicking him back. The next drink was a glass of red wine, so, one after the other, we threw it under the table on top of his white dinner jacket and gelled hair. Will started screaming, "Lads, let me out or I'll turn over the table." We all put our elbows on the table. We were laughing away and eventually Roger Uttley saw what was going on and dragged Will out from under the table. There were big red-wine stains dripping off his lovely white jacket. A few minutes later, Will gave his speech. Carling subsequently went on to make a fortune going around companies giving inspirational speeches but let's just say his address that night wasn't his finest moment!'

21

DON'T PICK WARDY

IN THE COURSE OF HIS CAREER, TONY WARD WOULD BUILD TWO reputations, one for his skill on the field and the other for the controversies which restricted his appearances in the green jersey. In fact, it is somewhat surprising that he never got the nickname 'the Judge' because he spent so much time sitting on the bench. Ward initially took the international world by storm, and in both 1978 and 1979 he was voted European Player of the Year by *Rugby World* magazine.

Just as Ward's career was at its height, his world came apart on Ireland's tour to Australia in 1979.

'My scoring achievements made headlines in the Australian papers. I found myself being sought out for interviews; rugby writers seemed to follow my every step. It was never my way to reject media representatives in such circumstances, as I feel they have a job to do and it's only right that one should cooperate with them. To simply run away or meet their queries with a bland, tight-lipped "no comment" was never my way. I hadn't thought that publicity about me in Europe – winning the European Player of the Year Award and so on – would have been so well known down under. I was rather naive in that respect. But they knew everything about me.

'In retrospect, I now realise – older and wiser – that if I'd wanted to make sure of my place on the Irish team for the First Test, I might have acted more correctly if I had gone to ground at that point and ignored the media. It would have spared me a moment that left an indelible imprint on my mind. I have pondered it again and again when reflecting on what developed into a most traumatic experience that shattered my confidence for almost two years.

'Earlier in the tour, we were in the dressing-room preparing to go out for a training session for the match against New South Wales when Jack Coffey, the team manager, came over to me and said, "This is absolutely ridiculous. It's crazy what's going on – all this media stuff. I suggest that you stay away from these fellows altogether." I looked at him aghast. I didn't know what he was driving at. It was later on the tour when my friend and teammate Pat Whelan told me I was going to be dropped for the First Test that the true significance of Coffey's remarks that day became clear to me.

'I knew before I left Ireland that I was under pressure and consequently made certain that I played well in the preliminary games on that tour. I suspected certain devious undertones. I was aware that the coach on that tour, Noel "Noisy" Murphy, was no fan of mine; when he was the Munster coach he used to call me "the soccer player" from the sidelines. I still feel that leaving me off the team was totally unjustified and unfair. It hit me like a thunderbolt – no warning, no explanation, nobody wanted to help me. It was extremely traumatic. The immature side of me wanted to go home immediately.

'I reacted like a spoilt brat. I wanted to get on a plane and get out of there. How dare anyone drop me?! In retrospect, I'm glad I didn't leave and I would like to think I learned a lot from the experience. That is what life is about – learning from experience. If we could all live with the benefit of hindsight, that would be great.'

News that he had been dropped sent shock waves through Irish rugby fans. It was like using the Shroud of Turin to clean somebody's porridge dish – sacrilege. It had a profound effect on Ward's life as a whole. Up to '79, he had led a sheltered rugby life, wallowing in the delight of a successful career which had made all his childhood fantasies reality. The greatest tragedy was that he lost his inherent faith in his own ability. Ward feels that as a result he can better cope with any adversity or cruelty life can throw at him. He is a much stronger character for the traumas he endured before finding blissful happiness through his marriage to Louise and the love of his children. He has less interest in raising a glass to the past than toasting the present and the future.

Although Ward has many sad memories from this time, there are also happy recollections of the friendships he formed during his international career. One of them was with his half-back partner, Colin

Patterson. As Ulsterman Patterson was not brought up in the Nationalist tradition, Ward was given the job of teaching Colin the national anthem. In the interests of political balance, Patterson sang the first half of the anthem and for the second half he sang the anthem of Unionism, 'The Sash My Father Wore'. Ward claims that listening to Patterson singing never failed to bring a tear to his eye. Patterson's singing really was that bad! However, he adds that Patterson was not the only Irish international whose singing put the 'c' into 'rap'.

In 1980, Ward was back in the limelight again when he was dramatically summonsed to play for the Lions in South Africa. One of the players on the tour was the Welsh centre Ray Gravell. They shared a few good moments in South Africa. Ray was famous for singing patriotic Welsh songs before big games. One day, he confided to Ward, 'Tony, I can't stop singing "The Green, Green Grass of Home".'

Ward replied, 'That sounds like Tom Jones syndrome.'

'Is it common?'

'It's not unusual.'

LIMERICK, YOU'RE MY LADY

Although Ward did famously play on the same Irish team as Ollie Campbell during the 1981 season, as Ireland were whitewashed in the Five Nations, the experiment was deemed a failure. For the remainder of his career he was generally second choice to Campbell and, later, Paul Dean. In fact, Ward's problem with the Irish selectors was to be celebrated by comedian Dermot Morgan, later to find fame as Father Ted in the TV series of the same name, in a song called 'Don't Pick Wardy'.

Ward did revive his soccer career, playing with Limerick, and won an FAI Cup-final medal. In 1981, he played for Limerick against Southampton in the UEFA Cup. Thrown in at the deep end, Ward did more than just play, he set the soccer-watching public agog with his performance. Although Limerick lost 3–0, Ward's display caught the eye of Southampton's Kevin Keegan, who was sufficiently impressed to remark, 'Some players have the ability to generate excitement merely by running onto the pitch. Tony Ward would appear to be one of them. It was a fine performance from a man who could have made a name for himself in top-class soccer. He could probably make a lot of money for himself. Money is not everything but it makes life a lot easier.'

Southampton manager Laurie McMenemy was generous in his praise for Limerick: 'They certainly hit us with everything in the first half and

Tony Ward buzzed around like he was at Twickenham. For a while I was half expecting Terry Wogan to come on!' He was also impressed by Ward's tremendous display of wing play and expressed the view that Ward had what it takes to make it in the big time: 'With full-time coaching, it would not take much to play him in higher company.'

Around this time, Ward appeared on *A Question of Sport* – the BBC's premier sporting quiz programme. Ward was on Emlyn Hughes' team and Liam Brady was on Gareth Edwards' side. Ward was to witness 'Colemanspeak' at first hand when presenter David Coleman asked Liam Brady, 'In what sport is a kamen used?' Both Brady and Ward were very surprised to discover that the answer was hurling. Coleman had mispronounced 'camán' as 'kamen'.

POACHER TURNED GAMEKEEPER

Since his retirement, Ward has made his living in the media, which can bring its own stresses and strains. When Ward's friend Gerry Murphy was Ireland coach, he was visited in his home by popular RTÉ broadcaster Des Cahill for an interview. Murphy was on the phone to Michael Bradley when Des arrived and he ushered his guest into the sitting room before resuming the telephone conversation. Des was waiting for 15 minutes for the conversation to end. He amused himself by looking at the pictures on the wall and then gazed out the window for a while. He then sat down and for the first time noticed that Murphy had what had once been a beautiful white carpet which was covered in mud. Des was thinking that Murphy would have confirmed all the stereotyped views many women have about rugby players being untidy. Then Murphy joined him. Des was unnerved when he saw Murphy constantly looking down at his guest's shoes. Eventually, Des looked down and was horrified to discover that his shoes were caked in mud. He remembered stepping in a puddle after he had parked his car but hadn't realised that he had accumulated so much muck. Destroying his host's exquisite carpet was not the most auspicious start to an interview.

Meanwhile, when Tony Ward's nemesis Ollie Campbell visited Ward for dinner in his home, he was pleasantly surprised to see Ward making his own salad dressing and that he was something of a genius at it, blending all sorts of stuff to ladle onto the lettuce, tomatoes, celery and other chopped-up things. When Campbell sampled the salad, he asked Ward what he put on it to make it taste so good. 'I'm sorry,' Ward replied, 'but as a journalist, I stand on my right never to reveal a sauce.'

22

THE WEST'S AWAKE

THE BEAUTY OF TELEVISION COVERAGE OF SPORT IS THAT IT CAN occasionally capture an image which offers a telling insight into a sporting hero. For the Irish rugby fan, an enduring example will always be Ciaran Fitzgerald's efforts to rally the Irish team as they appeared to be letting the 1985 Triple Crown slip from their fingers against England in the wake of their dazzling and stylish victories away to Scotland and Wales. Even those who had no experience of lip-reading could clearly make out his plea from the heart, as he temporarily put aside the good habits he acquired as an altar boy with the Carmelites in Loughrea: 'Where's your pride? Where's your f**king pride?'

TEENAGE KICKS

His record speaks for itself: Triple Crown and Five Nations championship in 1982, a share of the championship in 1983 and the Triple Crown again in 1985. Fitzgerald, however, was a rugby virgin until his late teens.

'As a boy growing up in Loughrea, the only social outlet available was the boxing club. I won two All-Ireland boxing championships. My heroes at the time, though, were the Galway Gaelic football team who won the three-in-a-row in 1964, '65 and '66, and I attended all three finals. At Garbally College, my main game was hurling. The highlight of my hurling career was playing in an All-Ireland Minor final against Cork in 1970. Our team had been together from the Under-14 stage and featured people like Sean Silke and Iggy Clarke. Initially, I played at half-back but for some reason for one match they moved me to the forwards and I scored three goals. The problem was that when I played at full-forward in that All-Ireland final, I was marked by Martin Doherty who subsequently made it big with the Cork Senior team. "Big" was the word for Martin. I would have needed a step-ladder to have competed with him in the air! I was moved out to centre-forward but who followed me? Only Martin. He destroyed me. That Galway Minor team went on to win an Under-21 All-Ireland and most of them formed the backbone of the Senior All-Ireland-winning team in 1980. After I left school, though, rugby became my main game.

'It wasn't until my final year at Garbally that I became a rugby player. The previous year, we had qualified for the All-Ireland Colleges hurling semi-final, losing to St Peter's, Wexford. In my Leaving Cert year, though, we went out of the competition early, so I had time on my hands. The school were stuck for a hooker and thought I looked the part. At the time, we did not take part in any competitions. The local bishop felt that the rugby ethos was a corrupting influence on our Catholic sensibilities. We just played friendlies. My first game was against Blackrock College. I remember spending the journey to Dublin at the back of the bus reading the rule book because I was still a rugby novice. I couldn't figure out this offside law.

'After I left school, I joined the cadets. We played in the Leinster Towns Cup for a season. In my first match, I made the fatal mistake of winning two balls against the head. The next thing I knew, I was being carried off. I quickly learned how to survive in the rugby jungle. I did my degree in Galway, where I played for UCG in the Connacht League and quickly found myself making my debut for Connacht against Ulster.

'In 1973 when my university days finished, I joined St Mary's because I enjoyed their style of play. This caused me some problems. My superior in the Army at the time was a great Monkstown fan. In almost our first conversation, I was marched into his office and he said in his most authoritarian style, "You're joining Monkstown, aren't you?"

'I answered meekly, "No, sir, I'm not." I was later interrogated by him again on the reasons why I hadn't joined Monkstown.

'My early years with Mary's were a bit of a disaster; I was constantly injured. There wasn't the specialisation in sports injuries then that you get now. Basically, there were three strategies: bandage it, rest it or give it up. I was so keen to play that I made things worse for myself because I would return far too early. I'd say, though, that when I did play, my teammate Sean Lynch was a great help to me. He was a great man to bind a scrum.'

BACK ON TRACK

It was not until 1977 that he got his career back into a groove, captaining the Irish 'B' team during the 1977–78 season. Then, on the controversial tour to Australia in 1979, he made his international debut, playing in both Tests, although he went out as number two to Pat Whelan.

'At the time, there was an incredible fuss about the fact that Tony Ward had been dropped and Ollie Campbell was chosen in his place. I was totally oblivious to it all. I heard my own name mentioned when the team was announced and nothing else registered with me. A tour is a great place to win a first cap because you're sheltered from all the hype, press attention and distractions that you get at home. I was able to hold my place the following season. I never felt threatened but I never felt comfortable either. All you can do is perform to your very best and forget about the lads who are challenging for your position.'

In the 1980–81 season, Fitzgerald sustained a serious shoulder injury in a club match.

'A bad situation was made worse by a doctor during the match. Immediately after the injury he tried to yank my shoulder back into place. Then I was assisted off the pitch. He put me flat on my back on the sidelines and tried a second time. As a result of the injury and the "cure", I missed the entire international season.'

A CAPTAIN'S PART

Not only did Fitzgerald regain his place on the team the following season, he found himself taking over the captaincy from Fergus Slattery. What was the secret of his success?

'I think I'm very sensitive to people and curious about them. I was still a relatively inexperienced player in comparison with most of my pack. I knew there was no way I could use my army style to deal with these guys. You have to remember there were a lot of world-class players in the forwards, like Orr, Keane, Slattery, [John] O'Driscoll and Duggan. The previous year, Ireland had won no match and those guys were fed up hearing from people who knew virtually nothing about rugby, "You're only a shower of . . . " That really annoyed them and they were fired up to prove just how good they were.

'Whatever you say to players of that calibre has to be effective. Every player is different. The most important thing is to find out how to bring out the best in each player, to find a strategy appropriate to his personality. In 1982, before the decisive Triple Crown match against Scotland, the *Irish Press* printed a very critical article about John O'Driscoll, who was a superb player and central to our success that season. The day before the match, I quietly went to him in the Shelbourne Hotel and expressed my sympathy about the article. He knew nothing about it and asked to see it. He read it but said nothing. The next day he played like a man possessed.

'The most difficult players to handle are those making their debut. They get distracted by the press and the hype. The worst influence on them, though, is relatives who want to socialise with them and fill their head with all kinds of nonsense. The best way around this is the "buddy system": get them to room with one of the more experienced players.

'As captain, no matter what position you play in, you can't see everything that is happening on the pitch. You need guys you can quickly turn to in the heat of battle who can read the game and tell what is needed in their area. Fergus Slattery was a great player in those situations. Ollie Campbell, apart from being an outstanding player, had a great rugby brain and I relied on him to control the game for us. His partner at scrum-half, Robbie McGrath, also played a crucial role. He was a very underrated player who never got the acclaim he deserved. Later in his career, Hugo MacNeill developed into a very tactically astute performer.

'Our coach, Tom Kiernan, was always two moves ahead of you. I often heard myself saying things and later realise that Tom had discreetly planted the thought in my mind either the previous day or a week earlier. He was a great man-manager. He was always prompting you because he wanted the ideas to come from the players themselves so that they would take more responsibility for their own decisions. Tom was not called "The Grey Fox" for nothing. I wanted the players to do more physical work but Tom always subjected everything to a cost–benefit analysis and asked, "Was it worth it?" He always said that what exhausted players was not training sessions but constantly travelling up and down to Dublin. P.J. Dwyer, as chairman of selectors, was also somebody who was a great prompter of ideas.

'My clearest memory of 1982 is of Gareth Davies limping off in the Wales game. We could see it in their eyes that they knew we were going to beat them. The England game really established that we were a side to be reckoned with. I remember, travelling back to the hotel on the bus when everybody else was ecstatic, Willie Duggan was sitting at the back of the bus working out the practicalities of what was needed for a Triple Crown decider in terms of extra tickets for players and so on. There were a lot of myths about Willie and Moss Keane at the time in terms of drinking and lack of training. That's rubbish. I was living beside Moss at the time and was training every other night with him. I'm not exaggerating one bit when I say I was going flat out just to keep up with him. Moss's contribution was crucial on many levels, in my view, not least of which was in telling Ginger McLoughlin, "I'm not going back." I know this is very technical but basically, to put it as simply as I can, if the prop-forward retreats the second-row normally has to as well otherwise the prop's back is arched up. Ginger knew that this would be his fate if he didn't hold his line, which meant that he went in there fighting like a tiger. It's things like that which make the difference between victory and defeat, and only someone of Moss's stature could have pulled it off.

'I believe we should also have won the Triple Crown in 1983. We should have beaten Wales but we lacked discipline. The French match was like World War Four. World War Three was the previous year. Both sides had a lot of physical scores to settle in the first ten minutes of the game.'

IN THE EYE OF A STORM

1983 also saw Fitzgerald selected as captain of the Lions.

'It was like a whirlwind. I first heard about the captaincy when I got a call from a journalist. I was very surprised to hear the news, because the strong rumour, coming from the English press, was that Peter Wheeler was getting the job. It was a tremendous honour and I didn't give a tuppenny damn about who was disappointed. There was so much hype it was hard to focus. It was like getting a first cap multiplied by ten with all the receptions and media interest. I had to take ten days off in Mayo to regain my focus and kept in shape by training three times a day.

'I underestimated the ferocity of the campaign that would be waged against me. I couldn't influence what was said about me, so I just tried to do all I could to get the best possible performance out of the team. It's part of the psychological war that goes on when the Lions tour New Zealand that the media on each side talks up their respective squads. However, in New Zealand they were stunned to see that the British media were trying to outdo each other in terms of rubbishing me. By the time we arrived, everybody wanted to know "Who is this fool of a hooker?" It got to the stage where I expected the first question of every interview to be "What kind of ape are you?" I was amazed that the New Zealanders knew everything about me. It shows how fanatical they are about the game.

'The tour was a roller-coaster for me. As captain, I was asked to attend all kinds of receptions and press events, which I was determined to do because the PR aspect is so important. The result, though, was that I never got a day off and couldn't get away from the press. There was one day I was determined to get away for a break. The Irish guys had arranged a game of golf, so I decided to join them. We pulled a fast one by having our team car parked outside the front of the hotel as a decoy and getting a car to pick us up and discreetly whisk us away. I'm not a golfer but was just managing to relax at last at the fourth hole when I heard a rumpus behind me. It was the media scrum!

'The press have to fill their columns. There were all kinds of stories about splits in the camp which were absolutely untrue. There was a story about fights on the team bus which was a blatant lie. At the end, the English players threw some of their journalists into the swimming pool, they were so disgusted by the untruths. As a result of all that was written about me, I developed a very tough skin. You are judged by your results and at the end of the day we didn't win our matches, which was a huge disappointment for me.'

The Lions got off to a bad start and never really recovered.

'The crucial Test was the first one. We had a few really good scoring opportunities which we didn't take, especially in the second half, when we dropped the ball a few times. If we had scored, we would have won the match and had we won the match, the momentum would have been with us. They would have been forced to change what was a fairly seasoned team because there was a lot of clamour down there to do that and a loss would have added to the pressure. They had an element of doubt going into that game but the Test win blew all that doubt away and, I suppose, put doubt in our minds instead. That First Test was probably our best shot but we didn't grasp it and ended up losing all four.

'They also had the advantage of having a more settled side throughout. They only had two changes in the back line in the whole series. Because we had so many injuries, we had to make a lot of changes, which is not what you want when you are trying to put patterns of play together and get cohesion into the side. We were particularly hard-hit at scrum-half. Terry Holmes got injured. Then Roy Laidlaw got injured. Then Nigel Melville flew out and he got injured. Finally Steve Smith had to fly out.

'I think we could have won the First Test, which would have changed the shape of the tour. I have to take part of the blame for that defeat because my throw-ins were poor. The only consolation for me was that the squad stuck together throughout, which is not easy when you're losing. The controversy over my selection as captain meant that we got off to a difficult start.'

There were other problems to be sorted out, including his relationship with the coach, Scotland's Jim Telfer.

'My style as a captain was more hands-on than some people's. I was very used to being involved in the preparation side of things. Jim Telfer had different views, for example in that he would have been used to the Scotland captain playing a different role. These were just things that had to be accommodated.'

PARADISE REGAINED

Happily, Fitzie's fortunes would be revived when he led Ireland to a second Triple Crown on 30 March 1985.

'Being successful with your country would always be the highlight of your career and from my point of view, winning Triple Crowns would always be the high point because they don't happen very often. Of course, on a personal level, the recognition of being selected as captain of the Lions was a lovely thing to happen, but doing well with Ireland meant the most to me.

'The best thing about '82 was the fact that we did it even though up to '81 Ireland had lost nine matches on the trot. I took over the captaincy in '82 and it was the fact that we won the Triple Crown against that sort of backdrop that made me most proud. It was something similar in '85. In '84, I had been dropped and Ireland had lost their matches and the next year, with a whole new team of young lads, Ireland won the Triple Crown against the odds. I think in sport it's the things you win when you're not expected to that are the great achievements.'

At first after the Lions tour, Fitzgerald's misfortunes had accelerated when he was dropped from the Irish team for the England match after the defeat to Wales in 1984. Was he a fall guy for Ireland's slide?

'I don't know why I was dropped. Nobody ever told me. Maybe I deserved to be axed. The one beef I had was the way the whole thing was handled. It was said that I was not available for selection because of injury but in fact I played for Mary's that day. I wish they had been straight about it and said I was dropped. I was determined I would come back and play for Ireland in 1985, though I had no thoughts about the captaincy.

'When Mick Doyle took over in '84, he brought me back as captain. Doyler made an enormous contribution to our Triple Crown win. He won the psychological war in terms of keeping all the media attention on him and away from the players. He was the crown prince making edicts but he was also very tactically astute. His chairman of selectors Mick Cuddy was a peculiar character. He was an insider in the IRFU but got on exceptionally well with Doyler and the players. His great gift was that he got things done. If we wanted new gear, he made the phone calls and got it for us. For my part, I got on exceptionally well with Doyler. Ours was much stronger than a rugby relationship. There was a deep friendship between us and we complemented each other in lots of ways.

'However, I would say that Doyler's contribution was not nearly as positive the following season. There were some crazy selection decisions. For example, dropping Phil Orr was madness. Doyler's focus was not as clear. I'm not sure why that was but I felt his heart wasn't in it as much. Having said that, I was not as focused myself because I had left the army and taken on a new, challenging job with James Crean.'

In the end, business commitments led to Fitzgerald's premature retirement, forcing him to reluctantly forego the opportunity to play in the inaugural World Cup, but he was back at the heart of the action as coach to the Irish team in 1991.

'If I had the chance to do things differently in terms of my time as coach, I would. I was reluctant to take the position but the IRFU pressed me. There was a good buzz early on in that we brought in a lot of new players and we played an exciting, expansive game. Although we played an attractive brand of rugby, we were always nearly winning. That's not good enough. Eventually you have to win, otherwise morale and confidence start to sap. The tour to New Zealand in 1992 was a bit of a disaster. We faced an impossible task because so many key players were unable to travel. Due to work demands, I shouldn't have travelled but out of loyalty I went, because there were so many defections. We made a superhuman effort and again nearly won the First Test but it was downhill all the way after that. Later that year, I had to step down for business reasons. It was not the ideal time to go because I would have liked to go out on a winning note.'

There is a note of reticence in Fitzgerald's voice for the first time when he is asked about the difficulties of balancing his rugby duties as Irish coach and his other commitments.

'The job of Irish coach is a full-time one. There was a *cost* to me in business terms. I'm not prepared to elaborate. Likewise there was a cost in terms of family life.'

23

JIM'LL FIX IT

IRELAND HAS PRODUCED MANY PLAYERS WHO WERE NOTED FOR their commitment to the green jersey. In this category was Jim Glennon, who always gave his absolute best to the team. To this day, Glennon continues to make the proud boast, 'Nobody ever used their arse better in the lineout than me!' Glennon was never a great lineout winner but was very hard to get a lineout ball from. He struck up a great relationship with George Wallace in the Leinster second row. Coach Mick Doyle went so far as to nickname them 'Urbi et Orbi'.

Strangely Glennon's memories of being capped for Ireland are not as happy as his memories of playing for Leinster.

'Tragedy struck my club, Skerries, just after I won my second cap in 1980 when one of our players in Skerries, Bernard Healy, got a bad neck injury, which devastated the club. In 1987, I broke A.J.F. O'Reilly's record for the longest gap between internationals when I got my third cap. But by the weirdest of coincidences, the joy of being recalled for me was shattered when another clubmate, Alan Boylan, sustained a serious neck injury on the eve of the game.'

Glennon played in Doyle's first and last representative games as coach: in Leinster's 1979 match with Cheshire and Ireland's World Cup match against Australia in 1987 respectively. He lays claim to an unusual distinction – he once saw Doyle speechless.

Glennon was reported not to be a big fan of Doyle's longer team talks and is said to have casually remarked, 'Doyler, the secret of a good speech is to have a good opening, a good ending and very little in between.'

THE PRODIGAL SON

After winning two caps for Ireland in 1980, Glennon spent seven years in the international wilderness. He came out of retirement to win his final four caps.

'I had genuinely given up on it in 1986. On 31 August that year, I returned from holiday in Kerry. The previous night, I had been out with my wife Helen and sister-in-law Aileen. Aileen is married to the former Meath footballer Brendan Murray. Brendan and I were having a great chat with the hotel owner about sport. At one stage, Brendan went to the loo and I told our host who Brendan was. A while later, I went to the toilet and Brendan told him my history. When I returned, the barman asked me how many caps had I won. I said, "Three: two in 1980 and one in 1987." No doubt I would have forgotten about that pledge but when we got home, Phil Orr and his wife called to see us. Phil bet me a tenner that I wouldn't play for Leinster that season. A weighing scales was produced and I was the wrong side of 20 st. I later learned that Phil's approach had been semi-organised, because Roly Meates, who was coaching Leinster at the time, was looking for an extra bit of power in the scrum. I can tell you, he didn't want me for my lineout ability! The season with Leinster went really well and I found myself back in the Irish team and flying off to the World Cup.'

Mick Doyle joked that after the tournament he paid Glennon a great compliment. 'I told him he was the most responsible player I ever saw. He was responsible for more disasters than anyone else on the team!'

CAL

Asked about the biggest personality he played with, Glennon does not hesitate for a second.

'Phil O'Callaghan. I toured with Philo to Zambia in 1977 with Clontarf. The previous November, I had won my first provincial cap for Leinster. I injured my knee in the last few minutes and was replaced by Jim Bardon of Clontarf for his first cap. At the time, I was one of the organisers of an annual beach game in Skerries to raise money for the lifeboats institution. I invited Jim to play the following year but we collided in the game and he dislocated his shoulder. He was due to tour to Zambia with Clontarf shortly after but his injury meant he couldn't travel, so Clontarf invited me to take his place. I then learned that Philo was also to be a guest of the club on the tour and was expected to be the entertainment content. Let's just say he didn't disappoint!

Everybody knows that Philo was one of the great characters of Irish rugby but what people sometimes forget is that even that late on in his career he was a superb player. We had a fantastic tour and I was billeted out in the bush for five days with Philo. We were staying with a former Scottish international and Lion, Peter Stagg, who had a massive ranch. Staggy was 6 ft 10 in. I learned more about touring in those five days with Philo than I learned in the remainder of my career – though I'm not prepared to elaborate!'

MANAGING MANUAL

In more recent years, Glennon made his mark as a rugby pundit in both the print and broadcast media, although the call of politics lured him away from the game. In 2002, he was elected to the Irish parliament.

However, he will probably be best remembered for his term as a rugby manager. In January 1996, he was chosen as the Philips Manager of the Month for his work with Leinster – guiding them to the Interprovincial Championship and to the Heineken Cup semi-final. One of the stories told about him from that time is the way he told a player that he was to be dropped from the squad: 'I've got good news for you. You won't have to worry about being late for training ever again.' However, serious fans remember him for his shrewd judgement, notably the way he fast-tracked the youthful Shane 'Shaggy' Horgan into the full Leinster set-up. Shaggy has publicly acknowledged his debt to Glennon.

Jim was also known for his shrewd man-management. One of the stories told about him in this regard is the way he dealt with a Leinster player who had a very high opinion of himself and a fondness for the good life but who was not noted for his intelligence. The team were flying off on tour to Italy and were travelling in economy class. The player in question saw that the first-class seats appeared to be much larger and more comfortable, and he moved forward to the last empty one. The stewardess checked his ticket and told the player that his seat was in economy. The Leinster player insisted he was not moving. Flustered, the stewardess went back to the cockpit and informed the captain of the problem. The captain went back and told the player that his assigned seat was in economy. A heated row developed. Seeing the commotion, Glennon assured the pilot he would handle the situation. He then briefly whispered something into the player's ear. He immediately got up, said, 'Thank you so much, Jim,' shook hands with

Glennon and rushed back to his seat in the economy section. The captain was watching with rapt attention and asked Glennon what he had said to the player.

Jim replied, 'I just told him that the first-class section wasn't going to Italy.'

24

NEAR ORR FAR

IRISH PROP FORWARDS HAVE ALWAYS BEEN GREAT CHARACTERS.
Tojo Byrne was a very good prop who played a number of games for
Leinster. However, he was small, and one of those guys who was always
at the final trials as a sub or on the 'B' team. He is a Dublin butcher and
has a marvellous sense of humour. At one stage, he was sub for a Leinster
final. Near the end, the 'A' side's number 8 went off injured. Tojo was
asked to go on as a replacement, even though it meant playing out of
position. As he shuffled on, a packet of cigarettes fell out of his pocket.
Then, as he took his place in the lineout, he looked at his opposite number.
Tojo, at 5 ft 8 in., was standing against Nicky Sweetman, 6 ft 7 in.
According to folklore, Tojo turned to scrum-half Johnny Moloney and
asked him, in a loud voice, if he wanted it off the top, or caught and driven.

Irish rugby has seldom produced a better prop forward than Phil Orr.
In fact, he became the world's most capped prop forward. Of his 58
caps, 49 were won consecutively (one short of the Scottish international
Sandy Carmichael's record for a prop forward of 50 caps), from 1976
to the match against Wales in 1986. He was recalled for the last match
of the 1986 championship.

PARISIAN WALKWAYS
In 1976, Orr made his international debut in Paris, coming in as a late
replacement for Paddy Agnew, as Ireland lost by a then record 26–3.

'It was a very strange experience for me. I don't think people
appreciate the culture shock Paris is for you, especially the first time.

If I was in charge of things, I would be inclined to bring the Irish team over on the Friday, not on the Thursday as is the norm. The food is so unfamiliar and the language barrier brings its own problems. Then, as you are driving through Paris, guys are looking at the shop windows and it's very hard to keep the focus that is needed. I feel we need better psychological preparation for the French matches.

'My clearest memory of the whole weekend is of breakfast the morning of the match. I was rooming with Stewart McKinney and he ordered breakfast in bed for both of us, scrambled eggs and toast. We were waiting for ages and ages but with no sign of any service. Stewart went out into the corridor and saw a few waiters walking up and down with trays of food. He simply grabbed one from a very surprised waiter, exchanged pleasantries and brought in the tray. I remember very little about the actual game except that it went very quickly and I was black and blue all over. I learned to react more quickly and to look after myself better after that.

'One thing I never could understand was the hassle that some players would put themselves through the morning of a match. We got only two tickets each at the time but there were lads who would be getting themselves in a rash worrying about tickets for family and friends. That's no way to prepare for a big match.

'The adrenalin is really flowing before an international, so it's crucial to keep your mind right. For home internationals, we always stayed in the Shelbourne. On the night before a match and on the day of the game, the lobby was a hive of activity. New players were told not to hang around because they would get too caught up in the occasion and their performance would suffer. In the early years, I followed that advice fairly religiously but at the end of my career, I would deliberately go down to the foyer just to get the adrenalin flowing.

'Something that always bugged me on those occasions was that on a big-match weekend Dublin goes rugby mad. On the Friday afternoon, evening, night and Saturday morning, everybody was going to some reception or party. It seemed that the only people not drinking were us!'

THE FAB FOUR

Orr was one of only three Irish players, with Willie Duggan and Mike Gibson, to be selected on the Lions tour to New Zealand in 1977. When Geoff Wheel withdrew from the tour, Moss Keane stepped in for him.

'The biggest shock for me about the Lions tour was the British press.

We would get on the team bus and there would be two busloads of journalists watching everything we did. All of these guys are looking for a different angle and would dig up any dirt they could find, or even a whiff of trouble. The pressure that puts you under is immense. I think that British sport is being destroyed by its journalists.

'I enjoyed the Ireland and Leinster tours more than the Lions tours. The 1977 Lions tour lasted three and half months, which is too long. One of the things I learned is that the Irish will talk to everybody. The non-Irish Lions won't. The Lions are not very popular in Australia and New Zealand because basically the British are hated, though they like the Irish down under. I particularly enjoyed Ireland's tour to Japan because it was such a different culture.

'I was lucky to play for a great Leinster side in the late 1970s and early 1980s. We never expected to lose and we could always shift into a higher gear whenever we were threatened in any way. One of the clearest memories I have is of touring Romania with Leinster in 1980. It was like entering a time warp. Most of the time we were starving because there wasn't enough food, largely because it all went up to Moscow. There was nothing in the shops except bare shelves. If you wanted an orange, for example, you had to order it the day before. One incident stands out for me. We stopped for a meal of sorts in a halfway house. As we got off the bus, what struck me most was that there wasn't the sound of a bird to be heard. I learned later that DDT had killed all the insects and the birds had migrated.

'The belief at the time was that one in every four people in Romania was an informer for the Securitate. It subsequently emerged that this was a lie deliberately put about by the dictator Nicolae Ceausescu to keep everyone in line.'

The high points of Orr's international career were the Triple Crown victories of 1982 and 1985. The low point came in 1986.

'I lost my place for the Welsh match to Paul Kennedy of London Irish, I think more because of the final trial than because of the drubbing we got from France in our opening match of the campaign. I was up against Dessie Fitzgerald on one side of the scrum and Jim McCoy was up against Paul Kennedy. Jim was pretty secure in his place and I don't think Paul thought he had any real chance of getting into the side, so they weren't trying too hard, but Dessie was mad keen to get picked and was wired to the moon that day, so I didn't give the "commanding performance" I would have liked.

'It would be a lie to say I wasn't very disappointed to be dropped. It made me even more determined to get onto the side. The hardest part of the experience for me was taking my place in the queue at the turnstiles to get into Lansdowne Road for the Welsh match. I played a club game for Old Wesley that morning and the lads were slagging me on the way to the match, asking me if I would be able to find Lansdowne Road on my own because I was so used to travelling there on the team bus.'

In the final match of the 1986 season, Orr regained his place for the home game with Scotland, which Ireland lost by the narrowest of margins. It was his 50th cap. The occasion was all the more memorable because he had the honour of leading the team onto the field. This event left an interesting legacy which today hangs proudly in Orr's home. Some of the Irish players penned a tribute to him and organised a singing telegram for him. He suspects Hugo MacNeill was the author. Hugo was one of Ireland's finest full-backs but on this evidence he is no Brendan Kennelly or Bono! The best line of this neatly typed, lengthy ode which Orr has had framed for posterity is 'The greatest prop among the Celts!'. However, it is the short handwritten message at the side which catches the eye: 'The next 50 is the toughest. Sam Torrance.' The celebrated golfer happened to be a guest at the Shelbourne Hotel that evening and was readily persuaded to join the festivities.

'The next season, the inaugural World Cup was taking place and I wanted to be part of it, so I trained that bit harder. To be honest, the tour was a great disappointment. The travel arrangements and the hotels were of a poor standard. I remember in Wellington it got to the stage where I would bring a book down to our meals because we would have to wait so long for food.'

PARTING SHOTS

Even when he departed the Irish scene, Orr still had time for a last hurrah on the international stage. Sadly, though, it was the greatest mismatch since the ultra-gorgeous Claudia Schiffer got engaged to the considerably less attractive David Copperfield.

'After the World Cup, I retired from international rugby, but later that year I was invited to play for a World XV in Japan as part of the All Blacks tour. They had Japanese players as hooker and scrum-half who couldn't speak a word of English between them. These are the two most important positions on the field in terms of making the calls on the pitch and giving instructions. It made absolutely no sense to have non-English speakers in those key positions in what was essentially a team of English speakers! We learned the Japanese for "one", "three" and "five", and limited ourselves to three calls. To confuse the opposition, I came up with the idea of using Japanese brand names so that our call would be "Honda One" etc. in Japanese. Then it was brought to my attention that one of the Japanese players worked for Honda and didn't like the company name being used in this way. So that ended my masterplan!

'We all knew the All Blacks were in a mean mood. They had defeated Japan 106–4 in the Test game. The mistake the Japanese made was scoring a try. If they hadn't had the cheek to score, I reckon the All Blacks would have let them off with a 50-point defeat. I can't remember much about the match except that we were murdered in the first half at tight-head prop. All I could say by way of tactical insight at half-time was "We're going to retreat carefully!"'

'I do remember that after the game the players said we wanted to be brought to the Japanese Disneyland. The All Blacks had already arranged to go and agreed to take us on their team bus. The problem was that the organisers hadn't got clearance for us. When we arrived, we went inside first but the Blacks were refused entry. They weren't used to this type of treatment and there were ructions about it!'

Orr is still heavily involved with Old Wesley and was club president for its centenary year. Indeed, such was his affection for the club that once when he played for Leinster against Italy, he did a rugby version of a 'Pieres dive' and rolled around in agony four minutes from time so that his clubmate Mick Jackman could win his first cap for Leinster. Observers were a bit puzzled about Jackman's psychic powers because he was warming up well before Phil got his 'injury'. So, now his playing days are over, what are his happiest rugby memories?

'Above all, I think of the guys like Willie Duggan. I love the story of him turning up for training with the Irish squad and when he was told to warm up he replied, "I don't need to. I had the heater on in the car."

'On Leinster's tour to Romania in 1980, we were soon fed up with the food on offer. On a bus journey, the two big jokers in the side, Paul McNaughton and Freddie McLennan, walked up the bus with a list taking the lunch orders. We were told we could choose between T-bone steak or grilled chicken, and we had to indicate whether we wanted chips, baked or sautéd potatoes, and select from a choice of vegetables, as it all had to be ordered in advance. All the players got very excited and great care was taken over the menu. We arrived at an impressive-looking restaurant for a big meal. There was a buzz of expectancy – which turned into a stunned silence when the food arrived. Each dish was the same: a big bowl of clear, greasy soup and in it a huge fish head complete with eyes. Nothing was eaten. McNaughton and McLennan had to be led out; they were laughing so much they couldn't walk.'

25

THE PERFECT TEN

RUGBY TOURS ARE NOTORIOUS FOR THEIR UNPREDICTABILITY. THE Irish tour to Australia in 1979 was no exception. More accurately, unpredictability was the order of the day. Consider the case of John Moloney who went on the tour as cover for the incumbent scrum-half Colin Patterson and won a shock call-up as wing three-quarter for the Tests.

But nothing could compare to the fairy tale of Old Belvedere's Ollie Campbell. Hans Christian Andersen could not have emulated his story. The 25 year old's international career had been launched and almost abandoned courtesy of one shattering appearance at Lansdowne Road against Australia three years earlier. He missed four penalties and was immediately written off by many who claimed to be judges of international players. Despite injury problems prior to the Australian tour – he had been out of rugby the previous season from September to February with ligament trouble – he had shown good club form and justified his recall to the Irish squad as cover for the out-half position. In the greatest selection shock in living memory, he displaced Tony Ward, the greatest superstar in Irish rugby since the emergence of Mike Gibson. Ollie's subsequent textbook performances were a revelation and he kicked Ireland to victory in both Tests. For Campbell all his Christmases had come at once but his dream was Ward's nightmare.

Following the sensational decision to drop Ward on that tour in favour of Campbell, the players found themselves unwittingly embroiled in the long-running Ward–Campbell saga. Records and adulation meant little to Campbell, a quietly spoken fly-half who would rather have melted into the background than become the centre of attention. A reluctant star, he was far from the norm, with no time for the arrogance or pretensions associated with such a label. Off the field, he tried to portray himself as an ordinary guy; on it, he could not disguise his skill.

Rugby features prominently in his family tree. His maternal uncles, Seamus and Michael Henry, won Leinster Cups with Belvedere College. Seamus (also Ollie's godfather) captained one of the famous seven-in-a-row Old Belvedere Senior Cup-winning teams in the 1940s, as well as captaining Suttonians to their last Metro Cup win in 1947 before they were a major force in the game. Ollie's father, James Oliver, was also on that team, as prop. His father played Minor football with Louth but after he left school, he went to live in Howth and joined Suttonians club, where he met his wife Joan. It was his father who bought Campbell his first leather ball.

'I was only five or six and he said, "If you can catch this, you can keep it." I did! He only missed one international between Ireland and Scotland in over 40 years. The gap was caused by the birth of my sister. I always thought it was a very weak excuse! My father was hugely supportive right through my career. It was he who taught me the skill of tackling.'

An impressive framed painting of Belvedere College graces Campbell's trophy-laden apartment and offers a tiny clue as to the affection he feels for his Alma Mater.

'To my shame, I mostly associate Belvedere simply with rugby. I remember when we lost a first-round Junior Cup match against Newbridge 6–3 I cried for three days. When I became an adult and played for Ireland, I was much more mature about the whole thing. Whenever we lost an international I only cried for one day! Winning the Leinster Cup in both 1971 and 1972 was an incredible thrill. After the first victory, I took the mud from Lansdowne Road off my boots and kept it in a plastic bag as a souvenir. I only threw it out a few years ago. Although she never missed her brothers playing, my mother only ever saw me play three times. I was small as a kid and the first time she saw me play she was afraid I would be killed. When I became an international, she would turn on the radio from time to time during the game to see if my name was mentioned. When it was, she knew at least I was still alive. That was really all she was concerned about.

'At school, not only was I not a kicker in terms of kicking for goal, but I hardly kicked in play at all and was not even responsible for 25-yard drop-outs or kick-offs or restarts. Times change! When I played my first game for Old Belvedere Firsts after I left school and we scored a try, the captain assumed that because I was playing fly-half, I was a kicker. So I just did what other fly-halfs do and it sailed through. And that's how it started. After that, it became something of an obsession to perfect the art of place-kicking and I practised endlessly. I figured everybody else had been taking place kicks right through their school days so I had to make up for ten years' lost ground. There is also a strong perfectionist streak in me, I have to admit.'

One of the few occasions when Campbell's kicking let him down was in his international debut against Australia in 1976.

'It was one of the biggest disappointments of my life. It was everything you want your first cap not to be. I was dropped from the side straight away. It was the only time in my career I was ever dropped off any team.'

It would be three years before Campbell regained his place on the Irish team, for the Australian tour at the expense of Tony Ward. The following season, he set a new points record (46) for the Five Nations championship. Campbell's next close encounter with Ward was on the Lions tour in 1980.

'With the First Test looming and with both out-halfs, Gareth Davies and me, injured, a fit one was needed. Who was flown out? A.J.P. Ward. Not only did he play in the First Test, he scored 18 points, which was then a Lions individual-points-scoring record in a Test match. Was there to be no escape from this guy?'

CENTRE STAGE

In 1981, Campbell was moved to the centre to allow for Ward's return as Irish out-half. How did he react to the change?

'I never minded the idea of playing in the same team as Tony – provided I was at out-half. The centre is a very different position and to be honest, I was never really comfortable there. In 1981, we lost all four matches, by a single score, after leading in all four at half-time. I remember at the time Tom Kiernan, our coach, repeatedly told us that whatever the results, if there had been a Lions tour that year, the country that would have had the most representatives would have been Ireland. I'm not sure if that was true but it certainly kept our morale and self-belief up. That summer, we toured South Africa. It was a non-event for me, concussion and a broken wrist keeping me down to about 50 minutes of rugby.'

The following season, things came together for the Irish side as they won the Triple Crown. One of Campbell's enduring recollections of the game is of the fans.

'Probably my abiding memory of that whole season is the reaction of the crowd during the whole of the second half of the Scottish game, particularly in the East Stand, because much of the half seemed to be played there. I think it was really the start of "Molly Malone" becoming the "anthem" of the Irish team. The atmosphere was just incredible. I heard a piece of radio commentary on the game for the first time a few years ago and it really sent chills down the back of my neck. An interesting postscript to the match came when my aunt in Scotland asked me to send on my autograph for a local lad who showed a lot of rugby promise. Later, he would be a star for both Scotland and the Lions. His name? Craig Chalmers.

'There were a lot of great moments that season, I suppose most famously Ginger's celebrated try against England. On a personal level, I remember a break I made which set up Moss Finn's first try against Wales; the virtual touch-line conversion of Ginger's try at Twickenham; and the drop-goal against Scotland. That score came from a special loop movement we had devised in January with David Irwin but kept under wraps. It should have led to a try but I gave a bad pass to Keith Crossan and the move broke down, so we had to settle for three points. Life for that team was never really the same afterwards. Most of the team had grown up with no international success. There was a huge sense of achievement and bonding that has lasted ever since.

'When we won our first match, all we were trying to do was bring a sequence of seven consecutive defeats to an end. Two weeks later, we won at Twickenham and suddenly we were in a Triple Crown situation. It was something that as a team we had never thought about. But we knew we were on to something big when we saw the huge crowds watching us in training. That was something we had never experienced before. It was a very exciting week, as we had a general election at the time following the fall of Garrett FitzGerald's first coalition government; but nobody seemed to care about it. Everybody was more excited about the possibility of a Triple Crown. Ireland had never won one at Lansdowne Road before.

'The tension mounted but when Tom Kiernan decided to have a closed practice session on the Thursday before the game, suddenly the Triple Crown match became just another game. I have never felt so at ease and comfortable going into a game. It was a masterstroke as far as I was concerned. Two weeks previously, I had missed a penalty against England that would have sewn the game up. On the Sunday afterwards, I went to Anglesea Road with my five balls and kicked for two hours from the same spot I had missed from the previous day. Ninety per cent of all the kicks I took in practice over the next two weeks were from that spot. When the first penalty arrived after just three minutes of the Scotland game, I relaxed. Amazingly, it was from exactly the same spot. I felt I could have kicked it with my eyes closed but I didn't take the chance. We were on our way and, for me at least, never before had the value of practice been more clearly demonstrated.'

After the Lions tour to New Zealand in 1983, in which he scored 124 points, Campbell's career never reached the same dizzy heights again. In his 22 appearances in the Irish jersey, he scored a then record 217 points. His retirement from international rugby was, through no fault of his own, shrouded in mystery. He is delighted with the opportunity to set the record straight about his decision to bid a reluctant farewell to the game he loves.

'The general perception was that New Zealand tired me out. Nothing could be further from the truth. New Zealand rejuvenated me. As far as I was concerned, I had achieved rugby's holy grail. When I returned, I was brimming with enthusiasm and new ideas about rugby. I did get some bug for a short time but that was a relatively minor setback. The real problem was hamstrings. I strained my hamstring in the penultimate game of the Lions tour and shouldn't have played in the final Test under any circumstances but we were so decimated by injuries that basically anyone who could walk was selected. In fact, I had to come off in the match after half an hour. We were losing 12–3 at the time but ended up losing 38–3. I asked the lads later, "What happened after I went off?"!

'I began the 1983–84 season feeling keen, healthy and eager, with the confidence of a mature player but the hamstrings got worse and worse and worse. My problems were compounded by the fact that both my hamstrings were affected but I struggled through that season. I trained harder than I had ever trained before in the summer of 1984 but the following season was a disaster because of the hamstrings. I trained even harder the following summer but my hamstring went in the first ten minutes of the season. By this time, I had a chronic problem and a lot of scar tissue. I visited practically every specialist in the business. It was even suggested to me that I should consider ripping them out completely or having them operated on. To be honest, if I'd thought it would have worked, I would have gone for it but I was not convinced.'

THANK YOU FOR THE MUSIC

Contrary to popular perception, Campbell has other interests apart from rugby. In 1995, the hottest ticket in pop music, the family group from Dundalk the Corrs, released their debut album, *Forgiven Not Forgotten*, which quickly rocketed up the charts. In the sleeve notes, 'special thanks' are expressed to Ollie Campbell. Is this the former Irish out-half?

'I'm afraid so. The thanks is there for the musical direction I've given them! Seriously, the Corrs are managed by one of my closest friends, John Hughes. With his brother, Willie, he formed the group Minor Detail, who attracted a lot of critical acclaim in the mid-1980s but never got the commercial success they deserved. As I don't have a note in my head, the truth is I'm probably the least musical person ever to have been mentioned on an album sleeve!'

After the Irish squad were awarded professional contracts, Campbell jokingly thought of establishing a petition of ex-international players asking that former internationals be rewarded retrospectively. Although he would appear an obvious choice, Campbell has declined to enter the media world as a rugby analyst. What is behind this reticence?

'Firstly, my main love is coaching. Secondly, when you are a media commentator you cannot sit on the fence. You have to be critical. That means that your relationship with any particular Irish team suffers.'

UNDER THE MICROSCOPE

Ollie is a big admirer of one of the biggest names in Irish rugby today.

'I remember Brian O' Driscoll was compared to God after scoring "the" try for the Lions in 2001. I think if Brian continues in the same style, that in time God will be very flattered by the comparison. I still get a shiver down my spine when I think about the try even now. What struck me was the words of Ian McGeechan, who coached the Lions on three consecutive tours. He said, "You can play for your country and become a hero but if you play for the Lions, you can become a legend."

I think when Brian scored that try, he became an instant Lions legend.

'Brian does have an unerring instinct for the essence of rugby, which is to score tries. He knows exactly where the line is. He's got an amazing strike rate at a time when defences are so well organised and I think that says more than anything else about Brian's ability.

'One of his great tries was the infamous one against France in 2001, which many people were surprised that the video referee awarded. What struck me the most was that as the camera was on Brian, as we were all waiting for the video to decide whether or not it was a score, there was the smile on his face. I think that one of the things that really appeals to me about Brian and his attitude to rugby is that he does play with a smile on his face and he really does seem to always have fun. This is particularly noteworthy in the modern professional era when the stakes are so high and it's a great example not only to children as to how the game should be played but also to his own contemporaries – he shows that it is still possible to enjoy yourself.

'Brian's qualities are too numerous to mention but I'll list some of them. He has a great work ethic and a healthy appetite for the more mundane aspects of centre play. Mike Gibson had that quality and Tim Horan, the great Australian centre, had it more recently. He doesn't shirk defensive responsibilities and in fact actually appears to relish them. He seems to enjoy the offensive and the defensive which is an unusual combination and only the great players have that. According to Mark Ella, the great Australian out-half in the 1980s, the essence of rugby is support. Brian does seem to have that instinct to be in the right place in the right time. There's an answer for everything in rugby except pace. Brian has that explosive speed off the mark, which he seems to be able to sustain for more than 15 yards. He is such a rounded player with pretty much all the skills in abundance, not least the extraordinary evasion skills. I've lost count of the number of times I've seen him be incredibly effective and creative in the most unlikely situations. Somehow, with his low centre of gravity, he has been able to dodge and weave, and offload to a supporting player, as often as not turning water into wine. Another of his great qualities is almost magical hands, hands that Paul Daniels would have been very proud of. One of his trademarks is his ability to offload in the tackle. He makes it look a very easy skill but in fact it is extremely difficult. I am reminded of a quote from my childhood idol Mike Gibson after the Lions tour in 1971. He said that they practised and practised, playing so often that the ball became an extension of their hands. Having watched Brian so often, it seems to me that the ball has become a mere extension of his body. Finally, I suppose another quality he has is a remarkable temperament.

'I think Brian has the potential to have an extraordinary career. If he can sustain the hunger, the enjoyment of the game and his freshness, and keep free from injury, he can go on to join that select band of sportspeople who became universal household names.'

ALL THE PRESIDENT'S MEN

Some sports personalities are renowned for their immodesty. Ron Atkinson famously said, 'I met Mick Jagger when I was playing for Oxford United and the Rolling Stones played a concert there. Little did I know that one day he'd be almost as famous as me.' Ollie, though, is known for his modesty. He is rugby's nice guy and is renowned for his good manners and clean living almost as much as his achievements in the game. The story is told that such is Campbell's legendary status within rugby that when Bill Clinton was president of America and wanted to promote the game in the States his first choice to spearhead the campaign was Ollie. Clinton flew over to Ireland and brought him back on Air Force One to the US. It was shortly after the Monica Lewinsky scandal broke. After they took off from Dublin, an air hostess came over to Ollie and Bill and asked them if they would like a drink. Bill replied, 'I'll have a Scotch on the rocks.'

She immediately got him his drink. Then she turned to Ollie and asked him if he would like a drink. Ollie replied, 'I'd sooner be ravaged by a loose woman than have a drink pass my lips.'

Straight away, Bill handed back his drink and said, 'I didn't know there was a choice.'

DREAM TEAM

On the basis of the interviews for this book, it would appear that rugby players judge their colleagues on the basis of four criteria: skill, contribution to the team, commitment to rugby and personality. For the older players who saw Jack Kyle in his prime, he scores a perfect ten on all counts. Most of the interviewees for this book had either played with or seen Campbell in action, albeit some only on video. Uniquely, he unites all the generations of Irish rugby in their total admiration for him. The most astute compliment paid to him was by Barry McGann, when asked, 'What's the secret of being a good out-half?'

'That's a big question but I think it boils down to taking the right options. There are some out-halfs who have all the skills but they're not good at adapting to varying circumstances. A guy who can take the right option eight out of ten times is top class. If I was asked to illustrate perfection in an out-half, I would go back to Ollie Campbell during Ireland's Triple Crown win of 1982. That season, Ollie seemed to take the right option ten out of ten times, especially when he set up that classic try for Moss Finn.'

Who then are the players Campbell would most have liked to play with? He prefaces his world dream team by pointing out that he could have picked out another equally strong one without choosing any of those who made it onto his dream side, including, for example, great players like Philippe Sella and J.P.R. Williams. The team he did choose, though, was: Serge Blanco (France); Gerald Davies (Wales), Tim Horan (Australia), Mike Gibson (Ireland), David Campese (Australia); Barry John (Wales), Gareth Edwards (Wales); Ray McLoughlin (Ireland), Tommy Lawton (Australia), Graham Price (Wales), Colin Meads (New Zealand, capt.), John Eales (Australia), Ian Kirpatrick (New Zealand), Murray Mexted (New Zealand), Michael Jones (New Zealand). Manager: John Hart (New Zealand), Coach: Carwyn James (Wales).

26

A ROLLING STONE . . .

IT IS ONLY WHEN YOU MEET MOSS KEANE THAT YOU REALLY understand the phrase 'giant of Irish rugby' – a huge hulk of a man, with a penchant for straight talking and a treasure trove of stories and jokes, surprisingly few about rugby, more about matters agricultural. The words 'hale and hearty' come to mind immediately. He has a nice line in self-deprecating humour: 'After I left university, I found I had no talent for anything, so I joined the civil service!'

He has a high resistance to 'rugbyspeak' and is as uncomfortable with reminiscing about his rugby days as he is with excessive compliments about his playing career: 'I won 52 caps – a lot of them just because they couldn't find anybody else.'

OH, HAPPY DAY

While Moss was lucky enough to be on the Triple Crown-winning side in 1982 and was also on the 1977 Lions tour, a famous Munster victory was the high point of his career.

'It's very hard to separate memories and say one match was more important than another. My first cap was a great feeling, so was my Lions Test appearance; Ginger's try in '82 was memorable. But the highlight was defeating the All Blacks with Munster. It was a great, great day, though my clearest memory is of the sadness we all felt when we heard that our captain Donal Canniffe's father died immediately after the match.'

Down through the years, Munster have turned in some remarkable performances against touring sides including the All Blacks, the Springboks and the Wallabies only to be narrowly defeated. When the All Blacks toured in 1978, the more senior Munster supporters could still remember the feeling of being robbed at the Mardyke in 1947 when Australia scored a last-minute try to win 6–5 despite the suspicion that the try came from a forward pass. 1978 was destined to be different.

The only biblical story which the four gospels share is the multiplication of the loaves and the fishes, when Jesus fed the multitude and managed to have twelve baskets of fragments left over. Munster's victory over the All Blacks has spawned a similar miracle. Although the official attendance at the match was only 12,000, since then hundreds of thousands of people have said, often with the benefit of generous liquid refreshment, 'I was there the day Munster beat the All Blacks.'

The Clare Hills provided a scenic background for the New Zealanders as they performed their traditional 'haka' before the game. Somewhat against the run of play, Munster took the lead in the eleventh minute: a delicate chip from Tony Ward was followed through and won by Jimmy Bowen, who made an incisive run and, as he was caught from behind, fed Christy Cantillon, who crossed the line beneath the posts. Ward kicked the conversion with ease. In the 17th minute, Ward dropped a goal.

The home side hung on to their 9–0 lead until half-time but they realised that a modern-day Siege of Limerick awaited them in the second half when the men from down under would do all in their formidable power to protect their unbeaten record. Their fears were justified as the All Blacks exerted enormous pressure. Literally and metaphorically, the tourists did not know what hit them as they were stopped in their tracks by a series of crunching tackles by such players as Seamus Dennison, Greg Barrett and, most notably, Colm Tucker. The All Blacks manager, Jack Gleeson, subsequently described them as 'kamikaze tacklers'.

As the seconds ticked by agonisingly slowly, the crowd became more and more frenzied, sensing that here lay history in the making. 'MUNSTER! MUNSTER!' rang out at a volume that rose to deafening levels. Ward got the only score in the second half – a drop-goal – and Munster held on. It was an extraordinary team performance.

The Munster team that day was: Larry Moloney (Garryowen); Moss Finn (UCC), Seamus Dennison (Garryowen), Greg Barrett (Cork Con),

Jimmy Bowen (Cork Con); Tony Ward (Garryowen), Donal Canniffe (Lansdowne, capt.); Gerry McLoughlin (Shannon), Pat Whelan (Garryowen), Les White (London Irish), Moss Keane (Lansdowne), Brendan Foley (Shannon), Christy Cantillon (Cork Con), Dick Spring (Dublin University), Colm Tucker (Shannon).

A Limerick man and his wife were making love that day. Suddenly she noticed something sticking in his ear. Not surprisingly, she enquired what it was. He replied, 'Be quiet. I'm listening to the match.'

One of Limerick's best-known sons, the late film star Richard Harris, swept away by the euphoria of victory, wired the following message from a movie set in Johannesburg:

> Your historic victory over New Zealand made roaring headlines in every South African paper. I've been on the dry for 10 months, but I can't think of a better occasion or excuse to reacquaint my liver with the drowning sensation of a drop. I wish I was there. I rang Richard Burton and although he extends his congratulations, I detected a tinge of jealousy.

One of the myriad of legends about Moss Keane goes back to that match, as Tony Ward recalls.

'The story goes that we were leading 12–0 with only minutes left and there was a scrum close to the sideline. Our lads wheeled the scrum and drove the Blacks over the sideline right up against the wall. The All Blacks were not very pleased about this and a scuffle broke out. One of their players, Andy Hayden, allegedly swung his arm out to have a swipe at Brendan Foley and Moss grabbed him by the arm and said, "Don't. You'll lose that one as well." Hayden turned, smiled and accepted it. The meaning was clear.

'Moss is one of the greats of Irish rugby. On the pitch he was a tiger but off the field a pussycat. I'll never forget when we played England in 1979 he took off on a run and the crowd started chanting "Mossie, Mossie". He was one of those characters who lifts the whole crowd and that in turn lifts the team.'

PARTY ANIMALS

Moss is one of the all-time greatest characters in Irish rugby and is often associated with his teammate Willie Duggan for the way they played on the pitch and the way they celebrated off it. In victory or defeat, Moss and Willie knew how to party after a game.

Rugby receptions involving the Irish team have tended to be boisterous. In 1980, after the official dinner for the Ireland and Wales match, the police stopped the party because of the high spirits of the players and summonsed them to attend Dublin District Court the following Monday morning. In February 1996, a leading doctor disclosed that the greatest demand for the morning-after pill in Dublin is on the Mondays following home rugby internationals. One of Moss Keane's most illustrious predecessors in the Irish and Lions second row, Bill 'Wigs' Mulcahy, laughs at the memory of one incident when he got into the spirit of things.

'After one of our trips to Paris, I was feeling very, very good at the reception thanks to a large amount of wine. At one stage, I went out to the toilet and returned to the top table. I was chatting away in my amazingly dreadful French before I realised that I had got my directions totally wrong and instead of returning to the rugby reception I was at a wedding!'

Like most of his contemporaries, former Irish hooker Pat Whelan has his own Moss story.

'I scored the first try of Ireland's 1976 tour to New Zealand when I flopped over from five yards. I really enjoyed that experience, especially the competitive way the New Zealanders played their rugby. There was also plenty of craic off the field. I was rooming with Mossie Keane the morning after a match. The *Irish Times* journalist Ned van Esbeck came into our room to call us for Mass at what seemed to us in our tired and emotional state to be an ungodly hour. All I can say is that Mossie escorted him out of our room in "typical Moss fashion". I'm not prepared to elaborate any further!'

SUGAR AND SPICE

Moss had originally made an impact as a Gaelic footballer. However, he was not known for being 'fleet of foot'. According to folklore, after a less than resoundingly successful career with UCC, Moss's conversion to rugby came when he overheard the current GAA press officer Danny Lynch saying in a pub that 'A farmer could make a tidy living on the space of ground it takes Moss to turn.'

When Moss went on his first tour to New Zealand with the Lions, he was the only player who the BBC had not interviewed in the first seven weeks, because they didn't think his strong Kerry brogue would work well with a British audience. Eventually the Lions players said they would refuse to do any more interviews for the BBC until Nigel Starmer-Smith interviewed Moss. Nigel reluctantly agreed to this demand and asked on live television, 'Well, Moss, you've been here now for two months and you've played in your first Lions Test, met the Maoris – what's been the best moment of the trip for you?'

In his thickest Kerry accent, Moss replied, 'When I heard that Kerry beat Cork in the Munster final.'

The myth surrounding Keane grows with every day and distinguishing fact from fiction is not easy. Moss was playing for the Wolfhounds and in the side was Charlie Kent, the big blond English centre. Charlie is a diabetic and at half-time this rather puffed-up ambulance man arrived in the players' huddle and tapped Moss on the shoulder. He asked Moss if he was the man who wanted a sugar lump; Moss said, 'Arra Jaysus, who do you think I am, Shergar?'

THOSE TERRIFIED MEN IN THEIR FLYING MACHINES

Like Willie Duggan, Keane has a fear of flying and generally the only way they got on a plane was with the benefit of a lot of Dutch courage. As he drove to the airport for the Lions tour in 1977, he was so nervous about the flight that he crashed his car. The story is told that he rang his mother just before he took off and said, 'The car is at the airport. It is wrecked. See you in four months.'

Keane was once asked, 'Are you afraid of flying, Mossie?'

He replied, 'Afraid of flying? No. Afraid of crashing? Yes.'

Moss habitually sat in the last row of seats at the back of the plane. Asked by Ciaran Fitzgerald why he always took the back seat he replied, 'I've never seen a plane back into a mountain yet.'

One of Moss's most famous trips was to Dubai, where he had a speaking engagement. According to legend he required so much Dutch courage before taking off that he had to be lifted off the plane. As he was carried off, people watching thought it was part of the ritual of a Muslim funeral. When he returned home he was asked about his most striking impression of life in a Muslim country. He replied: 'If you steal anything they cut off your hand. If you tell a lie they cut off your tongue. I didn't see one flasher in the whole place.'

He was also asked about the food and drink.

'The drink was fine but the food was mad hot. No wonder these people are called the Shiites.'

27

IS THERE A DOCTOR IN THE HOUSE?

HOW DID A MANCHESTER-BORN DOCTOR, WHO IS A LEADING dermatologist, end up winning 26 caps for Ireland from 1978 to 1984 and twice tour with the Lions? This is my obvious first question in a conversation with John O'Driscoll.

'My father, Florence, a GP from Skibbereen, played rugby at Roscrea and we got our passion for rugby from him. My brother Barry is 13 years older than me. As a boy I spent the weekends travelling to see him play. After he was capped for Ireland, my burning ambition was to emulate his achievement.'

When Ireland drew with France in their opening fixture of the 1971 Five Nations, Tom Kiernan broke a bone in his leg and he was replaced at full-back by Barry O'Driscoll who retained his position for the entire season.

'Even though he could have played for Leinster or Munster, Barry opted for Connacht, largely because of the influence of their coach, Joe Costello. Our grandfather was a Connacht man. When I went to medical school in London I joined London Irish where Mick Molloy was a great influence on me. I think the best thing that ever happened to me was to declare for Connacht. In my years with them, I never felt like an outsider. When I played my first game for the province, they hadn't won an interprovincial match for twelve years and I played with them for five years before we won a game.

'We were rarely heavily beaten because we played with such

enthusiasm. We had some great players like the McLoughlin brothers and Galwegians' Mick Casserly, who was one of the unluckiest players I know because he never played for Ireland. Our coach, Tony Browne, epitomised the Connacht attitude as did Irish selector and former Ireland prop forward P.J. Dwyer. There was never any backbiting or recriminations. I consider it a great education in the ethos of the game. Nowadays, there's no tolerance for failure. Just look at what happened to Jack Charlton when Ireland lost a few matches.'

In a curious way, it is often harder to break out of a settled side than it is to break into it. Whether it is regarded as stubbornness or loyalty, coaches and selectors rely on the tried and trusted rather than taking risks. The Olympic ideal of participation coming first does not feature prominently in sport today. In an atmosphere where winning is all-important, it is considered dangerous, even foolhardy, to take risks. Moreover, regular occupants of first-team jerseys do not cherish the hope that soon they will be looking down on the action with a panoramic, bird's-eye view from the terraces. Although O'Driscoll played in a final trial in 1976–77, he had to wait for another year before being selected for Ireland. The following season, he fractured his cheekbone in October which caused him to miss the interprovincials. Although his injury was not completely healed, he was selected for his second final trial.

'The selectors were basically experimenting with several different number 8s playing in different positions. I was chosen at number 8 and had a special mask made to protect my cheekbone. It was one of those days when everything went right for me. I won my first cap against Scotland in 1978. The problem was that I got knocked out during the game. When I came around the first thing I heard was a great cheer. My replacement, Stewart McKinney, had scored a try. That meant no more caps for me that season.'

The Australian tour in 1979 marked the rehabilitation of O'Driscoll's international career, though like Willie Duggan he was not chosen on the original touring party. Both made the trip down under by the back door when Mike Gibson the younger and Donal Spring were forced to cry off the touring party because of injury.

'The pundits were expecting Australia to hammer us, especially as the previous year they had destroyed the mighty Welsh. The Irish selectors took an incredibly brave decision in selecting Ollie Campbell at out-half. The Test results proved their decision was the correct one.

In terms of our Triple Crown victory three years later, Ollie's presence in the side was crucial.'

ER

With Rodney O'Donnell, Colin Patterson, Ollie Campbell and Shannon's Colm Tucker, O'Driscoll was chosen for the Lions tour to South Africa in 1980. Tucker was an interesting selection because he was unable to command a regular place on the Irish team. Tony Ward, Phil Orr and John Robbie subsequently joined the squad as replacements. O'Driscoll played in all four Tests. He has both happy and sad memories from his trip.

'It was a real education touring with the Welsh. That was the era when you paid for your own telephone calls home. They had three great tricks devised so they never had to pay for a call. Plan A was to charm the hotel receptionist into giving them the secret code they could use to make calls without having them charged to them. Plan B was to distract the receptionist and for one of them to sneak in behind the desk and steal all their telephone bills. Plan C was that when a journalist asked for an interview, they traded it for a phone call.

'Best of all though was when we went into the Adidas factory. We were allowed to pick a bag of our choice and stuff it with gear. Most of us selected the most stylish bags and filled them with gear. All the Welsh guys without exception took the biggest bags in the shop and walked out with half of the gear in the factory!'

It was a bad tour for two of O'Driscoll's Irish colleagues. Scrum-half Colin Patterson's career ended after a tackle.

'It was very sad and very bizarre. As Colin was stretchered off, they were so fanatical about their rugby out there that two fans rushed on. One took his discarded boot and the other his sock and he asked Colin if he would give him his shorts.'

Tragedy struck against Junior Boks in the penultimate game of the tour when the Lions won 23–19 and Rodney O'Donnell sustained a serious injury tackling the massive Danie Gerber. Although he walked off the field, when he was examined in hospital it was discovered that he had dislocated his neck between the sixth and seventh vertebrae and that he had come within a fraction of an inch of being paralysed for life. Prompt intervention by O'Driscoll on the pitch prevented more severe repercussions. To compound the problems, when the ambulance finally arrived, the driver got lost on the way back to the hospital, depriving the Irish player of the quickest possible care.

One person literally at the centre of the action was the great Welsh player, Ray Gravell. It was Gravell who rechristened John O'Driscoll 'John O'Desperate' on the tour. He takes up the story.

'It was such a shame that Rodney's career ended so prematurely on that tour. Rodney was actually lucky to still have the use of his limbs after breaking his neck. If Dr John O'Driscoll hadn't been playing and hadn't shouted to the ambulancemen not to move him, then he could have died or been paralysed. Moreover, John was only playing against the Junior Boks that day because Colm Tucker had sprained his ankle.

'Ireland also supplied two great wing-forwards on that Lions tour in Colm Tucker and John O'Driscoll. Colm was so committed that it was a pleasure to play with him. I would die for John O'Driscoll. What a player and what a man. Mind you, John and Maurice Colclough were always trying to get me pissed. They were forever pouring rum, without my knowledge, into my soup.

'I will never forget that we played a match a week before the First Test and they sprung this amazing kicker who could kick the ball 80 yards and was really crucifying us. Bill Beaumont said, "We must do something about him." The next time he kicked the ball, I tackled him ferociously and broke his shoulder. John said to me, "Grav, what the f**k are you doing?"

'I replied, "I caught him a late one, early."

'John was incredibly brave on the field. I still keep in touch with him. Of course, he is Brian O'Driscoll's cousin. Brian is a world-class player and I would have loved to have played with him. I'm not sure if I would have enjoyed playing against him as much, because he would be whizzing by me and I think I would be spending a lot of my time looking at the back of his jersey! Gordon D'Arcy is another great new talent to have come onto the rugby stage and it is great that Ireland have two such classy players in their back line.'

One of the occupational hazards John faces because of his medical expertise is that he has to put up with a lot of medical jokes like:

Q: Who are the most decent people in the hospital?

A: The ultrasound people.

AN UNHOLY TRINITY

In the early 1980s, O'Driscoll, Willie Duggan and Fergus Slattery firmly established themselves as the most effective Irish back-row combination since the days of the 1948 Grand Slam side.

'Fergus and Willie played hard on and off the pitch. The difference was that whereas Fergus never seemed to show any ill effects the next day, Willie did! It was an accepted fact that Willie was last in every exercise in training. Our recurring nightmare was that Duggan would beat one of us into second-last place! That would suggest that we were totally unfit and almost certainly lead to our demise on the Irish team.

'In June 1983, I went with "Slats" to Barcelona with the Wolfhounds to play an exhibition game against a French selection. The match was to be played at midday. The evening before the game, Fergus was looking for somebody to go out with him for a night on the town. Under the circumstances, nobody wanted to take up his invitation, knowing the tough conditions awaiting them the next day but eventually he recruited the replacement prop forward. The next morning, the two lads returned from their adventures as the French team were heading out to train! Fergus was not a bit fazed. On the bus to the game, Phil Orr was taken ill and to his horror the partying sub had to take his place. Slats played like a man inspired but I've never, ever seen anyone suffer on the pitch like his partner!'

After a disappointing season in 1981 when Ireland were whitewashed, the Triple Crown unexpectedly appeared on the horizon when Ireland played Scotland in 1982.

'I loved the adrenalin rush I got when I played for Ireland. I always found the tension helped me to perform. That Scottish game was an exception. Although we had done brilliantly against Wales and England, the communal tension in the dressing-room that day was striking. I felt it was very unhelpful to the entire team. The one exception was Ollie Campbell, whose kicking, even by his own high standards, was fantastic that day. He settled us down.'

OPPORTUNITY LOST

After Ireland won the Championship in 1983, O'Driscoll was selected to tour New Zealand with the Lions in the company of his Ireland colleagues Trevor Ringland, Michael Kiernan, David Irwin, Ollie Campbell and Donal Lenihan. Although he played in two Tests, it was not the experience he had hoped for.

'I was injured in the first match and didn't play for three weeks. You need to be playing on a tour like that. We were not as evenly balanced as we had been in 1980. The press were very unfair to Ciaran

Fitzgerald, which didn't help. By the standards of the time, the criticism of him was way over the top. Nowadays, that kind of sustained media assault has become commonplace.'

He was prematurely cast off the team that was whitewashed in the 1984 Five Nations.

'After the highs of '82 and '83, the following season was a disaster. The balance between success and failure is relatively fine. Ollie was injured, which disturbed our rhythm a lot. We lost confidence when we started losing. I was ill for the 1984–85 international season and never regained my place. Even though I was a few years younger than them, I was regarded as of the same vintage as Willie Duggan and Fergus Slattery, as part of "Dad's Army". In fact, I continued to play for Connacht for a number of years and hoped to make it back onto the Irish side. But it was not to be. I never actually retired.'

When Jonathan Davies switched from rugby league to rugby union, he was asked what the main difference between the two codes was. He said, 'In rugby league you pay your taxes.' O'Driscoll welcomes the fact that the new era of professionalism has at least ended the 'shamateurism' of previous years but is troubled about aspects of the game's future. O'Driscoll has watched the increasing mental and physical pressures on players, due in part to the more intrusive demands of the media and the escalating commercial pressures. There is also an increased requirement for peak physical fitness.

'American sport is all about money. I hope rugby will not go down that route. I think rugby people have to be careful about playing too many matches, not alone because of the physical aspect but because of the psychological preparation required. I see problems down the road for English players in this respect because the club structure is so strong. I'm also particularly worried about the future of the small clubs who have given so much to the game over the years. That is why the interprovincial structure is so important – it provides a platform for players from such clubs to show their wares.'

28

SUPERQUINN

'MINE HAS BEEN AN EVENTFUL CAREER.' THIS IS MICK QUINN'S summation of his life in rugby, which brought him ten caps for Ireland at out-half. His rugby potential was identified at an early age.

'When I was eight years old, I got three coaching sessions with Keith Wood's late father, Gordon, at school at De La Salle Churchtown. He was an absolute gentleman and very kind. He told me, "Never go home with your knees clean." So I would always rub dirt on my knees and go home and show my father my dirty knees. Gordon patted me on the head at one stage and said, "You'll play for Ireland one day." I never forgot those words.'

Yet his rugby career might have perished before it started.

'I played with the well-known Dublin soccer nursery Rangers and was offered a trial with Everton. For a few minutes, I dreamt of being the new George Best but my mother intervened and told me I was going to boarding school and not to Everton.

'I was playing for Ireland when I was only 20. I don't remember much about the build-up to my debut except that I fell asleep during Willie John McBride's team talk! Ray McLoughlin told me I was a cheeky bugger. Willie John was a wonderful captain because he had such a great presence. I remember when I first came onto the international scene I addressed him as "Mr McBride".'

CHAMPIONS

Quinn was an ever-present in Ireland's Championship success in 1974. That season provided him with his finest hour.

'My best game for Ireland was unquestionably against England at Twickenham in 1974. Although the final score [26–21] was deceptively close, we hockeyed them that day, scoring four tries. It was such a wonderful feeling after the game to know that I had played my very best and the team had performed its best. I have an unbeaten record against England and Wales – not many Irish internationals can say that. OK, so I only played against them once!

'I enjoyed every minute of my international career. I don't think I ever played a bad game for Ireland, which is a good feeling to have. The great thing about rugby is the friendship, even with your rivals for the Irish jersey. I get on brilliantly with Tony Ward, even though he was the main impediment to my international career. In his biography, *The Good, The Bad and the Rugby*, he jokes that if it wasn't for Ollie Campbell, he would have got 40 caps. When I read that, I rang him up and said if it wasn't for him, Mike Gibson, Barry McGann, Ollie and Paul Dean, I would have won 80 caps!'

For his part, Barry McGann jokes, 'I got Mick Quinn his 10 caps for Ireland because I was his only competition and I wasn't up to much at the time! Syd Millar was the coach then. I had the reputation of being a very laid-back player but I was serious when I needed to be. One time, because of work, I was late for a training session at Anglesea Road, although I genuinely got there as quickly as I could. The session was in full swing when I got there. I went over and apologised to Syd for being late and asked him what he wanted me to do. I had a strong feeling he didn't believe I had made much of an effort to be there but he told me to warm up. Instinctively, I rubbed my hands together and blew on them, and said, "OK, coach, I'm ready." Moss Keane was in stitches but I'll never forget the look on Syd's face. I think that incident probably cost me ten caps and gave Quinn his international career!'

Quinn relished his rivalry with both Ward and Campbell.

'Wardy's great champion was Ned van Esbeck of the *Irish Times*. When I kicked a great penalty, it was just "a great penalty" but when Wardy kicked one, it was "a wonder strike from the master craftsman". Whenever I was kicking exceptionally well I would shout up at Ned and ask him whether or not Wardy could have bettered that.

'There was a time I got one up on Ollie. I am good friends with Chris

De Burgh and was with him in Rome for the World Cup quarter-final in 1990 when Ireland lost to Italy. It was incredible to see the way all the Italians mobbed Chris before the game but we went into the middle of the crowd just as ordinary fans. I saw some of the U2 guys up in the stands with their bodyguards away from the riff-raff but Chris wasn't like that. After the match, Jack Charlton and the players got on the team bus but the Irish fans were still in the stadium yelling for Jack. I ran out and asked him to come back out on the pitch which he did. I walked out behind him and when I looked up there was Ollie in the stands. So I waved at him, knowing full well he would be wondering to himself how that so-and-so Quinn managed to get on the pitch with Jack Charlton!

'One of the highlights of my career was winning the three-in-a-row of Leinster Cups in 1981 with Lansdowne. We beat Old Belvedere in the final and it was nice to put one over on Ollie on the pitch.'

THE LIONS ON THE LINE

After the high of the Five Nations victory in 1974, Quinn was quickly brought down to earth.

'The one great disappointment of my career was when I was a standby for the Lions tour to South Africa. The English fly-half Alan Old got injured near the end of the tour. I got a call at home from one of the Lions' management team, Albert Ager, who told me to get ready for the trip to South Africa. An hour later, I had my bags packed and by the front door. Then another call came from Ager, a name I will never forget, telling me that in fact I would not be travelling and asking me did I mind. What a question to ask! Of course, I lied and said no but it was devastating. It turned out that after he had called me someone else rang Mike Gibson, who had initially declined the invitation to tour.'

Quinn did get an opportunity to play in South Africa, though.

'At one stage, Willie John McBride and I were invited there to play for a World XV against the Springboks. I was interviewed on South African TV and asked what I thought of the main contenders for the Springboks number 10 shirt and if any out-half had impressed me. I mentioned that I was taken with this new kid called Naas Botha who I had seen play on television. The next day I was training when this fella came over to me and I recognised him as Botha. He wanted to thank me for my compliments.

'Naas was a hugely controversial figure in South Africa. They either loved him or hated him. We got on very well and I subsequently invited him to come over and get some experience with my club, Lansdowne. I thought nothing more about it until some months later I got a phone call at home. It was Naas. He said he would like to take up my offer of hospitality. I told him he would be welcome and asked him when he would be travelling over. Then he told me, "Well, Mr Quinn, I'm ringing you from a place called O'Connell Street in Dublin!" He brought his brother Darius with him who has since became a Dutch Reformed minister. He used to organise prayer meetings in my house!'

A STITCH IN TIME . . .

Quinn was also given the chance to tour New Zealand with Ireland in 1976. The experience provides him with some happy memories.

'On that tour Jimmy Davidson was called into the Irish side as a replacement. He was so happy to be selected that he jumped for joy when he got on the team bus for the first time. He jumped so high that he smashed his head against the roof and needed six stitches.

'For his first game on the tour, we were worried about things getting out of hand on the pitch. At one stage, there was a mêlée in the ruck and Pat Whelan mistakenly stamped Davidson on the head. Initially the lads thought one of the New Zealand guys had done it and there was bedlam for two minutes. When order was restored, the first thing we heard was Davidson shouting, "You f**king idiot, Whelan!" He needed plenty of stitches after that game.'

Quinn is happy to laugh at himself, too.

'After one international match, a young autograph hunter said to me, "Can I have your autograph please, Johnny?" I didn't have the heart to tell him he'd got the wrong man, so I just signed it. "To Bert. Best wishes, Johnny Moloney." As he was leaving he looked up and said to me, "How do you keep playing with Mick Quinn. He plays like sh*t!"

'Johnny did me a favour when we played Wales in 1974. We drew 9–9. I had bad flu before the match and was puking all over the place. The only one who knew about it was "Shagger". I told him if he told anyone about it I would kill him.'

Through his involvement with the Wolfhounds, Quinn continues to have plenty of contact with the legends of international rugby.

'The former England international Gareth Chilcott earns a fortune from making speeches. I played him once in a golf match during the Lions tour of New Zealand. At one point, my ball trickled into a pond. I could see it and asked him to hold my hand as I leaned over to retrieve it.

He said he would but deliberately let me go and I toppled in. I had to take off all my clothes and try to squeeze the water out of them, much to the amusement of the women who were playing on the other greens!

'Dean Richards is the nicest guy of them all. He's loved by all rugby folk in the UK because he's such a down-to-earth guy. O'Carling (he got that name on the Lions' tour in 1993, when he started drinking Guinness at a time when Mick Galwey ruled the roost on the tour in terms of social activity) had buckets of character.

'Campo was a great guy. He says outrageous things, especially about the English team. Yet he took the game very seriously. His contribution to Australia's win in the 1991 World Cup was the decisive one, notwithstanding the roles of Nick Farr-Jones and Michael Lynagh.

'Tony O'Reilly is a legend. He was a big hero of mine. When I was a kid, I went to a party at Eamonn Andrews' house and I remember the thrill it was when Tony patted me on the head. I like the fact that he has no airs or graces to him and he will talk to anybody. He has a touch of class about him and great charisma. I was giving a speech at an event organised by the Munster branch of the IRFU. A young player from Limerick had sustained a horrific injury and I was told to instruct everyone present to put five euros in an envelope for a fund that had been set up for him. I told the crowd that I was going to stand over O'Reilly to see if he had anything as trifling as a fiver in his wallet. He had a great laugh at that and I like people like that who can laugh at themselves.

'Peter Clohessy and Mick Galwey are as thick as thieves. They are a special breed and really go out of the way to help us in the IRFU Charitable Trust. They'll never let you down.

'Hugo MacNeill is a great character. He has an amazing ability to do African and Australian accents, and he often used them to great effect to tease his Ireland teammates. My favourite of his stories is about Donal Lenihan. When Donal was captain of Ireland and Munster, Hugo rang him and pretended to be a chap called Fritz Voller from the South African Rugby Board. He said, "I'm ringing you in connection with permission we got from the IRFU to allow you to play in a special match we've arranged between the Springboks and a World selection. The match will be played on 14 October."

'Donal replied, "I'm sorry. I'm totally committed to my responsibilities with Munster and Ireland, so I'm unable to make the trip but thank you for the kind invitation."

"'But we would like you to captain our World selection.'"

"'I'm sorry, I can't make it because of my commitments to Munster and Ireland.'"

"'But you could have a nice holiday and your wife could come with you. You could stay on for an extended holiday before you return to Ireland.'"

"'No. I can't because of my commitments to Munster and Ireland.'"

"'OK, I hear what you're saying. I don't want to put you under undue pressure. Thanks for listening. I suppose there's no point in saying that your match fee would be £30,000 sterling.'"

'There was a pregnant pause.

"'Sorry?'"

"'Oh, I was just mentioning that your match fee would be £30,000 sterling. It would be lodged in a Swiss bank account. But I wouldn't want to compromise your commitment to Munster and Ireland.'"

"'That's OK. Sorry, what date in October did you say again? Let me recheck my diary. Now that I think of it, my poor wife, Mary, needs a little holiday!'"

'At which point Hugo rapidly reverted to his own accent and said, 'Lenihan, I've got you by the balls.'"

THE YOUNG ONES

Ollie Campbell would probably be seen as the crown prince of his generation of Irish rugby. Quinn is more likely to be seen as the clown prince. Yet he has a serious side.

'I would like to think I have an eye for a young player of promise. The first time I saw John Robbie play was when he played for High School. I went over to him after the match and said, "You'll play for Ireland." Years later, I won £100 for him. I was playing a club match and there was a guy slagging me all through the match, saying I was useless. We got a penalty fifteen yards inside our half and ten yards in from the touch-line. I had the wind behind me. John bet a pound at 100–1 that I would score and I did.'

While Quinn's gregarious personality has won him many friends in rugby, it has not always helped his career to advance.

'In general, I have great memories of playing with Leinster. One of the people I played with was Brian O'Driscoll's dad, Frank. Like Brian, he was a great tackler. I played my final match for Leinster in the Sports Ground in Galway in 1984 when we were going for the championship. It was an awful day with the wind and the rain, which made it impossible for me to run the ball. There was only a handful of people in the stand, one of whom was Mick Cuddy, "the Cud", former Ireland and Leinster selector. The only thing I could hear was a constant chorus from the Cud of "Run the bloody ball, Leinster." I got so fed up I shouted up at him, "Cuddy, shut your f**kin' mouth." He was furious and roared down at me, "That's the last time you'll play for Leinster"!'

Quinn enjoys the humour in other sports.

'One player I always admired was Manchester United's Denis Irwin. I attended Irwin's testimonial dinner. Jack Charlton brought the house down there with his unconventional tribute to Denis. Jack said, "Denis was the consummate professional: the best full-back to play for Manchester United, the best full-back to play for the Republic of Ireland; he was always our most consistent player, he never made mistakes, he never gave the ball away; he was always on time for training, always first on the bus for training; he never let you down or ever once caused a problem. What a boring f**king bastard"!'

29

MR VERSATILITY

WHO PLAYED AT LANSDOWNE ROAD, DALYMOUNT PARK AND
Croke Park in the one year? For years, this has been a standard pub-quiz
question. The answer is former Ireland centre Paul McNaughton. In
1974, he played rugby at Lansdowne Road, played for Shelbourne in an
FAI Cup final and played for Wicklow against Louth in the Leinster
Senior Championship. As an international, 'Macker' was a class apart
because he had the lot: good hands, strength in the tackle, exceptional
in the air, elusive on the break and most importantly the self-belief to
'go for it' from anywhere. He, more than anyone, put Greystones on the
rugby map. Initially he showed promise as a Gaelic footballer and
hurler, and later as a soccer player. But then rugby entered his life.

'When I was 15, my father sent me to boarding school at Rockwell
– sent being the operative word. The emphasis there was on rugby and
I wanted to be part of the major team in the school. Father Lavelle
coached the school Junior Cup team and saw me playing Gaelic
football. He was passionate about rugby and asked me if I had ever
played. When I told him no, he took me out and tried to coach me the
right way to catch a ball. He explained the difference between catching
the ball Gaelic style and catching the ball rugby style. He threw three
balls over my head and each one I caught beautifully – but like a Gaelic
footballer. He again patiently explained the difference and threw a
fourth ball at me and again I caught it like a Gaelic footballer. Father
Lavelle said: "Ah, shite, Paul." It was the first time I'd ever heard a
priest curse and I suppose it spurred me on to catch the ball properly

after that. With some personal coaching from Father Lavelle, I made it onto the Rockwell team and my rugby career was up and running.'

TORN BETWEEN THREE LOVES

After he left school, however, soccer was his main game for a while when he attended Trinity College.

'Gerry Doyle, Shelbourne's manager at the time, saw me playing and asked me to sign for them; essentially I was semi-professional for them for three years. But as well as playing Gaelic football during the summer, I also started playing rugby for a great Wanderers team that the former Ireland centre Kevin Flynn put together, with a back line that featured Kevin and future internationals like Robbie McGrath, Freddie McLennan and myself, as well as Tony Ensor at full-back and we went on to win the League and Cup Double. It wasn't always easy to keep both going simultaneously. There was one weekend when on the Saturday, I played rugby in the Leinster Cup semi-final and on the Sunday, I played in the FAI Cup final. The following weekend, on the Saturday I was due to play in the Leinster Cup final on the Saturday and the replay of the FAI Cup final on the Sunday. As a result of an ankle injury, I missed out on the rugby game but as it was the last game of the season, I had a cortisone injection and played in the soccer match only for us to lose 1–0 to Cork Hibs.

'One of the most memorable moments was playing for Shelbourne against Manchester United. They had signed Paddy Roche from us and part of the deal was that they would travel over to Dublin to play us in a friendly. My immediate opponent was Gordon McQueen and Martin Buchan was playing alongside him. Gerry Daly was in their midfield and Stuart Pearson was up front. He got their goal in a 1–1 draw.

'I suppose another highlight was playing against Vasas from Hungary in the UEFA Cup though I remember it more for off-the-field activities than for the actual games. Before we went to the away leg, the one bit of advice we got was that we shouldn't change our money at the official centres because we would get twice the amount on the black market. When we got to the team hotel, we decided we would make a killing. As I was six months into my Economics course at Trinity, the players decided I would be the guru, even though guys like Eric Barber could buy and sell me, so I was mandated to do the negotiating on their behalf. The official rate was £1 sterling for 100 forints. I got an offer of 350 forints for £1 and reported back to the lads. They asked me if we would get even more if we pooled our money. Most of us had brought £100 spending money, which was a lot of money back then. So I went back and agreed a deal where we got 500 forints per pound. We had piles of forints on the table and we distributed them out among the squad and had a great chat about all the presents we would buy.

'After our training session, we went into the city only to discover that there was absolutely nothing in the shops we could buy. Hungary back then was a very different place to what it is today. The only things they had were bread, bacon and chicken, and clothes none of us would be seen dead wearing. We decided that we would hold on to our money until after the match, then we would go to a nightclub and have a night to remember. We went to the nightclub only to discover that they wouldn't accept forints! We ended up giving one of the waitresses 450,000 forints. She thought she had won the lottery but we all went home with empty pockets and not a present between us! It would be fair to say that my first venture into financial engineering was an unmitigated disaster!'

McNaughton was not the first Irish rugby international to have distinguished himself in the League of Ireland. Although Barry McGann won 25 caps for Ireland between 1969 and 1976 he has an ecumenical background in a sporting sense. His brothers, Seán and Diarmuid, played Gaelic football for Cork. Barry is the son of a Galway man and a Tipperary woman, and being born in Cork, he could not but be interested in sport. He played everything in Cork: golf, cricket, soccer, Gaelic football, hurling and rugby. He grew up at the back of the Mardyke. It was the golden half-mile because it produced so many sports stars, like Irish soccer international Noel Cantwell and of course Tom Kiernan. He played soccer for Young Elms. They won the Under-15 and Under-18 national titles, which helped him get a place as inside-forward on the Ireland Youth side. He was the only Cork player on a side which included future international Terry Conroy. They were one of 24 teams in the UEFA finals and finished sixth in the tournament. The highlight for McGann was when they beat Holland. It was a major achievement since the Dutch side included no less a person than Johan Cruyff!

THE NEARLY MAN

The realities of working life meant that McNaughton had to make some hard choices.

'After college, I decided to restrict my sporting activities and concentrate on rugby – though not to the total exclusion of soccer. I won my first rugby cap against Scotland in 1978. The Irish side that day was: Tony Ensor; Tom Grace, me, Alistair McKibbin, Freddie McLennan; Tony Ward, John Moloney (capt.); Phil Orr, Pat Whelan, Mick Fitzpatrick, Moss Keane, Donal Spring, John O'Driscoll, Willie Duggan, Fergus Slattery.'

Four weeks later, it was off to France. The Irish were handicapped by the presence of just one specialist second-row player when Emmett O'Rafferty, due to make his international debut, was forced by a cruel twist of fate to withdraw four hours before the kick-off, having sustained a calf-muscle injury in training the previous day. Harry Steele was called into the second row and John O'Driscoll was brought over from London to act as a cover player.

'Emmett O'Rafferty was a hard, aggressive lock. I played with him at Wanderers and I'd seen how good he was at close quarters. He was finally picked for his first cap against France in Paris. At the last training run, the day before, he pulled a muscle. The management knew he was hiding something but they couldn't pin him down, so they appealed to Emmett's love of Ireland and guaranteed that if he withdrew from the French match, he would definitely be selected for the next game. With this guarantee, Emmett admitted that he had this sore muscle but his replacement, Harry Steele, performed brilliantly and Emmett never got the chance to play for Ireland. We lost 10–9. Effectively, we were playing on ice, in conditions more suited to skating than rugby.'

Who was his most difficult opponent?

'If you leave out Australia, the best team I played against was the great Welsh team. Their back line was awesome. I used to have great physical confrontations with Ray Gravell. He was a wonderful character off the field as was Scotland's Jim Renwick. Against England, my immediate opponent was generally Clive Woodward – before he became a Sir! He was skilful and tricky but not very physical. He showed the same confidence as a player as he does as a manager – which is saying something! One of the most exciting players I ever encountered was Scotland's Andy Irvine. He could really thrill a crowd when he was on his game.'

THE BIG SLEEP

The high point of Paul's career in the green jersey came down under.

'Winning the two Tests in Australia in 1979 was an incredible achievement, especially when you consider our track record of defeats in the southern hemisphere since. With all the fuss about the dropping of Tony Ward, people may have missed out on how good our performances were.

'The tour provided the funniest moment in my rugby career. The night before the First Test we had a team meeting. Our coach, Noel "Noisy" Murphy, always got very worked up when he spoke at these meetings. The problem was that he generally said the same thing each time. He always started with, "This is the most important match you will ever play for Ireland." The night before the First Test, sure enough, Murphy's first words were, "This is the most important match you will ever play." We were just after eating dinner and the room was very warm because there were twenty-five of us. Murphy was talking away for about five minutes and just as he said, "Jesus Christ, ye're wearing the Irish jersey and do you realise this is the most important f**king game you will ever play?", there was a massive snore. It was, of course, Willie Duggan. Murphy said: "F**k it. I'm not doing this." Then he stormed out.'

After he had won 15 consecutive caps, outside events prematurely ended McNaughton's international career. He worked for a government-affiliated company which would not release employees to play on the tour with the Lions to South Africa in 1980 given the apartheid regime in the country at the time.

'In 1981, at the start of the season, I announced that I was emigrating to America at the end of the Five Nations. I'm not sure what the Irish selectors thought about this but although I had played well in the first match in the Five Nations, I was dropped to the bench for the remaining three as the selectors went for the "great experiment" of playing both Tony Ward and Ollie Campbell in the Irish side. I was working with the Industrial Development Authority and I was offered a great job in the States. In the bleak days of the Ireland of the '80s, there was no way I could pass up on the opportunity. I was only 27 and at the peak of my playing career, so my friends could not believe I was turning my back on my playing career.

'I felt lousy the following year when Ireland won the Triple Crown. It was minus 25 degrees in Chicago and I listened to the decisive match against Scotland on the BBC World Service. I felt awful missing out on that, because Triple Crowns don't come along very often in Irish rugby; but it was the right career move for me.

'I actually played a lot of rugby in America. One of the players I came up against was the legendary South African out-half Naas Botha. One of my coaches was a then unknown South African, Kitch Christie, who steered his native country to their World Cup victory in 1995. When I returned to Ireland in 1985, I immediately started playing Junior rugby with Greystones. In my first game, my brother threw me a hospital pass, literally, and I fractured my skull!'

PARTING IS NO SWEET SORROW

Sadly, that was not the darkest rugby moment for McNaughton.

'I am lucky in that my three sons have played representative rugby. Conor has played for Ireland at Under-21 level, Cormac has played for Leinster at Under-21 level and Cian has played for Ireland at Under-19 level. I went to South Africa in 2004 for the Under-19 Rugby World Cup. Cian was playing for Ireland the day John McCall died. Being on the sidelines knowing that somebody has died on the pitch is just horrific. In the dressing-room afterwards, the Irish players were distraught. None of us had ever experienced anything like it. His father came out and spoke to the lads afterwards and was brilliant. He made a very emotional speech at a barbecue for the boys. He said he was very proud of his son and that John loved life. He emphasised that John had died as a result of a condition that had nothing to do with rugby and that his death had nothing to do with the game itself. His speech had a great impact on the players at such a traumatic time.'

Later that year, Paul unexpectedly found himself back in the centre of rugby action.

'I had just retired from Deutsche Bank, having negotiated the sale of their business in Ireland. I had a few directorships lined up when suddenly I was approached by Declan Kidney and Mick Dawson, the chief executive of the Leinster Branch of the IRFU, and they asked me to become Leinster manager. I accepted it on condition that it be a part-time position and that I would have a meaningful role. They wanted a Leinster person with business acumen.'

THE PAST IS A DIFFERENT COUNTRY

Change is inevitable, except from a vending machine. Paul has noticed big changes in rugby since his playing days.

'The game is so different now, particularly in the way the ball is recycled so much. I met up with some of my fellow Irish internationals recently and we all agreed that a back today gets more of the ball in one game than the entire Irish back line got back then over a full season. In fact, I remember coming off the pitch with Moss Finn after one international and he turned to me and said, "Christ, I never saw the f**king ball at all."

'During the late '70s and early '80s, the backs would spend half an hour in training working on the most fantastic moves with triple loops and everything. It was great but the problem was that we never got to use them in games. As soon as we got on the pitch, the instruction from the captain Fergus Slattery was to keep the ball tight. All our great moves were abandoned. During team meetings, Ollie Campbell and myself used to have a bet on how long it would take Noel Murphy to say, "Jesus, Ollie, put a few high balls up in the air because there is no better man in Ireland under a high ball than Paul McNaughton." Sure enough, it came in every speech.

'We were playing against France in 1980 and we lost 19–18. The backs were playing well, and we got a bit of confidence and decided to run the ball from our own 25. It was unheard of in England, let alone Ireland, to do this at the time. The Irish fans were completely perplexed at this sudden outpouring of adventure, seeing the ball going through hands across the pitch. Then the ball hit Rodney O'Donnell on the shoulder and France got possession and scored a try. All the backs were terrified we'd be dropped for the next match because we'd run the ball! The next time we got a scrum, Ollie Campbell asked us which move we wanted to play. As one, we all said, "Boot the f**king ball into touch as far up the pitch as possible!"

'Roll the clock forward ten years and we were playing in a golden oldies match in Bermuda for Ireland against America under lights. The back line included Mick Quinn, Freddie McLennan, Terry Kennedy and myself. Donal Spring was the captain but he got sick, so Pat Whelan took his place as skipper. When he gave us our tactical talk, it was as if we'd been caught in a time warp, because his tactical instruction was simply, "We're going to keep the ball tight." The backs all looked at each other. I knew the others were thinking the exact same thing as me: "For f**k's sake, we're nearly 40. We're playing America. Let's run the f**king ball at last." Moss Keane was our number 8. At the first scrum Pat said, "OK, Mossie, you take the ball on." Mossie made a break but one of the Americans nearly cut him in half. The Americans had very little skill but they were ferocious tacklers. At the second scrum, Pat said, "OK, Mossie, you take the ball on." Again, Mossie made the break and this time one of the Americans nearly killed him with a tackle. The third time we got a scrum Pat said, "OK, let the ball out to the backs." I'll never forget Mick Quinn screeching at him the immortal words, "Hold on to the f**king ball. Ye wanted it. So keep it f**king tight!"'

30

I'VE LOOKED AT LIFE FROM BOTH SIDES NOW

Q: WHICH LIONS PLAYER WHO WAS NEVER ON A LOSING LIONS
side had a record of played nine, lost nine for Ireland?

A: John Robbie.

Rugby does not distribute success according to some overarching principle of fairness. It tends to single out certain players for repeated kicks in the teeth. John Robbie fell into that category in the Irish jersey. A Greystones native, Robbie made the rapid journey from college games to international rugby star and then on to radio journalism in South Africa. He played for Trinity College, Cambridge University, Ireland and the Lions. In South Africa, he played a record number of times as the Transvaal scrum-half and in the Springbok jersey without getting full Springbok colours. Unusually for a scrum-half, he was also an accomplished place-kicker.

Robbie was a child star.

'When I was very small, I was chosen to do a Christmas TV advert for Raleigh bikes. A friend of Mum's was in the advertising business and cheeky small blond kids were always top of the shopping list. Anyway, I had to race down the stairs of a house, gaze at the presents around the tree, gasp as my eyes picked out the new bike, turn to my "parents" and utter the stunningly imaginative words "It's a Raleigh!". The ad ended with me riding the bike around the tree. All great fun for a ten year old but the trouble was that it kept reappearing each Christmas. As a gawky 14 year old, about to crash into the nightmare of adolescence, the nightly appearance of the advert made me blush scarlet. However, for doing the ad, I received the princely sum of £21. That really was big bucks in those days, and I was most irate when Mum suggested that some of it should go to the coal bill!'

EDUCATIONAL MATTERS

On the rugby field, Robbie first came to prominence as captain of Trinity College. There he had some unusual motivational ploys. Before a colours match with bitter rivals UCD, when Trinity were hot favourites and he felt the team were over-confident, John decided that a different type of tactic was necessary. He started with a real gut-wrenching speech. As he got to the part about how none of the team would ever forgive themselves if they lost, he made a conscious effort to start weeping. When he started to cry, the effect was electric – total concentration – and the atmosphere changed dramatically. It stayed that way and the next day they beat UCD fairly easily. Robbie was chosen to tour New Zealand with the Irish Senior team in 1976.

'The tour was a marvellous experience. I was the youngest in the party and looked it. On one boat trip during the tour, some New Zealander glanced at me and remarked in all seriousness that it was nice of the New Zealand Rugby Union to allow the Irish manager to bring his son along on tour.

'It was all rugby at the start but loosened up a little at the end. On the way home, we stopped in Fiji for a few days. We travelled throughout the island in an old bus with no glass in the windows. I'd got a bit drunk in Auckland and told the team about the current craze of "lobbing moons" – pulling one's trousers down, bending over and displaying the bare backside to all and sundry. The trick was to choose the time and place with care to get the greatest effect. The Fijian bus without windows was too much of a temptation and so I lobbed a moon out at a village through which we were passing. The locals were totally amazed and we all had a great laugh until I couldn't find my wallet. It looked like I had lobbed all my travellers cheques out of the window too. In the end, we discovered that they had just fallen down the side of the seat – but it was a close call.'

He went on to study at Cambridge University where he was elected skipper of the rugby team ahead of Eddie Butler, who was destined to become a legend of Welsh rugby. Robbie was a bit taken aback by the side's preparation for the glamour fixture against Oxford. A few days before the big game, they had a nuts and port dinner and toasted Oxford in the traditional way. They stood and said 'GDBO' – God damn bloody Oxford. He scored 17 points in the game, including a spectacular try. He jokes that his one regret was that he missed out on Alastair Hignell's record for a Varsity game. He had instructed the team to run a penalty from in front of the posts at one stage but had he known he was just two points off the record, he would have kicked it.

While he was at university, he also played for Pontypool, the famous Welsh club, the result of a drinking session with Eddie Butler. One of his clearest memories of his time with the Welsh giants is of an occasion when, after a match against Cardiff had been stopped due to snow, he got involved in a snowball fight in the middle of Pontypool with some of the greats of Welsh rugby, like Graham Price, Bobby Windsor, Charlie Faulkener and Eddie Butler.

AT THE CAPTAIN'S TABLE

After Cambridge, he returned to play for Greystones and was made captain of Leinster by the new coach, Mick Doyle, and his chairman of selectors, Mick 'the Cud' Cuddy.

'I'm afraid we didn't think much of Doyler at first. We had a Wednesday evening practice two weeks before our annual game against Llanelli. The Cud drew me aside, punched me in the arm and said, "We've made you captain, get the lads going." I lost my temper. Looking back, I cannot imagine why. The team, including a number of very senior players, some of them Lions, was starting to get changed when I stormed in. I told them that there would be a delay and that I would be chatting to the brace of Michaels, Cuddy and Doyle, for a while. We went into an adjoining room and I told them I was cheesed off. First of all, I would not be told in that manner of my captaincy; I expected to be asked. Second, before accepting, I wanted an assurance that I would not just be there to toss the coin but that I would have a major say in the running of the side. Third, I felt that a philosophy for the side had to be agreed upon by the players, otherwise it would be the same old rubbish of the interprovincial side being used solely as a stepping stone to the final Ireland trial. It was the start of two fantastic years. That night, the team never did get changed. We talked it out, and agreed on our strengths and just what we were going to do.

'We took Llanelli apart. We won something like 21–0 and they had guys like Derek Quinnell, Ray Gravell and J.J. Williams. It was a good start. Apart from a game on tour to Romania, we lost no other game in two years. It was a great side and I must say that eventually Mick Doyle won the respect of the players. He was that rare breed of coach who allowed the players a major say but could always give us a valuable overview of how things stood.'

Although he was substitute to Colin Patterson on the Irish team, Robbie was chosen as Terry Holmes' replacement for the Lions tour to South Africa in 1980. He had some bizarre experiences on the tour. Tony Ward was sub to Ollie Campbell in the Third Test in Port Elizabeth. Just before the match began, he realised with mounting panic that he had forgotten to bring his boots and it was too late to go back to the hotel and get them. His problem was exacerbated by the fact that nobody had a spare pair of boots to lend him. At least, he thought, he was unlikely to need them. As the match was starting, Ward heard someone calling his name. Campbell was bleeding heavily from an injury. Robbie managed to get hold of a pair of boots for Wardy from a ball boy. They were much too big for him and worse still, the studs were moulded – not ideal considering the muddy conditions that day. Under the circumstances, though, they were a lot better than nothing.

'Wardy asked me what the hell he should do now. I said, "Pray as hard as you can." It must have worked, because Ollie somehow continued and to this day I don't think Noel Murphy, our coach, knows how close he was to learning that his replacement fly-half and goal-kicker in a series decider between the Lions and the Boks had arrived with no boots. I don't think Noel's heart would have survived.'

The Lions lost the series 3–1. Why?

'One day, I think it was before the Third Test, we were training in Port Elizabeth. The Lions side was practising winning the ball from a set phase, moving it to first centre and then hoofing it up in the air. Our main tactic seemed to be simply to draw up the defending line and then turn them. I noticed that sitting on the grandstand deep in conversation were Carwyn James, Chalkie White and Ian Robertson. They were three of the best back-line coaches ever produced by British rugby, watching the cream of the current players practising booting the ball up in the air. I must say I felt a little ashamed.

'One of the problems, I believe, was that all the big guns on the tour – manager Syd Millar, Noel Murphy and captain Bill Beaumont – were all forwards as were the senior players – Graham Price, Peter Wheeler, Geoff Squire and Derek Quinnell. I have read books about the tour which blame the back line but I blame the decision-makers who framed our tactics. We had backs of the calibre of Colin Patterson, Ollie Campbell, Dai Richards, Ray Gravell, John Carleton, Clive Woodward and Andy Irvine. To say, with the amount of ball being won by the pack, that this back line, or one with a few of the other players, was incapable of using it is nonsense. Instead of moving all balls early in the tour, thus developing a pattern of movement and support, the team kicked for position and drove excessively with the pack. It was good enough against the provinces, but in the Tests it was different.'

LAUGHTER IS THE BEST MEDICINE

Robbie retains many funny memories from that time.

'Jean-Pierre Rives, the French flanker, was there as well at the end of the tour. I was in Pretoria with Noel Murphy at some function or other and we got a lift with some bloke in a sports car who was taking Jean-Pierre back to Johannesburg. We got hopelessly lost and I recall that as we sped at breakneck speed down a backroad we could see a fork ahead. "Go left," said Noel to the driver.

'"Please go right," said I.

'"Please go fuckccng slower!" screamed Rives, who could speak little English, from the back seat. The driver, a South African, was laughing so much he nearly crashed.

'One day, I went fishing with Ollie Campbell in Durban. Ollie got as sick as a dog and was hurling his guts overboard. He also caught a whopper of a fish, a barracuda. As he was feeling so ill, he asked one of the crew to help him reel in the fish. He was promptly told, "The rule of this boat is that you pull in your own fish." At the best of times, Ollie looks pale but that day he looked whiter than a sheet!

'But the funniest moment, I think, came after the Third Test in Port Elizabeth. The Lions had gone into the game two down, so it was a crucial match. In shocking weather, we lost 10–12, and thereby the series. The Lions were very disappointed; it was a game that had been won everywhere but on the scoreboard. Still, there was no sulking. In the best tradition, the Lions decided to drown their sorrows and so a monumental piss-up was held. A few equally drunk South African fans got into the hotel's off-limits area, and a bit of a skirmish developed. At one stage, our tour manager Jack Matthews chucked a couple of the intruders down the stairs from our floor. He picked a watch up off the ground and flung it down after the guys with a cry of "And take your blasted watch with you!". Then he saw his bare wrist: in the excitement, he'd flung his own watch down the stairs.

'Quite near the end of the tour, we were all called in to a special meeting. Syd Millar addressed us and asked if we were unhappy, as he had read reports to that effect. We all said we were having a whale of time. He then asked us if we would all return to tour South Africa if selected. Ironically enough, I was the only player who indicated that I would have to think about it; everyone else said they would. In fact, Peter Morgan, the young Welsh utility player, who had played in only a few games on the tour brought the house down by saying that he'd love to come back again, as next time they might let him have a game!'

MONEY TALKS

The tour opened Robbie's eyes to the sham amateurism that operated in rugby at the time.

'Almost all the Lions were sponsored, with kit from their local agent of a major footwear firm, the Irish players as well as those from Britain. Well, we heard that the British guys had actually received some cash as well. It now seems a very small amount – £300 each, I think. The Irish convened a meeting one evening in one of the players' rooms. We were all there: Ollie Campbell, Tony Ward, Colin Patterson, Phil Orr, Rodney O'Donnell, Colm Tucker, John O'Driscoll and myself. The meeting was to decide whether we should contact the firm and insist on our cash. Despite two players wanting to do so, the rest of us felt that this would infringe our amateur status and so the motion carried was that we would say nothing. We actually threw away £300!

'Another time, Ollie and I were approached by a sports firm in South Africa. They offered us a four-figure rand fee if we would wear their make of boots in a game for the Lions. We explained that we were amateurs but, as a favour, we wore their boots in many practices. Can you believe it! The tour was generating millions, the players were making money on the normal team pool arrangement – against the amateur laws but that was as much a part of major touring as team courts or duty boys – and here we were chucking it away.

'I was also approached by a senior Lions player, a Scot, who said that the boot firm sponsoring him wanted me to sign for them the following season. He started talking cash that I couldn't believe and I said no. Although I had never received a penny for wearing kit, I was very grateful to my sponsors, who always gave me free boots. I can still remember the look of disbelief on his face and he told me that one day I would look back and laugh at my attitude. He was wrong – I now look back and cry.

'When I moved to South Africa, I discovered that one of the benefits of being a high-profile sportsman there was sponsorship. I was given a car at a time when I had been dropped by Transvaal. The panel on the door read "Opel supports John Robbie". Some wit suggested that the lower panel should read "Transvaal doesn't".'

WHAT IT SAYS IN THE PAPERS

Colin Patterson's international career ended on the Lions tour and Robbie was back as Ireland's number 9. Given his record as a captain, some suggested that he would become Ireland captain but he had equivocated in an interview with Ned van Esbeck in the *Irish Times* when asked if he would tour with Ireland in the forthcoming South African tour in the summer of 1981 and Fergus Slattery retained the captaincy.

'During the run-up to the tour, I met the journalist Eamon Dunphy by chance in a Dublin pub. I admired his writing but as soon as we met he informed me that in his view rugby had done more to harm Ireland than anything else in history, including the Crown of England. I was a bit stunned and said nothing. Eamon was like an opened tap and went on to give his opinions on the tour, interspersed with expressions of his own hatred of rugby as an elitist sport.

'The Irish soccer team had recently played in Argentina and this had coincided with a lot of his articles about human-rights abuses there. I asked him his views on this and the question seemed to throw him a bit. He didn't answer, instead launching an attack on me because as a university graduate I was automatically a member of the oppressing upper classes etc. I started to get annoyed; I thought Eamon was a stupid little chip-shouldered troublemaker. I told him that my father had started his working life labouring in a coal yard after the Great Depression and through his hard work at sea, his after-hours study and later his work as a marine engineer, he had made enough for his kids to have the chance of a university education. I told him that, far from feeling guilty about this, I was extremely proud. Then I realised that Eamon had a few drinks on board and he disappeared somewhere. I enjoyed reading Eamon's articles subsequently but he took himself extremely seriously. Our meeting must have done something, because the next weekend he wrote a rambling article castigating everything to do with rugby.'

Before the tour to South Africa, Robbie was called into his bosses' office (he worked for Guinness) and told that he would not be allowed to go. Robbie resigned, although he was married with a young child to support. He did retain his sense of humour through this difficult time.

'The great departure day arrived and we learnt about the cloak-and-dagger methods that we were going to use to get to South Africa. I suppose it was necessary; we were getting worried about running the gauntlet at Dublin airport, as we'd heard that a massive demonstration had been planned. I rang one of my fellow players Terry Kennedy and in my best Peter Sellers Indian accent I told him that I was Kadar Asmal, the high-profile leader of the Irish anti-apartheid movement, and could I talk to him? Terry was very worried and when I asked him to confirm the secret arrangements for our departure, I could almost see the beads of sweat pouring from his brow. He was gibbering like an idiot and nearly collapsed in relief when I told him it was me.

'I was super-fit because of my extra training when I was on the dole. Remembering how I had played with the Lions, I was confident that I could play the best rugby of my life. As things turned out, it was a disaster. I got sick and only played a game and a half in the month or so we were away. However, by the time I returned to Ireland, I would have decided along with Jennie that we were off to live in South Africa, a decision that would have seemed ridiculous three months earlier.'

RITE OF PASSAGE

After making the momentous decision to take his family and strike out for the shores of the promised land in South Africa, Robbie's introduction to provincial rugby was not what he expected.

'I made my debut for Transvaal away to Griqualand West. We won well and I assumed it was drinks and bed just like at home. But I was told that all new caps had to wait outside the team room until summoned. I got called in. The room had been altered and for all the world it was like a courtroom. All the players were dressed immaculately in their number-one blazers, ties and trousers, and there were three "judges" sitting at the front. Everyone was deadly serious and there wasn't a sound. I made some wisecrack as I walked in and I was quickly told to shut up. It was all serious and I got nervous. I had to remove my shoes and stand on a chair in front of the dock. I was asked what I thought of playing for the team. Again I made a joke but no one laughed. I was asked to sing a song which I did, no one clapped or did anything. Suddenly I was grabbed, turned upside down across one of the lock's shoulders with my backside up, and each member of the team with the flat of his hand gave me, in turn, a real smack across my bum. I couldn't believe it. The pain was excruciating. After they had stopped, I was angry and nearly lost my temper. Luckily one of the judges told me this was just tradition and to say nothing. Then I was turned up and hit again. I was actually crying in pain and anger. But when it stopped, the judge made a genuine speech of welcome; I was told that now I was a true Transvaal player and each player shook my hand. During this episode, I also had to drink four or five glasses of beer. At the end, it was actually quite emotional. I gather it was a fairly tame initiation – known as the "borsel", or brush – by some provincial standards but I must say I still hated it.'

RADIO DAZE

After his rugby career ended, Robbie began a new career in radio, working for Radio 702. He has become South Africa's answer to Joe Duffy. By 1995, with his unique insight into the host country, he was ideally placed to observe the World Cup as a commentator for RTÉ. This was reflected in the accuracy of his predictions, particularly when the host nation were involved. Against the weight of popular opinion, he called the fairy-tale ending that saw Nelson Mandela's Rainbow Nation upset the favourites on their World Cup debut, leaving the All Blacks to blame food poisoning.

'To be here was marvellous. That World Cup and South Africa winning the African Nations Cup in soccer for the first time the following year had a huge bonding effect on the country.'

1995 was also a significant year because rugby turned professional. It is something Robbie has mixed feelings about.

'Professionalism exploded onto the scene very quickly and very quickly turned a lot of players into millionaires. It led to a lot of greed, which is understandable. The money side of rugby bores me silly. I am only interested in the game once the whistle goes.

'Professionalism has changed the sport. The level of fitness and training has risen dramatically. Many of the players who flourished in the amateur era would not do so now. I don't think I would have been tough or hard enough for the professional game, though the money would have been nice! I was a dedicated, passionate rugby player and it was probably payment enough that I had great fun in my playing days.'

THE GREEN, GREEN GRASS OF HOME

Although he is unable to get back to Ireland as much as he would like, Robbie still keeps in touch with some of his rugby friends back home, like Ollie Campbell, Peter Boyle and Paul McNaughton. In 2004, he got the chance to see the Irish team at close quarters.

'I was very proud of what Ireland had done in the Six Nations that season, especially winning the Triple Crown. I was really looking forward to their two Tests that summer here in South Africa but I was disappointed in the way Ireland played. Before the tour, there had been the threat of a players' strike over appearance money and, whether it was that or the fact that the players were tired after a long season, you could pick up that things were not quite right. The only consolation for me was the chance to see Brian O'Driscoll in the flesh. I think he's a wonderful player. After Danie Gerber and Mike Gibson, he's the best centre I've ever seen.'

On his rare trips back to Ireland, Robbie enjoys the chance of seeing the Irish team play if the opportunity presents itself. He doesn't always get the reception he expects.

'I left Ireland in 1981 after Ireland were whitewashed! In '82, Ireland won the Triple Crown and in '83 the championship. I timed my first trip home to Ireland in '84 to coincide with Ireland's Five Nations game against Wales. Ireland were whitewashed again that season. I had missed out on two glorious years for Ireland and come home to see them losing again, an experience I was all too familiar with from my playing days. After the Welsh game, I was still in the stand as the crowd was thinning. I heard a voice shouting, "Robbie, Robbie!" I looked around until I found the owner of this voice. When I eventually met this stranger's eye, he said, "John Robbie, I'm addressing you." I was very flattered to be recognised and gave him the royal wave. After all the drama, though, he took the wind out of my sails when he said, "You're some f**king good-luck charm!"'

31

PEER PLEASURE

TALK TO ANYBODY WHO PLAYED INTERNATIONAL RUGBY FOR
Ireland in the 1970s and two constants emerge: firstly, at the very top
of the list of players they most admired will be the late Shay Deering;
secondly, they will be totally bemused that such a talented sportsman
with so many great attributes as a player and as a man should have
relatively speaking so few caps. In the past, such blunders from the
Irish selectors were even easier to predict than Keith Wood's latest
hairdo.

When Ireland drew 9–9 with Wales in 1974 Shay Deering, 'Deero',
made his international debut. His selection continued a great family
tradition. His father, Seamus, was a distinguished Irish forward of the
1930s and his uncle Mark also played for Ireland. Deero was a colossus
of a forward with awesome power, who had the honour of captaining
his country. He had the knack of leading a team with a mixture of
humour, charm and lordly aggression. Leadership by example and his
special presence were matched by the loyalty and respect he inspired in
others. A fiercely competitive streak, though well controlled, burned
inside him. Few people have made a greater impression on and off the
field on those who knew him.

PERSONAL TESTIMONIES
For former Irish captain Johnny Moloney, Deering was a brilliant
constellation in an otherwise gloomy sporting sky.

'He was a very sympathetic personality off the field but hard as nails on it. In 1995, I saw his son Shane helping Westmeath win the All-Ireland Minor football title. At one stage, he brought off a rugby tackle which his father would have been proud of. I was glad Shane kept the Deering name in lights.'

Moloney's admiration for Deering is shared by Mick Quinn.

'He was such a charismatic man. His smile signalled friendship but when he hit you in a tackle, friendship went out the window. He was a great teacher and leader, and you would have died for him. We all knew about his cancer, so we organised a golf Classic to help him out a bit. Four days before he died, he carried around his bag and played nine holes of the course. I remember Stewart McKinney who was his rival for the Irish jersey was in tears and how upset Slats and people like that were. His funeral will live with me forever. I gave the homily at the Mass. "Gracer" [Tom Grace], who wouldn't be my biggest fan by any means, told me afterwards that it was the best speech I ever made. I think it was because of the emotion as much as the content.'

The legendary Phil O'Callaghan was yet another huge fan.

'The best wing-forward I've ever seen was Shay Deering. He was such a wholehearted, committed player and one of the greatest characters I've ever met on or off the field. I have a lot of great memories of Shay. One of my strongest memories of my playing days is of an incident involving him. The night before an Irish squad session, Barry McGann, Shay and I had frequented a few pubs. In fact, we were even thrown out of one of them! The squad session the next day started with some laps around the pitch. Shortly after we started off, I heard Barry shout at me, "Cal, don't leave me." I dropped back with him and we were lapped once or twice. The cruel irony of the situation was that after the session McGann was selected and I was dropped!'

Like so many others, former Irish out-half Mick English is totally bewildered by the fact that Deering didn't win at least 50 caps, particularly since Ireland were trawling along the rocky bottom of international rugby that was their all-too-familiar habitat when he was in his prime. In fact, he won only eight. 'He was one of the best forwards I ever saw. No one could surpass his commitment. He was one of the few genuinely unforgettable people I ever met.'

Another in the long queue to praise Deero is Paul Dean.

'Shay was my mentor when I went to St Mary's. He taught me the rights and wrongs of rugby. He was very committed but very fair and he never threw a punch. As I was the out-half at Mary's, I'd make the breaks and he'd be on my shoulder to take the ball. I think the first year I came up into the Seniors he was the top try-scorer. He was a mountain of a man, with a huge heart – a true legend.'

Former Ireland hooker and later team manager Pat Whelan was also an ardent admirer of Shay Deering.

'I was fortunate in that my international days coincided with that of three of my Garryowen friends, Shay Dennison, Larry Moloney and Shay Deering. It's very difficult to talk about Shay Deering to somebody who never met him. Anyone who played with him or against him will never, ever forget him – as a rugby player or as a man. He was a breed apart, someone you would walk on water for. It's one of the great mysteries of Irish rugby that he didn't win scores of caps. I'd say most players of his era who were asked about the legends of Irish rugby would have him at the very top of their list. The four of us, me, Larry and the two Shays, travelled up to Dublin together for squad sessions. On the way home, we had a number of stops for "light refreshments". We came home at all hours of the day and night. My wife could never understand how a training session could last 24 hours!'

For his part, another former Irish captain, Tom Grace, finds it very difficult to talk about his great friend's death. His respect for Shay both as a player and as a man knows no limits: 'If someone asked me for a definition of the player's player, I would simply have two words to say – Shay Deering.

'I played with him at UCD. Strange things happened there! The classic for me was the case of Joe Comiskey, who became doctor to the Irish Olympic team. He was picked once, scored three tries and dropped for the next match. The next year he was selected again, scored four tries and was dropped again!

'Deero was such a presence. He epitomised somebody who brought 110 per cent to everything he did, whether it be singing a song or training. He had a gift which very few people possess. He was a natural leader rather than a follower. You felt ashamed not to be trying your best when you knew he was giving everything. When we trained at UCD, we went for a two- or three-mile cross-country run. Deero would always try to be first one home. There was never any doubt in my mind that I could beat him, because I had a better sprint but he never accepted this. He refused to concede that he would lose.'

A TONY AWARD

A new range of emotions come into Tony Ward's voice and facial expressions as he talks about the man who was, and is, his inspiration. He speaks with even more intensity than normal.

'For me, the best Irish player by far in his position was Shay Deering. He was the ultimate personification of bravery. His biggest problem was his lack of fear. He would stick his head in where most people would stick their boot. Fergus Slattery would be the first to admit that the way he and Shay complemented each other for UCD and Leinster was a significant factor in Slats' progression to the top.

'His caps were a paltry return in relation to his ability and commitment. He was one of those players who oozed, and I mean oozed, physical presence and charisma. He was the original gentleman off the pitch but, boy, was he a hard man on it. He particularly loved showing a gap to an outside-half or scrum-half and then when the player took the bait he pounced on him. My favourite rugby player of all time is Gerald Davies, but my all-time hero is Shay Deering. He will always have a special place in my heart.

'I first got to know Deero as a starry-eyed schoolboy at St Mary's in 1966. Shay was in sixth year and captain of the Schools cup-winning Senior side. He became my hero instantly and he has remained so to this day. With the arrival of his twin brothers, Kevin and David, in my class, I was to get to know Shay on a more intimate basis and many times, as the years progressed, not only were our paths to cross but they became very much one and the same. We played together for club [St Mary's and Garryowen], for province [Munster] and for country, and I will be forever grateful that it was with rather than against him that I played.

'He won eight caps for Ireland between 1974 and 1978, captaining his country in his final appearance. He won Munster and Leinster cup medals, a Leinster League medal and was capped for both provinces. He had a most distinguished career but long after the cups and caps have been counted, it is the friendships he made along the way that mattered the most. Shay was quite simply the player's player.'

Deering's heady mixture of athleticism, speed, aggression, power, skill and bravery won him incredible respect from his peers but in his final years, it was his courage that made the greatest impression on Tony Ward.

'That he was brave on the field is beyond dispute but in his final years, his bravery was stretched to the limit in the face of his battle against terminal illness. He displayed the courage and fighting qualities that one would expect only of him. His passing has left the game he loved much poorer.

'In recent years, I think of him regularly, particularly whenever I hear the Bette Midler song "Wind Beneath my Wings", from the film *Beaches*, because of the line "Did you ever know you were my hero?" Every time I hear that song, Deero flashes into my mind.'

CELTIC COUSINS

Irish rugby in the past has sometimes been accused of being too insular. In compiling this book, I thought it would be useful to get a more detached perspective, so I spoke with one of the stars of the great Welsh team of the 1970s, Ray Gravell. I contacted him initially as a total stranger but as soon as he heard my accent, he launched into a glorious recitation of lines of Irish poetry. He then dazzled me with his knowledge of Irish history. Who does he think are the legends of Irish rugby?

'When I think back to all the times I played for Wales against Ireland, I would characterise all the games we played as ferocity without malice. We would kill each other on the pitch but we loved each other off it. I remember the first time I travelled to Ireland with the Welsh team we stayed at the Shelbourne Hotel. Although I was far from Wales, I felt so at home. It took me a while to figure out what was so special about Ireland and then of course I realised it was the people. Over time, I discovered that there was some kind of affinity between the Welsh and the Irish because of our shared Celtic heritage. I made a number of conscious efforts to get to know Ireland outside rugby and explore all the wonders of Ireland, like the library at Trinity College, and to get to know people outside the rugby community, such as musicians like the legendary Dubliners. I remember when my mother died 15 years ago, the Dubliners sent me a bouquet for her funeral. I'll never forget the message they put on it, a classic Irish phrase: "Keep it going, Patsy". It meant a lot to me. When I got married I even had an Irishman as my best man.

'On the pitch, I have been fortunate to play with and against some of the greats of Irish rugby. Straight away, I think of Willie John McBride. I played against Willie John during his last game for Ireland in the centenary year of the IRFU. We beat Ireland well, though Willie John scored a try. Late in the game, Phil Bennett chipped through and I was chasing it. You don't think in the clamour of Cardiff Arms Park you will be able to hear any one voice in the crowd but I could hear perfectly this marvellous Irish accent shouting, "Kick ahead, Ireland! Kick any f**king head!" In that moment, I realised that, despite the intensity of the competition, it is really only a game.

'I got to know a number of the Irish players well on the Lions tour in 1980. In Wales, we had two great out-halfs at more or less the same time in Barry John and Phil Bennett. The difference between the two is that Phil made space whereas Barry made time. In Ireland, you had the amazing situation where you produced two great out-halfs in Tony Ward and Ollie Campbell, whom I got to know well on that Lions tour. Tony I would describe as a big man with short legs. I would describe Seamus Oliver Campbell as the bravest of the brave. He was so pale and slight looking but he really put his body on the line in the tackle. People talk about his kicking but there was so much more to his game than that. Another superb kicking out-half I came across for Ireland was Barry McGann. Barry was the fastest out-half I've ever seen over five yards. The problem is that he was completely f**ked after five yards!

'Fergus Slattery was a brilliant player and a great mix of the verbal and the physical. Mike Gibson is a complex man but he formed a great centre partnership with Dick Milliken. Because he was such a star of the Lions tour in 1971, Welsh rugby fans have huge admiration for Sean Lynch. Every time I come over to Ireland, I head to York Street to visit Sean in the Swan Bar. He never lets me buy a drink though. Willie Duggan was another awesome player and a great man to knock back a pint! I would probably say the same thing about Moss Keane. These guys were legends on the pitch and legends in the bar! Sometimes too much drink is not enough! It only took one drink to get them drunk. The problem was they could never remember if it was the 24th or the 25th! I always remember playing against Leinster in a club match and they had a 17 year old in the centre who just flew by me at one such stage. Already he was a class act and Brendan Mullin certainly became a great player after that.

'When I think of the legends of Irish rugby, though, I have to reserve a special place for Shay Deering. He was "the man", for me. He was a superb wing-forward and a wonderful leader because he led by example. He was so brave. I always felt very comfortable and secure in his company. He was very intelligent and he "got" things very quickly.

A formative influence on my career was one of my first coaches, Bert Peel. He was a coalminer and when I was young, he and Carwyn James told me I would play for Wales. In my teens, I was playing a club match and made a crushing tackle on my opposite number. I think I cracked his ribs but in the process I broke my shoulder. Bert came running onto the pitch and started rubbing my forehead with his sponge. I was in great pain and roared at him, "Bert, it's my f**king shoulder that's broke not my forehead." He calmly told me, "Yes, but your real problem now is up there." When I told that story to Shay, he knew immediately where Bert was coming from.

'He also enjoyed a story I told about another of my friends. His car was unreliable and he called me sometimes when it broke down. One day, I got yet another one of these calls.

'"What happened this time?" I asked.

'"My brakes went out. Can you come and get me?"

'"Where are you?"

'"I'm in the supermarket."

'"And where's the car?"

'"It's in here with me!"

'I just loved Shay and it was such a sadness when I heard that he'd passed away. Not just the rugby community but the world at large is a much poorer place without him.'

HAPPY DAYS

Shay had a keen sense of humour. He described the scene when one of his Garryowen teammates got married in the late 1970s. He laid down the following rules: 'I'll be home when I want and at what time I want – and I don't expect any hassle from you. I expect a great dinner to be on the table unless I tell you that I won't be home for dinner. I'll go playing rugby, training, hunting, fishing, boozing and card-playing when I want with my teammates and don't you give me a hard time about it. Those are my rules. Any comments?'

His new bride said, 'No, that's fine with me. Just understand that there will be sex here at seven o'clock every night . . . whether you're here or not.'

At a party to mark his wedding anniversary, Shay was asked to give his friends a brief account of the benefits of marriage. Deero replied, 'Well, I've learned that marriage is the best teacher of all. It teaches you loyalty, forbearance, meekness, self-restraint, forgiveness – and a great many other qualities you wouldn't have needed if you'd stayed single.'

Shay always enjoyed a good laugh with his fellow players. The size of the waistline of former Irish fly-half Barry McGann was the subject of many a quip during his playing days. Shay joked that Barry joined an exclusive gym and spent about 400 quid on it. He didn't lose a pound. He didn't realise that you have to show up to lose weight.

Former Irish full-back and later leader of the Irish Labour Party, Dick Spring, was initially a lawyer by profession. Deering went to him in a professional capacity and stated, 'I would like to make a will but I don't know exactly how to go about it.'

Spring said, 'No problem, leave it all to me.'

Deero looked upset as he said, 'Well, I knew you were going to take the biggest slice, but I'd like to leave a little to my children, too.'

Shay enjoyed a joke about lawyers at Spring's expense.

An engineer dies and reports to hell.

Pretty soon, the engineer gets dissatisfied with the level of comfort in hell, and starts designing and building improvements. After a while, they've got air conditioning and flushing toilets and escalators, and the engineer becomes hugely popular. One day, God calls the devil up on the telephone and says with a sneer, 'So, how's it going down there in hell?'

The devil replied, 'Things are going great. We've got air conditioning and flushing toilets and escalators, and who knows what this engineer will come up with next.'

God replied, 'What??? You've got an engineer? That's a mistake – he should never have gone down there. Send him up here.'

The devil said, 'No way. I like having an engineer on the staff, and I'm keeping him.'

God said, 'Send him back up here or I'll sue.'

Satan laughed uproariously and replied, 'Yeah, sure. And just where are you going to get a lawyer?'

As a vet, based in Mullingar, Deero had a passionate interest in animal welfare. At one stage he met a rugby player from, of all places, Mexico. He explained to Shay that rugby was a tiny minority sport in Mexico but that the number-one sport was bullfighting.

The horrified Shay said, 'Isn't that revolting?'

'No,' the Mexican replied, 'revolting is our number-two sport.'

One of Shay's favourite stories was about the dog who went into a hardware store and said, 'I'd like a job, please.'

The hardware store owner said, 'We don't hire dogs, why don't you go join the circus?'

The dog replied, 'Well, what would the circus want with a plumber?'

A client took his Rottweiler to Shay.

'My dog's cross-eyed, is there anything you can do for him?'

'Well,' said Deero, 'let's have a look at him.'

So he picked the dog up and examined his eyes, then checked his teeth. Finally he said, 'I'm going to have to put him down.'

'What? Because he's cross-eyed?'

'No, because he's bloody heavy.'

32

THE MAGNIFICENT SEVEN

LIKE LOVE AND MARRIAGE, HORSE AND CARRIAGE, RUGBY AND nicknames go hand in hand. Perhaps one of the most surprising omissions from the Irish rugby landscape is that Fergus Slattery was not known as 'Tow Truck', as he was always first to the breakdown and first to the out-half.

Fergus Slattery won 65 caps for Ireland over 14 years as an open-side wing-forward (a world record for a flanker), between 1970 and 1984, scoring 3 international tries. He was part of a 19-match-record back-row combination with Willie Duggan and John O'Driscoll. It is recognised worldwide that Slats at his best was great because of his presence on the field. His angles were so good that he always managed to put the opposition under pressure, forcing either the centre or out-half to release the ball. The significance of this is that when this happens, it is the wing-forward's play that is dictating what happens in the game and not vice versa. Although Slattery played his best rugby on the Lions tour of 1974 (when with Roger Uttley and Mervyn Davies, he formed one of the finest back rows in Lions' history), as he got older he read the game tremendously well. A master of mayhem, he put his body through extraordinary punishment. The great Phil Bennett famously said that he would rather play against any other open-side flanker than Slattery. The doyen of rugby commentators Bill McLaren picked him for his all-time dream team.

In the boardroom of his business premises at Northumberland Road in Dublin, Slattery's rugby brain is spinning into overdrive recalling the many golden moments in a glittering career. His first cap came against the Springboks in 1970 in an 8–8 draw. The terraces behind the goals at Lansdowne Road were empty and the playing surface cordoned off by barbed wire to prevent protesters from invading the pitch.

'It was a very controversial match. I was at UCD at the time and there was a forum before the game to debate whether or not Ireland should play South Africa. I spoke in favour and Kadar Asmal, the human-rights campaigner, spoke against. The weather was very bad before the match and they put straw on the pitch. It was like running into a barn. Having said that, the game lost none of its impact for me because of that. Things went pretty well for us that season. We beat Scotland 16–11 and then defeated a Wales side seeking the Triple Crown 14–0.'

TOURIST DISTRACTIONS

Slats played a pivotal role in the famous Barbarians match against the All Blacks at Cardiff Arms Park in 1973, scoring a try and setting up another for J.P.R. Williams. Although he distinguished himself in arguably the most stylish match of all time, Slattery was a hard man, which always stood him in good stead on tour.

'Selection for the Lions tour of New Zealand in 1971 was a natural progression. I was disappointed that I did not make the Test side but it was a terrific education. You're playing against the same guys every week, and of course you're living and breathing rugby.'

It was not a tour for the faint-hearted given the ferocity of the physical exchanges. One of the Lions forwards, Sandy Carmichael, suffered a multiple fracture of his cheekbone and had to return home. Slattery was decked by Alister Hopkinson but, typical of Slattery's guts, he played on, despite being so stunned he did not know where he was after the 'incident'.

'For me, touring was the best part of rugby. The best tours were the short ones. I loved touring in the south of France with Leinster. I found playing in the interprovincals nothing but drudgery. I would have traded all my interpro appearances for one tour to France. Even though we had such great success on the Lions tour to South Africa in 1974, it got very boring towards the end. You're packing your bags every three days and everything becomes very repetitive. I decided that I would never take part in a Lions tour again.'

In '74, he captained the team against the Proteas, the Lions' first match against a non-white team in South Africa. On the tour, he played in twelve of the twenty-two games, including all four Tests, and scored six tries. In fact, Slats was involved in the most controversial incident of the tour when the Lions needed to win the last Test for an unprecedented clean sweep of the Test series. With the score tied 13–13, the South African referee Max Baise failed to award him what looked a clear and fair touchdown in the last minute. Although the Lions were certain that it was a try, Slats is philosophical about the decision now.

'I don't think it would be fair to say Baise cost us the victory. Roger Uttley didn't touch down his try in the first half and in both that case and mine, Baise was very badly positioned, he couldn't see what was going on. He made a call but was just in the wrong place. I suppose the result was probably fair, because we didn't play well. I think you could sense it in the build-up: guys were packing their bags and preparing to go home, one or two guys played with injuries and we had lost a little focus. Above all, we probably paid the price for the euphoria of having won the series and annihilated the Springboks in two of the three previous Tests.

'After that tour, I came back and played a lot of matches. I pushed myself too hard and my blood count went down. I see my career in two phases: before and after that tour. Up to then, rugby was everything for me but after that, it wasn't. I had to look after my career.'

CONQUERING THE AUSSIES
Slattery led Ireland on the successful tour down under in 1979.

'Before the Australian tour, I thought we would have our work cut out to win the Tests. I think it's fair to say Australia underperformed in the first match; we caught them on the hop. But we beat them on merit in the second game.'

Surprisingly, an apparent low point in his career elicits the greatest passion.

'The 1981 tour to South Africa was a landmark in the development of the Irish side. We played out of our skins. I had captained the Irish team to Australia in 1979 but that was an experienced, powerful squad that convincingly won the series. Those who went to South Africa were very young, as in only two years we had virtually changed the entire side. It was literally a 'B' team, with 12 uncapped players in the party. And then we lost John Murphy, the full-back, and Ollie Campbell, whose absence was to prove very significant. Micky Quinn flew out the week before the First Test and in mid-week we played a racially mixed team, scoring a lot of tries. I will always remember that we missed about 17 kicks at goal. Still, it was the best investment in Irish rugby that could possibly have been made. We gave a number of young players a chance to show their wares.

'We played well in the First Test and lost 23–15 but we went into the Second Test without two senior players of Campbell's and Murphy's calibre. In the First Test, South Africa had outplayed us in the lineout with three giants, Stofberg, Malan and De Klerk, winning everything. All three were over 6 ft 5 in., whereas our tallest men were only 6 ft 2 in. and 6 ft 3 in. So we decided to revert to Plan B – in other words, play many three-man and four-man variations. We played the lineout quickly and did all sorts of things, using every trick in the book. We said that if we won 50 per cent of the possession, we would be satisfied. We also realised that South Africa's immense forwards tend to kill you when they go forward but if you turn them around, put the ball behind them and keep turning, they struggle. And we made every effort to disrupt their wheel and put-in to prevent them from getting quick ball. We were supposed to be very destructive on their ball and very creative on our own. And we certainly didn't go into the game without hope. Our loose forwards came out on top in both Tests. We knew that Rob Louw was their most potent loose forward but we managed to keep him out of the game.

'In the end, it was Naas Botha who beat us. He was only the fourth man in history to drop three goals in a Test and we were out. We'd had no luck at all, missing a conversion and having a bloody good try disallowed. We were leading 10–9 when Botha got his last with a few minutes left. It left us too little time to do anything and although we tried desperately, we just could not score. I really felt sorry for the guys, their achievement was spoilt at the very last moment.'

Ireland's fine performances on the tour tempted Slattery to engage in what was to be a lucrative speculation.

'When we left South Africa, Willie Duggan asked me, "Fancy a bet on the Triple Crown?" The odds were a generous 14-1. It was the first time I had ever bet on myself. Of course, I was delighted to win.'

He relinquished the captaincy to Ciaran Fitzgerald before the 1981–82 season. What prompted the move and how did he evaluate his successor?

'We had lost seven matches on the trot and needed a change. I was worried about Ciaran before the Australian tour in 1979 because he had a reputation for getting injured but he held his own there and grew in stature from then on. He was made to lead and his record as captain speaks for itself.

'The only disappointment I had in 1982 was the Paris game. We went there as favourites but they hockeyed us. There is something wrong with the Irish psychological preparation. Our forwards in particular seem to be too easily intimidated there.'

THOSE WERE THE DAYS

Asked about the Irish players he admires most, Slattery's reply is immediate.

'I loved playing with Mossic Keane because of his great commitment. I also admired Ollie Campbell's wholesale commitment to making himself what he became – a top-class player.'

However, he has special plaudits for his great friend and clubmate Willie Duggan: 'Willie was both a superb player who gave it all on the pitch and a wonderful character.'

In one match, Duggan was playing for the Public School Wanderers when his cousin and fellow Irish international, Ned Byrne, was clobbered in the eye. Byrne turned to his relative for comfort but was instead sharply reminded, 'I told you when you hit a guy don't be watching him. Watch the guy who's coming in behind him.'

33

CENTRE OF EXCELLENCE

WHEN IRELAND TOURED AUSTRALIA IN 1979, PRESS ATTENTION centred on the elder statesman of Irish rugby, Mike Gibson, then the most capped international of all time. Gibson was 36 at the time but still feared, because although his flesh was not as willing as in the golden days of his prime, his keen brain and polished skills still functioned unimpaired. He ended his international career on the tour having won 69 caps.

Asked about Gibson, his Ireland teammate Fergus Slattery is effusive.

'The giant of Irish rugby is C.M.H. Gibson. He is the role model you would want to hold up to younger players, because of his endurance and because he developed his skills to the very maximum.'

AMAZING GRACE

Former Irish captain Tom Grace has an unusual memory of touring with Mike Gibson.

'One of my first experiences of touring as an international was in 1972. A fella came up to me in a pub and asked me if I would like to go to Bermuda. I wasn't sure if he was joking or not. Mike Gibson and Fergus Slattery were the other Irish internationals travelling. One of the Bermudan players, to use a Barry McGann expression, "looked very strong". That meant that he was about 18 st.! He had two speeds – slow and very slow.'

For Mick Quinn, Mike Gibson was Ireland and the world's greatest player.

'Today, I hear players talking about all the sacrifices they make. I don't begrudge them the money they get in this professional era but I really get sick when I hear it suggested that the current players are more committed than we were. I doubt if any player today, professional or not, trains harder than "Gibbo" did. I certainly learned a lot just by watching him train and playing with him was an education too.

'Another thing I learned from Gibbo was what you might call a philosophy of the game. One statement in particular stands out and it's one I constantly repeat when I'm coaching kids: "The guys who are the best are the guys who can do the simple things – kicking, passing, running – better than anybody else. Work on the basics, everything else will fall into place."

'I remember telling a ball-boy that once in a dressing-room when I played in a charity match for Public School Wanderers at West Hartlepool. I didn't think much more about that incident until 1984 when I was in Cardiff with my close friend Brendan Mullin, who was playing for the Lions selection against a southern hemisphere selection. I was in the lobby of the Angel Hotel with him. Brendan I would have considered then to be the best Irish player since Mike Gibson. Who walks in but Rory Underwood. I was dumbfounded when he walked up to me and said, "Hello, Mick." I asked him how he knew me. He told me that he had been the ball-boy I talked to all those years before and that I had been the only player to talk to him that day. We became good friends. Some years later, I got mini-rugby going in Lansdowne. We would have 150 kids every Sunday. At one stage we organised an Under-12 tour to England. Rory is a pilot with the RAF and I got him to arrange a tour of the RAF base for the kids. It was great for them to see all the fighter jets and have the guys at the gate salute them and address them as "Sir". Rory also arranged for us to be taken into the briefing room before the pilots went on a mission to Scotland. Rory told me that he never forgot what I told him about doing the simple things well. I suppose Gibbo and myself must take some of the blame for all of those tries Rory has scored against Ireland!

'Gibbo was such a meticulous, single-minded player. I think the only player who could match him in that respect was Ollie Campbell. Mind you, Ollie has lightened up since he retired. Ollie is married to rugby, though there were many girls who would have been happy to be Mrs Ollie Campbell. He's brilliant with kids and would be a fantastic father.

To get to the highest level you have to be very dedicated and both Ollie and Gibson had phenomenal dedication.

'Gibbo had a great temperament. The only time I ever saw him rattled was on the tour to New Zealand in 1976. We were really up against it in some of the matches. I remember Tom Grace saying at breakfast, "Quinner, do you think we'll get out of the place before they realise we're afraid of them." We laughed at the time but I wonder! Barry McGann did not share the general concern. He was playing at out-half that day and was kicking everything, and I mean everything. Gibbo was yelling for a pass but Barry said, "Listen, Mike, when I meet a player who can run as fast as I can kick it, then I'll think about passing it!"

'Phil O'Callaghan had been recalled for that tour. He looked a bit older than the rest of us in '76. A journalist asked him who he was and Philo answered, "I'm Ireland's secret weapon." There was a lot of surprise that he was selected but he played a very significant role on that tour. He earned his cap on merit. I would describe him as the traditional Irish rugby tourist. When we were being intimidated on the pitch, he wasn't found wanting.'

SLEEPING BEAUTY

Ireland's tour of Australia in 1979 provided one particularly amusing memory of Gibson for former Irish captain Johnny Moloney.

'I was sharing a room with Terry Kennedy. Rodney O'Donnell was rooming with Mike Gibson. I can't think of a greater contrast of personalities, unless you put Tony O'Reilly rooming with Moss Keane! Mike was very dedicated, prepared meticulously and normally went to bed by ten. Rodney was very laid back and an early night for him would be midnight. He went to Australia as a 22-year-old St Mary's full-back, an uncapped unknown, and returned as a hero.

'Rodney's middle name could have been "Superstition". He had a huge fear of anything connected with the number 13. On tour, not only did he refuse to stay in a room numbered 13, or 213, or a room on the 13th floor, but he would not even stay in a room in which the numbers added up to 13, like 274.

'When he believed in something, there could be no deviation. He always insisted on being the last man on the team bus and would patiently wait for everyone to assemble and get on the bus, regardless of the climatic conditions. He refused to walk over a line. On a stone pavement, he would make the most bizarre movements to avoid treading on a line. Such an event could only trigger tragedies of apocalyptic proportions. With all this practice, some of his fellow players said he could have been world champion at hopscotch.

'A Friday the 13th fell on the Lions tour in 1980. Ollie Campbell and John Robbie rose at 6.30 a.m. that morning and taped lines right across the corridor outside O'Donnell's room and stuck up signs with the number 13 on them all over the corridor and the elevator. As a result, Rodney was afraid to leave the room for the entire day.

'He had an interesting theory about the psychology of the rugby ball. When an opponent had kicked a goal against his team, he felt much better if the ball came down in such a way that he was able to throw it back over the crossbar, his theory being that the next time, the ball would either be unsure where to go or would lose the habit of travelling in the right direction.

'Yet another ritual was preparing to tog out before games. He had to put on his togs in such a way that the material did not touch his skin on the way up. Should such a calamity occur, he would begin the whole process again – and if necessary again and again until he got it exactly right. The second part of this operation was that he would never button up his togs until he was running onto the field.

'He was preoccupied with exactitudes to the point that he went around every room adjusting pictures so that they hung straight on the walls. This tendency was dramatically illustrated on Ireland's tour to Australia in 1979. In the middle of Noel Murphy's team talk, he jumped up to the astonishment of all present to adjust the position of the telephone.

'One of his most famous idiosyncrasies was his desire to get into bed each night without touching the bottom sheet. The task had to be executed with military precision. If he failed the first time he tried, he kept trying, until he got it exactly right. Only then did he allow himself to relax.

'Rodney dropped into our room for a chat one night on that Australian tour and later we were joined by Paul McNaughton. Paul asked Rodney who he was rooming with. When he answered that he was with Gibbo, Paul pretended to be very sympathetic, which made Rodney a tiny bit uncomfortable, because Paul had shared with Gibbo the week before. He told Rodney that when he went back to the room, he would discover that the sheets and blankets on his bed would be neatly folded back, the light would be left on in the bathroom and the bathroom door would be slightly ajar. Then when he went into bed he would be asleep about half an hour when Gibbo would jump on top of him in the bed. Rodney was very sceptical but a couple of hours later when he went back to his room, he saw everything just as Paul described: the light on in the toilet, the bathroom door slightly ajar and the covers folded back on the bed. The next morning, he came down for his breakfast like a zombie. He told us he hadn't slept a wink all night because he was waiting for Gibbo to jump on top of him!'

34

OBSERVE THE SON
OF ULSTER

IT IS INCONCEIVABLE THAT A DISCUSSION ON GREAT IRISH forwards could begin without reference to Willie John. The fact that it is unnecessary to use his surname says it all. To say that his rugby CV is impressive is an understatement: 63 caps, 5 Lions tours, 17 Lions Test appearances and captain of the most successful Lions side of all time. Born one of six children in Toomebridge, County Antrim, he lost his father at the age of four and was brought up by his mother on a small farm. The hardships he experienced give the lie to the perception that rugby in Ireland is only a game for those born with a silver spoon in their mouths.

On the eve of his departure for the Bermuda Classic, the rugby memories roll off his tongue. He is spoilt for choice when asked about the highlights of his career.

'Beating Australia in 1967 in the Test at Sydney Cricket Ground was a great achievement, particularly as we had to strap up three players because of injury to get them onto the field. Our win over Wales in 1970 was also a magic moment. We had an amazing pack of forwards then, with world-class players like Ray McLoughlin and Fergus Slattery. We haven't turned out as good a pack of forwards since. The team was probably at its peak in 1972 but politics may have cost us the Triple Crown because Scotland and Wales refused to travel to Ireland because of the Troubles. It was great towards the end of my career to lead Ireland to the Championship in 1974.'

Asked about what it was like to play in '*the* game' for the Barbarians against the All Blacks in 1973, he laughs.

'When you say I played in it – I was there. I don't think I actually played in it. The match was played at 100 miles an hour, which is unsuitable for a guy like me whose game is not based on mobility. Phil Bennett passed to me three times in the one movement. I remember at one point getting the ball and it was hot!'

THE LION KING

Pride of place in Willie John's trophy cabinet goes to a silver water jug presented to him by the players on the 1974 Lions tour to South Africa, engraved with the words 'To Willie John. It was great to travel with you.'

The Lions won all eighteen of their provincial games and three of the four Tests, with the other drawn only because the referee disallowed Fergus Slattery's match-winning try. They scored a record 729 points. McBride's philosophy was that the Lions would 'take no prisoners' and 'get our retaliation in first'.

'South African rugby was always physical and we had always been dominated, played second fiddle, in years gone by, and they just couldn't believe that we could stand up to this. Of course we were physical but we were definitely not dirty. In fact we went out of our way not to be dirty because we knew we were the better players and the better team when we played rugby football. You can't be a good team and a dirty team at the same time.'

McBride was responsible for a tactic that has now become part of rugby folklore: the infamous '99' call used by the captain as an emergency measure when things looked like getting out of hand. On his signal, all 15 Lions would 'take on' their nearest opponent, not only to show the South Africans that they were not going to back down but also to reduce the risk of a sending-off, as the referee was highly unlikely to dismiss an entire team. The call was used twice in the bruising Third Test, but only as a last resort.

'The whole thing about the 99 call has been overplayed. I would say there were possibly four incidents in all the games and that was about it. It was a good thing because it showed South Africa that the Lions were going to stand up at last and weren't going to take any nonsense. On previous tours, there is no doubt about it, they were bullied and there was no way we were going to accept it in 1974.

'My experience on previous Lions tours had taught me that in provincial games you tend to have a bit of thuggery to soften up the tourists. Before the match against Eastern Province, I told the side that I was expecting trouble. I said to them, "Tomorrow, if anything happens, we are all in it together – and I mean all. You hit the guy that is nearest to you as hard as you can whether he has done anything wrong or not. If that doesn't stop it, you haven't hit him hard enough." My attitude was, hurt one of us and you hurt us all, so we'll stop it there and then. Initially, the signal I came up with was "999", the traditional alert for all emergency services, but the feeling among us was that 999 was too long, so we cut it down to 99.

'There is no question but that Gareth Edwards was one of the best players in the world at the time. So if there was any thuggery, he was always likely to be targeted. At one stage during the game, he got a thump on the back of his head after he had passed the ball. Within seconds, about half the Eastern Province team were sprawling on the ground. They didn't know what had hit them, literally. An important marker had been put down for the rest of the tour.

'The 1974 tour was like all my Christmases at once. Winning became a habit and we liked it. I suppose the sad thing was that there was such controversy about the drawn game, which was the final match. None of us could understand why Fergus Slattery's try was disallowed. The main thing was that we didn't lose the game because of it. If we had, it would have taken some of the gloss off the tour. To beat them on their turf was incredible.'

The tour itself was shrouded in controversy.

'You might say we were under house arrest even before we left home. We came under tremendous pressure, spending three days in London where the anti-apartheid movement asked us to pull out of the tour. I met the players and told them, "If you don't want to come, please leave now." There wasn't a sound. It seemed like forever but after a couple of moments I could wait no longer and said, "OK, then, we are all in this together." Once we were in South Africa, we discovered that the British Government, who were against the tour, had instructed the Embassy to boycott us. The opposition helped to weld us together, to mould us into one big family.

'That was the biggest challenge of my life, trying to get coalminers from Wales and solicitors from London to mix together. Cracks could have appeared in the squad when we divided into a Test side and a midweek side, but those problems never arose because we kept on winning. We only used seventeen players in the four Tests: one change was caused by injury and the other was when we brought Andy Irvine in on the wing. Although he was out of his position (full-back), he was too good a player to leave on the bench. I especially remember after Alan Old broke his leg, Phil Bennett came along to say to me, "Don't worry, I'll play as often as you need me." Those guys had a great attitude to life. They trained hard, played hard but were always a good laugh. When we won the first two Tests, we had the Springboks reeling. I think they made ten changes in all for the Third Test. That was the big one because if we won that match, we won the series. We trained every day, concentrating on scrummaging, and no quarter was asked or given. Those workouts were much tougher than anything we could have encountered in a match.

'The day before, we travelled on a coach to a little village outside Port Elizabeth and had tea and scones on a very English lawn. We told stories, and laughed and joked a lot. We really managed to relax and the game was put to the back of our minds. As the old man of the party, I was anxious to get to bed early because I needed my rest. But that night it was not easy to sleep. I told the players that evening, "There is no escape. We will take no prisoners!"

'The following day, when I walked into the room where the team had gathered, the air was full of electricity. There were five minutes to board the coach and they stood up. Usually, I would talk about the importance of the game and the reasons for wanting to win. But this time I simply asked, "Men, are we ready?" They looked up. They were ready.

'The first 20 minutes or so were probably the toughest of the whole tour. The pressure on us was terrible. People expected us to win, which can be fatal for any team. We made it hard on ourselves by making mistakes we'd never made before. However, we finally got it together and won 26–9.

'The feeling of greatness in that side was unbelievable. We had the best back row I have ever played with – Fergus Slattery, Gareth Edwards, Phil Bennett and J.P.R. Williams. The real strength of that team, though, was its togetherness, loyalty and bravery. There is a bond between that team that will never die.'

In 1975, in his final home international, McBride scored his first try for his country when Ireland defeated France 25–6. Such was the emotion generated that the crowd ran onto the pitch to celebrate the try. To mark the centenary season of Irish rugby, the IRFU arranged a match between Ireland/Scotland and England/Wales in April 1975. It was to be the last time the Ballymena man would lead out a side at the home of Irish rugby. Events took an unexpected turn after the match when he was hijacked by the late Eamonn Andrews and whisked away to become the subject of an edition of *This Is Your Life*.

HARD TIMES

When asked about his most difficult opponent, McBride does not hesitate for a second.

'Colin Meads was as hard a man as I ever came across, though I also played against his brother Stan, who was a tough nut too.

'Another tough man was the South African forward Mof Myburgh. It is difficult to describe just how imposing this man was. I will never forget my Test debut for the Lions in 1962, largely because of Mof. We were playing in the famous Newlands ground at Cape Town but there were great patches of the ground that had no grass on them at all, and, just to illustrate how naive I was, I said, "Mof, there's not a lot of grass on the pitch."

'No answer.

'Louder this time, I said, "Mof, there's not a lot of grass on the pitch."

'Mighty Mof continued to look straight ahead but replied out of the side of his mouth, "I didn't come here to f**king graze."

'Thus began my experience of Test rugby for the Lions. If I was nervous before, that exchange was not what I needed to soothe my anxiety.

'For me, the crucial person in transforming the Lions into a more professional outfit was Carwyn James, the Welsh coach who took charge of us on our tour to New Zealand in 1971. I can still remember him telling me, "I see rugby as a piece of opera, a piece of music. It is something that can flow like music and opera, and can be beautiful to watch." He wanted his players to play, to enjoy the experience, to take responsibility and to have the courage to make decisions for ourselves. He really brought us together as a squad and got us to be the best we could be, which is what the great coaches do, and as a result we won that series.'

Willie John had the opportunity to put his own vast reservoir of experience playing for the Lions to good use when he managed the

Lions side that toured New Zealand in 1983. However, the Lions were whitewashed in the Test series. What went wrong?

'A lot of things, like injuries to key players. I suppose the dynamics were wrong. Our captain Ciaran Fitzgerald was under a lot of pressure, especially from the British media, who felt he wasn't up to the job. The problem was that Ciaran wasn't really allowed to do his job by our coach, Jim Telfer. Don't get me wrong, Jim was a great coach and extraordinarily committed but he intruded into Ciaran's space and didn't allow him to display his talent for leadership, which he had already shown for Ireland and showed again in 1985 when he captained the team that won the Triple Crown. The other problem was that Jim overtrained the team so that they were too tired to play. This was most obvious when we lost the final Test 38–6, which was a right hammering. It is fair to say that when I look back on my career, that series, like my season coaching Ireland in 1983, was not my happiest experience. But when I reminisce, it is the good days I choose to remember.'

Not surprisingly, there is much folklore about Willie John. One of the stories told about him goes back to the Lions tour to South Africa in 1974, when he and Andy Irvine went into a diner that looked as though it had seen better days. As they slid into a booth, Irvine wiped some crumbs from the seat. Then he took a napkin and wiped some mustard from the table. The waitress, in a dirty uniform, came over and asked if they wanted some menus.

'No thanks,' said Andy, 'I'll just have a cup of black coffee.'

'I'll have a black coffee, too,' Willie John said. 'And please make sure the cup is clean.'

The waitress shot him a nasty look. She turned and marched off into the kitchen. Two minutes later, she was back.

'Two cups of black coffee,' she announced. 'Which of you wanted the clean cup?'

35

DOYLER

IRISH RUGBY WAS SHOCKED IN 2004 BY THE UNTIMELY DEATH OF
Mick Doyle in a car accident. I first met Doyler in 1993, through our
mutual friend Tony Ward. I had the good fortune to bump into him on
a number of occasions subsequently and in 1996 I interviewed him
about his life in rugby. Doyle's first love was the GAA, though when he
began his secondary education as a boarder at Newbridge College,
rugby became his number-one sport.

'In a strange way, it was only after I went away to school that my
father became the biggest influence on my rugby career. Whenever I
was at home, I would have big question-and-answer sessions with him
about what options should be taken in specific situations during a
match. It was from him I got my philosophy of the game and in those
sessions my "give it a lash" approach was born. As we had such a small
pool in Newbridge and there were no subs allowed in a match at the
time, I played in a wide variety of positions: in the centre, wing-
forward, out-half, full-back and as a number 8.'

He made his international debut against France in 1965 and scored a
try. He had many memories of that game and of his international career.

'Noel Murphy and Ray McLoughlin helped me a great deal in
adjusting to the demands of international rugby. I always looked up to
Bill Mulcahy. He made you aware of what it was to be an Irish player
and the standard you had to reach to do justice to the green jersey. I
loved every single game I played for Ireland. The highlights for me
were beating South Africa in 1965, playing against England with my

242

brother Tommy also playing on the other flank for Ireland, scoring a try against Wales in the ninth minute of injury time in 1968 and touring with the Lions to South Africa in the same year.

'The great thing about my rugby career was that it gave me the opportunity to meet so many wonderful characters, like Ken Kennedy. He has a great irreverence. I would describe him as a macho David Norris. I have great respect for him as a person. Of course, you could write a book about Phil O'Callaghan. He's a panic. The late Jerry Walsh was a great Irishman and a fabulous tackler. Willie John has a great sense of humour and I love Syd Millar's ready wit. Both of them could take it as it came.'

On tour with the Lions, Doyler was as well known for his off-the-field exploits as for those on it, particularly in exposing the gap between 'The Wreckers' and 'The Kippers', the latter being those who liked to get an early night and the former those who chose to get as late a night as possible.

1968 marked his retirement from international rugby. The decision was prompted by non-rugby factors.

'I was 28. I had been a perpetual student up to that time. It was time for me to settle down and to build up my veterinary practice.'

The rugby bug bit again and he made a comeback with Naas, initially as a coach and then as a player. 'I got so hoarse from shouting on the sidelines that I used up less energy joining in on the pitch.' As Leinster coach, he took them to five interprovincial titles between 1979 and 1983 (1982 shared). There was controversy about the manner in which he was appointed Irish coach, with Willie John McBride being cast aside after just one year. He was prompted to throw his hat into the ring for the position by members of the team.

'After Ireland lost to Scotland in 1984, Moss Keane and Willie Duggan came to me and persuaded me that I should run for the job of Irish coach, because they felt we were going nowhere fast.'

CROWNING GLORY

There was no disguising the pride in Doyle's voice as he talked about the Triple Crown in 1985.

'I had built up a huge dossier of information about each player. I had made up my mind if ever I was made a coach of a representative side, I would give players responsibility for their own performances. The only thing I would not tolerate was players not trying. I think it is fair to say I gave straight answers to players and there was honest selection, which helped to build up the right spirit.'

Doyler had many stories about his players from that team, notably his full-back Hugo MacNeill, who was famous for his good looks.

'One evening Hugo went into a seafood disco and pulled a muscle. Another time, he took his blind date to the carnival.

'"What would you like to do?"

'"I want to get weighed," she said.

'They strolled over to the weight guesser. He guessed 130 pounds. She was delighted and was given a teddy bear as her prize. Next, the couple went on the ferris wheel. When the ride was over, Hugo asked her what she would like to do.

'"I want to get weighed," she said.

'Back to the weight guesser they went. Again Hugo guessed correctly and they won another teddy bear.

'The couple walked around the carnival and again he asked her where she would like to go. "I want to get weighed," she responded.

'By this time, Hugo figured he should cut his losses and dropped her home.

'Her flatmate, Laura, asked her about the blind date.

'The girl responded, "Oh, Waura, it was wousy".'

In fairness, Doyler told more stories against himself than anybody else. He frequently joked about his weight: 'I have flabby thighs but fortunately my stomach covers them. We have a tradition of walking in our family to fight the battle of the bulge. My uncle started walking five miles a day when he was 60. He's 97 now and we don't know where the f**k he is. I like long walks myself, especially when they are taken by people who annoy me.'

The highs of 1985 were dramatically reversed the following year when Ireland were whitewashed in the Five Nations championship. 1987, too, was a year of missed opportunities and some rumours of discontent within the Irish camp.

'We should have won the Triple Crown in 1987. We let the game against Scotland slip through our fingers. Things were sometimes misinterpreted. After we lost that match, the then chairman of the selectors, Eddie Coleman, asked if he could sit in on our team meeting. I told him I would prefer it if he didn't but because he was chairman of selectors, I couldn't stop him if he really wanted to. During the meeting, I was very critical of the players' performances and told them so in forthright terms and outlined what I expected of them. I also said that what I had said was not for repeating outside. Some people obviously thought I was putting on a macho display for Eddie's benefit and was trying to show them up. Within a week, a journalist, David Walsh, had the story. I don't think the affair did any lasting damage. The mood was brilliant after we beat Wales in Cardiff and the guys, in a show of affection, threw me in the bath!

'I think that it's probably fair to say that I was less tolerant towards the end, particularly during the World Cup in 1987. My period as Irish coach cost me about £750,000. Before we left for that tournament, my business was going down the tubes. I didn't have time to keep my eye on the ball in terms of my work. I had never experienced stress until then but literally up to the last minute before going down under I was frantically trying to salvage my business. I was also hitting the bottle too hard and it wasn't doing me any favours. It was the darkest hour of my life because everything I had worked for was disappearing before my eyes. Of course, what made it much worse was that I was worried about not being able to provide for my family.

'I suppose we didn't have the same off-the-cuff attitude we had in 1985. On the rugby side, things were not going right in the build-up. We lost Nigel Carr from the team when he was injured in a horrific bomb blast, which was a huge blow. I always take too much on and I was trying to do everything I could for the players on the organisational side. Philly Orr told me I was doing too much.

'Within 24 hours of getting to New Zealand, I had my coronary "incident". I should have been sent home after that. I was on tablets to sleep, tablets to wake up, tablets for hypertension and God knows what else. Most of the three or four weeks I was there, I was edgy and irritable and in no way a suitable candidate for being a coach. The guys deserved a better coach than I was. I was less understanding than I should have been. Syd Millar and Mick Molloy were probably too kind to me at the time. They should have shaken me up a bit.

'When I came home, I was on the point of having a nervous breakdown but I never quite went over the brink. That phase lasted for about six months, until I started to put the pieces back together.

'I learned a lot about myself in that period. I discovered I wasn't invincible. The one thing I will say is that if you can't control stress, it will control you. Two exercises which I found helpful were, firstly, to think of the blackest possible scenario that could happen to me in my worst nightmare. Once that wasn't happening, I was already winning. Secondly, I learned to live in the moment, in other words to forget worrying about yesterday or tomorrow and just worry about today.'

GONE BUT NEVER TO BE FORGOTTEN

Every meeting with Doyler was memorable. My final encounter with him was a few months before his tragic death. He had just been listening to a report that Greece might not be able to finish building all the facilities for the 2004 Olympics. Doyler joked that as a result, the 2004 triathlon would combine running, swimming and pouring concrete.

However, what had really put a spring in his step was a joke that he had heard that morning about a visit by President George W. Bush to England.

While visiting England, Bush was invited to tea with the Queen at Buckingham Palace. With an eye on the forthcoming presidential election, Bush was keen to pick her brain and asked her about her leadership philosophy. She told him it was to surround herself with intelligent people. Bush asked how she knew if they were intelligent.

'I ask them the right questions', said the Queen. 'Let me show you.'

Bush watched as the Queen phoned Tony Blair and said: 'Mr Prime Minister, may I ask you a question? Your mother has a child and your father has a child, and it is not your brother or sister. Who is it?'

Blair replied, 'It's me, ma'am.'

'Correct. Thank you and goodbye, sir,' said the Queen. She hung up and said, 'You see what I mean, Mr Bush?'

Bush nodded. 'Yes, ma'am. Thanks a lot. I'll definitely be using that!'

Bush, upon returning to Washington, decided he'd better put his administration to the test. Bush summoned his vice-president, Dick Cheney, to the Oval Office and said, 'I wonder if you can answer a question for me.'

'Why, of course, sir. What's on your mind?'

Bush posed the question: 'Uhh, your mother has a child and your father has a child, and it is not your brother or your sister. Who is it?'

Cheney scratched his head, 'I do not know, sir. That's too tough for me. You will need the most intelligent member of your administration for that.'

That evening Colin Powell was summoned to the West Wing. The president asked, 'Uhh, your mother has a child and your father has a child, and it is not your brother or your sister. Who is it?'

'It is me, Mr President.'

President Bush hung his head. 'You dumb sh*t. You're so wrong. Of course it's not you. It's Tony Blair.'

36

THE RED FELLOW'S THE BEST

THERE ARE GOOD PUBLIC SPEAKERS, THERE ARE GREAT PUBLIC speakers and there's Tony O'Reilly. Watching him in action, it is difficult not to feel overwhelmed by the sheer strength of his personality. Every word is carefully chosen, every pause and gesture is carefully orchestrated. The atmosphere is electric, like a revivalist meeting with a touch of fanaticism. The crowd wait for him to come up to the podium as if he were a presidential candidate. As he speaks, all eyes are on him, seemingly transfixed. It appears that if he asked them to try walking on water, they would be happy to do so. His little asides are priceless gems: intimate, wry, and chatty by turns, but always drawing his audience into moments of shared experience.

After listening to O'Reilly give a lengthy speech at his Alma Mater, the Taoiseach, Bertie Ahern said, 'I'd like to congratulate Belvedere College on the great job dey did in teaching Tony O'Reilly to speak so well. A pity dey didn't teach him to stop!'

Such is O'Reilly's flair with words, it is difficult to imagine that he was once out-quipped – but miracles do happen. England beat Ireland 20–0. As he walked off the pitch, O'Reilly turned to Tom Reid and said, '20–0! That was dreadful!'

Reid responded, 'Sure, weren't we lucky to get the nil!'

At the height of his playing career, O'Reilly held the distinction of having broken the records for the most tries ever scored for the Lions and the most tries ever scored by a Barbarian. Coached at Belvedere

College by the legendary Karl Mullen, he played his first match when he was six years of age. His mother asked the priest what he thought of the small players on show. The Jesuit, who had no idea who she was, answered, 'The red fellow's the best.' She glowed with pride. The red fellow was her son.

OUT OF AFRICA

O'Reilly is very much the Roy of the Rovers of Irish rugby. Having first been capped against France as an 18 year old in 1955, he was the undisputed star of the Lions tour to South Africa in the same year. The Lions were captained and managed by Irishmen, Robin Thompson and Jack Siggins respectively. The squad featured five Irish players, Thompson, Tom Reid, and Robin Roe in the forwards and O'Reilly and Cecil Pedlow among the backs. O'Reilly scored no less than 16 tries, a record number, and emerged as top scorer.

O'Reilly's achievements on the field do not seem to square with his own assessment of his playing style: 'I suppose you could say I was a slightly furtive player. I hung back waiting for the game to show itself to me rather than show myself to the game.'

In 1959, O'Reilly performed even better on the Lions tour to New Zealand and Australia, amassing a staggering 22 tries. It is a testimony to his importance to the team that he played in more matches than any other player, 24 in all. However, this time it was another Irish player, David Hewitt, who was top scorer with 106 points.

O'Reilly celebrated his 19th birthday on the 1955 Lions tour to South Africa. In the opening Test, the Lions won 23–22 in Johannesburg. It was the biggest attendance ever seen at a rugby game. The Springboks led 11–3 at one point and to compound their misfortune the Lions lost their flanker Reg Higgins with a broken leg. At the time, no replacements were allowed, so they had to play with 14 men in front of over 100,000 partisan South Africans. Then, 3 tries from Cliff Morgan, Cecil Pedlow and Tony O'Reilly gave the Lions a 23–11 lead. The Afrikaners replied with a vengeance. In the final minute, Chris Koch crashed over for a try to cut the deficit to just one point. As van der Schyff faced a relatively easy kick to give the South Africans victory, the Irish Lions turned to religion. The Limerick lock Tom Reid said, 'Jesus, if he kicks this, I'm turning Protestant.'

To the horror of the home fans, van der Schyff pushed his kick left of the post.

The late Tom Reid saw rugby as a 'little refreshment of my spirit' and was a great diplomat. On the tour to South Africa, O'Reilly and Reid were in a group of Lions tourists who were asked during an offical reception about the political situation. An awkward silence descended on the party until Reid piped up, 'Well, sir, I think nothing of it. I come from Limerick in southern Ireland and I have my own political problems.'

Reid suffered from bad eyesight and went to live in Canada after that tour. In 1959, he memorably linked up with O'Reilly again. After the southern hemisphere tour, the Lions stopped off to play a Test in Canada. O'Reilly was standing in line before the match when he heard a loud Limerick accent booming out over the ground, 'Hello, O'Reilly, I know you're there. I can't see you but I can hear you all right!'

O'Reilly could have been a film star. The acclaimed Irish actor Noel Purcell recommended him to Al Corfino, the casting director of the film *Ben Hur*, for the role that was eventually played by Charlton Heston. O'Reilly's physique made him ideal for the scenes in the galleys. Purcell arranged for a meeting between the director and O'Reilly but the rugby player never showed up. The story of O'Reilly's possible role in the film made headlines as far away as South Africa.

HUSBANDS AND WIVES

O'Reilly is one of the greatest raconteurs world rugby has ever produced. When Éamon de Valera was in his final few years as Irish President, he was virtually blind. But he was persuaded to attend one of Ireland's home internationals. Watching the game in the stands, Tony O'Reilly was unhappy with some of the referee's decisions. When he was asked afterwards to comment on the match he said, 'Dev saw more of it than the referee.'

He once told the story of an unnamed Irish international whose wife arrived home from work early one day and found her husband in bed with another woman. 'That's it!' she shouted, 'I'm leaving and I'm not coming back!'

'Wait, honey,' the Irish international pleaded. 'Can't you at least let me explain?'

'Fine, let's hear your story,' the wife replied.

'Well, I was driving home when I saw this poor young lady sitting at the side of the road, barefoot, torn clothes, covered in mud and sobbing. I immediately took pity on her and asked if she would like to get cleaned up. She got into the car and I brought her home. After she took a shower, I gave her a pair of the underwear that doesn't fit you any more, the dress that I bought you last year that you never wore, the pair of shoes you bought but never used and even gave her some of the turkey you had in the refrigerator but didn't serve me. Then I showed her to the door and she thanked me. As she was walking down the step, she turned around and asked me, "Is there anything else your wife doesn't use any more?"'

Another of the stories attributed to O'Reilly is about the Irish international who was having an affair with an Italian woman. One night, she confided in him that she was pregnant. Not wanting to ruin his reputation or his marriage, he paid her a large sum of money if she would go to Italy to have the child. If she stayed in Italy, he would also provide child support until the child turned 18. She agreed, but wondered how he would know when the baby was born. To keep it discreet, he told her to send him a postcard, and write 'Spaghetti' on the back. He would then arrange for child support. One day, almost nine months later, he came home to his confused wife. 'Darling,' she said, 'you received a very strange postcard today.'

'Oh, just give it to me and I'll explain it later,' he said.

She obeyed and watched as the Irish international read the card, turned white and fainted.

On the card was written, 'Spaghetti, spaghetti, spaghetti. Two with meatballs, one without.'

LADIES' MAN

One of the many tributes paid to A.J.F. O'Reilly over the years was, 'Never have you satisfied so many women in the one day.' Despite O'Reilly's erstwhile reputation as something of a ladies' man, this is not what it seems. The source was Irene Johnson, president of the Hockey Union, rejoicing at his generous donation towards the running of the 1994 Women's Hockey World Cup.

O'Reilly gained a reputation as a lover of wine, women and song. Many stories are told about his exploits. They often score low on veracity but high on entertainment value. One of the many stories told about him goes back to his time on the Lions tour to South Africa. O'Reilly thought it was raining and put his hand out the window to check. As he did so, a glass eye fell into his hand. He looked up to see where it came from in time to see a young woman looking down.

'Is this yours?' he asked.

She said, 'Yes, could you bring it up?' and the Irish star agreed.

On arrival, she was profuse in her thanks and offered O'Reilly a drink. As she was very attractive, he agreed. Shortly afterwards she said, 'I'm about to have dinner. There's plenty, would you like to join me?'

He readily accepted her offer and they enjoyed a lovely meal. As the evening was drawing to a close, the lady said, 'I've had a marvellous evening. Would you like to stay the night?'

O'Reilly hesitated, then said, 'Do you act like this with every man you meet?'

'No,' she replied, 'only those who catch my eye.'

Another story about O'Reilly from that tour is that he was having dinner in a fine restaurant with a beautiful young woman. Their waitress, taking another order at a table a few paces away, noticed that O'Reilly was slowly sliding down his chair and under the table, with his dinner partner acting unconcerned. The waitress watched as O'Reilly slid all the way down his chair and out of sight under the table. Still, the woman dining across from him appeared calm and unruffled, apparently unaware that her date had disappeared. After the waitress finished taking the order, she came over to the table and said to the woman, 'Pardon me, ma'am, but I think your boyfriend just slid under the table.'

The woman calmly looked up at her and replied firmly, 'Ohhh no, my boyfriend just walked in the door.'

37

BIG TOM

NO ONE ENCAPSULATES PASSION FOR RUGBY BETTER THAN TOM Clifford. He was first capped for Ireland against France in 1949 and won the last of his 14 caps against France in 1952, a match that also saw the end of the international careers of Karl Mullen, Des O'Brien and Bill McKay. Clifford was a key part of the '49 Triple Crown victory and toured with the Lions to Australia and New Zealand in 1950. He was one of nine Irish players to make the tour with Karl Mullen, George Norton, Michael Lane, Noel Henderson, Jack Kyle, Jimmy Nelson, Bill McKay and Jim McCarthy. Clifford was famous on the tour for his singing. One of his favourite ditties went: 'When I was a wee wee tot, they put me on a wee wee pot, to see if I could wee or not.'

According to legend, Tom's rugby affiliation was evident at an early age. When he was in primary school he got a new teacher who came from a different part of Limerick and as a result, she was a fanatical Shannon fan. On her first day she asked Tom what team he supported.

Tom replied, 'Young Munster.'

'And why do you support Young Munster?'

'Because my mum and dad support them.'

'And I suppose if your parents were Shannon fans, you would be a Shannon supporter.'

'No, Miss. If my parents were Shannon fans, I would be an idiot.'

CLASS BOUNDARIES

Rugby is and always has been a middle-class, if not an upper-class, pursuit in Ireland. The vast majority of the rugby-playing population began their careers in the most prestigious fee-paying schools in Ireland, like Clongowes and Blackrock College. Hence it cannot compete in terms of popularity with the GAA, where banker, priest and small farmer come together to celebrate the magic of a Munster hurling final between Cork and Tipperary or an All-Ireland football final between Dublin and Kerry.

This point is reflected in Brendan Behan's observation, 'I never heard rugby was a proper game for anyone except bank clerks. It was a game for the Protestant and the shop-keeping Catholic and I never thought it had anything to do with me.'

All this changes, however, on the days of international matches, when Ireland becomes a rugby nation and each pass and kick is not just passively observed but lived like a heartbeat. This applies particularly to matches against England at Lansdowne Road, which are matters of national pride – bearing in mind that unlike the soccer team, the rugby team is an All-Ireland side. Victory, when it comes, is a huge bonus. There is always a generous allowance for honourable failure, as in the case of the day when Ireland nearly beat Australia in the 1991 World Cup.

The exception to the rule of rather tepid enthusiasm for rugby is Limerick, where rugby is like a religion, touching a deep nerve in the psyche of the people of the city. It is recognised worldwide as one of the great cathedrals of rugby.

From the outset, the Limerick observers took Tom Clifford to their hearts because they were positive that he would willingly shed his last drop of blood for them. They knew instinctively that if defeat pained them, it would hurt him even more.

In Limerick, they appreciate style but equally they are quick to see through a veneer if there is not substance to match. From his earliest games, as he lengthened his stride towards maturity, the gossip in Limerick was about how good a player Clifford would become. Nobody had any doubt he had enough class to go all the way. Reared on a diet of good, sometimes very good players, they responded to somebody with something extra.

A GOOD PROP-OSITION

For his Ireland and Lions teammate Jim McCarthy, Clifford was not only one of the great props but perhaps the biggest personality in Irish rugby.

'When I look back, it's the matches with Munster that stand out for me. Rugby is everything in Munster, especially in Limerick. For me, the person that encapsulated that feeling was the late, great Tom Clifford.

'I was on the Lions tour with Tom in 1950. Tom was a larger-than-life figure, especially when he sang his party piece, "O'Reilly's Daughter". Another typical Munster forward was Starry Crowley, a hooker. We were playing in a ferocious match when he "made contact" with a player. He explained his motivation to me afterwards: "I was running across the pitch and I saw a head lying on the ground and I kicked not to maim but to kill."

'That kind of commitment is essential if you are to win matches. There's no doubt in my mind that if you look back to the 1995 World Cup, South Africa were the fourth-best team after the Wallabies, the All Blacks and France, but they were that bit hungrier, which allowed them to win the tournament. No one I knew played with more hunger than Tom Clifford.'

Jack Kyle also has reason to remember Tom fondly from the Lions tour in 1950.

'We were given two blazers and our jerseys, and two pounds ten shillings a week for expenses. If you adjusted that figure to allow for inflation, I can't see chaps playing international rugby accepting that today! From our point of view, the trip was a very enriching experience.

'We were gone for six months. Although we had journeyed to France to play an international, it was our first real experience of travel. We went out via the Panama Canal and home by the Suez Canal, so it really was a round-the-world trip. We kept fit by running around the ship. Every afternoon, we had great discussions about rugby. I learned more about the game in those conversations than I ever have before or since.

'Our champion was Tom Clifford. Apart from the normal luggage, Tom brought a massive trunk onto the ship. We were all puzzled about what he could have in it. As cabins were shared, players were instructed to only store essential items there but Tom insisted on bringing in his trunk which immediately caused a lot of grumbles from his roommates, who were complaining about the clutter. They changed their tune the first night, though, when some of us said we were feeling peckish. Tom brought us into his cabin and opened his trunk which was crammed with food which his mother had cooked. So every night we dined royally in Tom's cabin. Someone said that we should all write a letter to

Mrs Clifford because she fed us so well on that trip! Tom had a very healthy appetite. To break the monotony on the journey, we had all kinds of competitions. One night we had an eating competition. Tom won hands down because he got through the thirty courses that were on the menu!'

Having successfully negotiated the Lions tour, Clifford was immediately involved in an accident when he returned to Ireland. He took a taxi in Dublin and, anxious to ask the taxi driver if he knew what time the next train to Limerick was, he leaned forward and tapped the driver on the shoulder. The driver screamed, lost control of the cab, nearly hit a bus, drove up over a footpath and stopped just inches from a large plate-glass window. For a few moments, everything was silent in the taxi. The startled Clifford apologised to the driver, saying he didn't realise a mere tap on the shoulder would frighten him so much.

'No, no,' the driver replied. 'It's all my fault. Today is my first day driving a taxi. For the last 25 years I've been driving a hearse.'

THE KILLING FIELDS

Clifford died in 1990 and was honoured by Young Munster when they renamed their Greenfields stadium Tom Clifford Park, a ground which has been nicknamed 'The Killing Fields', 'The Garden of Get Somebody' and 'Jurassic Park'. Hence the joke told by visiting teams from Dublin: Why does the Shannon run through Limerick? Would you walk through Limerick?

Tom's legend lives on in rugby folklore. On the Lions tour, Clifford warned some of the Welsh players about the hazards of going out with an Irish Catholic girl on the basis that you could take the girl out of Cork but . . .

He also explained to them that he considered playing against the Welsh a dangerous activity. 'The last time I played against Wales, I went onto the pitch and punched somebody in the face.'

Clifford was adept at psyching his team up for England games in particular. He once told the team about the three young children who go to heaven, but God says they are too young to die. He tells them to take a run off the cloud and on the way back to Earth to shout out what they want to be. The first lad jumps and says he wants to be a successful teacher. Twenty years later he is the youngest head teacher in the country. The second wants to be a successful lawyer and twenty years later, he is the youngest judge ever appointed. The third young lad trips over his own feet jumping off the cloud and involuntarily shouts out 'Clumsy bastard!' Twenty years later, he's playing scrum-half for England.

Tom was way ahead of his time in his capacity to outpsyche his opponents. Before an international against England, he went up to the two English props and said, 'I'm very sorry. I just heard the news. You don't deserve that – either of you.'

The two English players were puzzled: 'What do you mean?'

'I've just heard what everybody's calling the two of you.'

'Really. We haven't heard anything. So what are people calling us behind our backs?'

'Sim-bolic.'

'Symbolic? Why are they calling us that?'

Tom paused theatrically before replying, ''Cos one of you is simple and the other is a bollix.'

38

BREAKING THE MOULD

CORK-BORN WING-FORWARD JIMMY MCCARTHY IS A PRODUCT OF CBC Cork. He won a Munster Senior Schools Cup medal with the school in 1943. With his club, Dolphin, he won Munster Cup medals in 1944, '45 and '48. He was capped twenty-eight times for Ireland between 1948 and 1955, captaining the side four times in 1954 and 1955, and scoring eight international tries. He was also ever-present in the Irish team which won the Five Nations championship in 1951, and toured Argentina and Chile in 1952 with Ireland.

He is best remembered as a breakaway forward of the highest quality, playing in all four matches in the 1948 Grand Slam year and for the entire season of 1949. He brought a new dimension to wing-forward play, particularly in relation to helping the out-half breach the opposing half. A flying redhead, he was an invaluable ally to Jack Kyle, combining with him to devastating effect. His back-row combination with Old Belvedere's Des O'Brien and Bill McKay in those years was among the finest in Irish rugby history. Where did his involvement in rugby begin?

'My father was interested in rugby and sports in general. My sister Aileen became an international golfer before she became a Mercy nun. She was a real tomboy. I always felt she should have played rugby for Munster. She would have been the ideal partner for Tom Clifford!'

A TEAM OF ALL THE TALENTS
He attributes Ireland's success in 1948 and 1949 to the fact that so many great players came onto the scene at the same time.

'As any of the older generations of players will tell you, the best thing about rugby is the friendships. Some years ago, I was at a dinner to mark the 40th anniversary of one of Dolphin's Munster Cups. Strangely, that team won their six rounds without ever scoring a try. I was making the speech and sitting beside Norman Coleman, a great servant of the club. Since his playing days, he's had, I think, three hip replacements and a heart bypass operation. I began my speech by saying, "I now find I only half know Norman."'

Ireland's Grand Slam victory in 1948 prompted McCarthy to engage in what the IRFU saw as extravagant behaviour.

'After we won the Triple Crown in Belfast, I sent in my expenses to the IRFU. I claimed four pounds and ten shillings but only got four pounds and seven shillings. They deducted three shillings because I had rung my family to tell them we had won the Triple Crown and because I had gone outside the de l'hôte menu. I had ordered two raw eggs to eat on the morning of the match. That was part of my ritual. I also took glucose. It probably did me no good physically, but psychologically it gave me an extra edge.'

FOREIGN AFFAIRS

McCarthy toured with the Lions to Australia and New Zealand in 1950.

'It was the last of the six-and-a-half-months tours. When you go along on a tour like that, it's years later before you really appreciate it. It's amazing how quickly people get used to the star treatment. Welsh coalminers who were reared on anything but the silver spoon quickly assume a new star persona. After a few weeks, we were all cribbing about the waitresses.

'Looking back, there were some great players on that team. Scotland's Graham Budge was a peculiar case. He had come from nowhere to play in the final Scottish trial, in the four matches in the Five Nations and then went on the Lions tour, and after that was never heard of again. In 1980, I was holidaying in Pebble Beach in America and I went to a local rugby tournament. My eye was caught by a headline which read "Rugby player dies with his boots on". It reported how the previous year a player had dropped dead playing a match on the same ground. It was Graham. He would have been in his 50s then but was still playing rugby when he grabbed the ball and made a run. He dropped dead on the halfway line.

'The other great find of that 1950 Lions tour was Lewis Jones of

Wales. He was only in his teens but he looked much older because he was losing his hair like lightning. With his big bandy legs, he was the first running full-back. That's the big difference between our time and now. Then, every player's first instinct was not to get tackled. Today, their instinct is to make sure they get tackled, with all this talk about recycling the ball. The first people to start this were the All Blacks. It's very effective but not very pretty to watch. It's not so much "win" rugby as "no loss" rugby. I'm certain it's not the running game which William Webb Ellis envisaged. For me, the only keepers of the true tradition of rugby are France. Why France don't win the Six Nations every year is a mystery to me. They do the extraordinary as if it were the ordinary.'

There is one big regret from his playing days.

'We should have won the Triple Crown in 1951. We had the beating of Wales but our penalty kicker, George Norton, was injured and we let the game slip through our fingers. We drew 3–3. They sprung a new kicker, Ben Edwards, who kicked a wonderful penalty and we equalised with a fantastic try from Jack Kyle. We missed the conversion from in front of the posts. Jack's opponent that day was Cliff Morgan, who went on to become one of the greats himself. We won the championship that year but it should have been the Grand Slam.'

McCarthy held the record for most tries scored by an Ireland forward. What was the secret of his success?

'Wherever the ball is, you be there. When I was playing for Ireland, the best place to be was two feet behind Jackie Kyle.'

A number of players have caught McCarthy's eye in the green jersey since his retirement.

'In my position, Fergus Slattery was the greatest player of recent times. He was so energetic and chased all over the place. I always felt that Colin Patterson was a great loss to Ireland when he got injured. He had a great ability to score tries, which is always a big problem for an opposing side because they don't know what he's going to do next. Of course, Ollie Campbell was a superb player and would be a wonderful asset to any team.'

THE LIFE OF O'REILLY

McCarthy has a long association with Tony O'Reilly.

'Tony came down to take up his first job in Cork and joined us for afternoon tea, which led him to stay a few days, which became two years and in the process he became one of the family. When he first came, he would say "your house, Jim", and "your children and your wife", but he quickly changed the "yours" to "ours" I had no problem with "our kids" and "our dog" but when he started saying "our" wife I showed him the door!

'I knew the first time I saw him that he would be a success in anything he turned his hand to. He had it all and more. Having said that I don't envy him.

'I believe he was never fully exploited on the Irish team. I think he should have been selected at full-back to get the best out of his attacking abilities. There are two sayings which I think apply to Tony: "The bigger the reputation, the smaller the gap," and "To be good, you've got to be twice as good." Everybody wants to cut the guy with the big reputation down to size.

'I was best man at both his weddings! I only played one season with Tony at international level. When he arrived on the scene he was the darling of the media and could do no wrong. After his first match against France, the *Irish Independent* said that I had played poorly and had not protected Tony well enough even though I wasn't playing in the centre! I was dropped for the next match after that report and never played another international. Twenty-five years later Tony put me on the board of the *Irish Independent* just to make up for their injustice to me all those years ago!'

As a gentleman to his fingertips, Jim will also not reveal who Tony O'Reilly's roommate was the night before Ireland took to the field against England at Twickenham. O'Reilly was out having a good time and his bored roommate was sitting in the room alone when the phone rang. A young woman's voice came over the line.

'Can I speak to Tony, please?'

'I'm sorry, he's not in right now. Can I take a message?'

'Do you know what time he'll be back?'

'I think he said he'd be home around ten.'

Silence. Awkward silence.

'Do you want to leave a message for Tony? I'll be happy to pass it on to him as soon as he comes in.'

'Well . . . he said he would be in at this time and asked me to call him.'

'Well, he went out with Karen about an hour ago and said he would be back at ten.'

A shocked voice now: 'Who the fu . . . who is Karen?'

'The girl he went out with.'

'I know that! I mean . . . who the fu . . . who is she?'

'I don't know her last name. Look, do you want to leave a message for Tony?'

'Yes . . . please do. Tell him to call me when he gets in.'

'I sure will. Is this Mary-Kate?'

'Who the f**king hell is Mary-Kate?'

'Well, he's going out with Mary-Kate at ten. I thought you were her. Sorry. It was an honest mistake.'

'Tony's the one that made the mistake! Tell him that Liz called and that she's very upset and that I would like him to call me as soon as he gets in.'

'OK, I will . . . but Samantha isn't going to like this.'

The phone was slammed down with venom.

39

CAPTAIN MARVEL

RUGBY IS THE ONLY GAME WHERE A MAN STICKS HIS HEAD UP another man's bum and the referee allows it. Yet Irish rugby players have often had more specialist knowledge of human anatomy. Doctors played a prominent part in the golden era of Irish rugby. Apart from the peerless Jackie Kyle, there was Ireland captain Karl Mullen of Old Belvedere. Mullen was Ireland's most successful captain, leading them to their only Grand Slam, in 1948, the Triple Crown in 1949 and the Five Nations championship in 1951. He also led the Lions in Australia and New Zealand in 1950.

For Jack Kyle, Mullen was an inspirational force.

'Karl was a wonderful captain. His greatest gift was to let the men play to their full potential. There were times, though, when he showed great tactical awareness. Before we played Wales in Swansea in 1949, he gathered us around and said, "We're going to run them into the ground." We had such a fit and fast back row in particular at the time that he knew we could wear them down and we did. There's a lot of talk today that "forward supremacy is the key" but at that time, we were always able to win the battle of the packs, which made our job in the backs that much easier.

'I especially remember the 1948 game against Wales at Ravenhill in front of a capacity crowd of 30,000. I'd say they could have taken four times as many had there been space for them. We were all understandably a bit apprehensive but deep down felt we could win. Karl made a point of getting the team to discuss tactics, and the strengths and weaknesses of our opponents before matches. He made sure that every man had his say and it was an important part of the pre-match preparations from the point of view of contributing to the great team spirit. We also had a "council of war" at half-time and Karl kept us on the straight and narrow.'

REID ON

One of the centres on that team, Paddy Reid, recalls that New Year's Day in 1948 saw the opening of an unexpectedly glorious chapter in the history of Irish rugby when Ireland pulled off a shock 13–6 victory over France at Stade Colombes. Reid was literally at the centre of things.

'A great character in the team was Barney Mullan. The night before the game in Paris, we had a team meeting as usual. Barney came up with the idea that if we were under pressure during the game and got a lineout, he would call a short one and throw it out over the forwards' heads and lift the siege. As predicted, we got a lineout on our own 25. The French players were huge. They looked like mountains to us, so we needed to out-think them. Mullan threw it long and Jack Kyle grabbed it, passed it to me, I fed it to Des McKee and he returned the compliment for me to score under the posts. The glory was mine but it was Barney's tactical awareness that earned us that try.

'Travelling to Paris for us at the time was like going to the edge of the world. We were as green as grass. After our win, we were invited to a reception at the Irish embassy. Of course, champagne was the order of the day, which was a very novel experience for most of us. We were knocking it back as if it was stout! To me, the incident that best illustrated our innocence was when the Dolphin pair Jim McCarthy and Bertie O'Hanlon asked for red lemonade!'

The following Valentine's Day saw Ireland beat England 11–10 at Twickenham. The Grand Slam decider against Wales at Ravenhill was the critical one. The date –13 March – was not to prove an unlucky one as Ireland fought a tense battle with their nerves as much as with the opposition before emerging victorious. Reid's memories of that year are vivid. He believes that the decisive moment came when Ireland laid the Welsh bogey to rest.

'We were fortunate to have a wonderful captain in Karl Mullen. He was great for letting everyone have their say. The night before the Wales game, we had a meeting. One of the people who had given us advice was Dave O'Loughlin who had been a star Irish forward just before the Second World War. To all of us on the '48 team, he was an idol. He had played against the great Welsh scrum-half Haydn Tanner, who was still calling the shots on the Welsh team in 1948. [The previous year his late break had set up a try which robbed Ireland of the Triple Crown.] Dave told us that Tanner was the man to watch and assured us that he would make two breaks during the game. At the meeting, I suggested that Des O'Brien should be appointed as Tanner's shadow, whose job it would be to ensure that when the Welshman broke, he would be quashed. I went so far as to suggest that if he didn't do his task properly in this respect, he should be dropped. Des was not too happy with this part of the plan at the time but he was given the assignment nonetheless.

'Sure enough, as Dave had promised, Haydn broke twice. Both times, Des tackled him superbly. In fact, so frustrated was Tanner on the second occasion that he slammed the ball to the ground in frustration. These things can turn a match. I'm convinced it was the difference between victory and defeat for us in the Grand Slam.

'Karl Mullen was a great leader but we also had the great fortune to have Jack Kyle in the side. He was a wizard. I'd be struggling to describe him, he was such a classy player – a man apart. The strange thing about him is that for all his greatness, he was such a humble man and a real team player. I would also have to say, though, that we were no one-man team. There was great camaraderie and spirit in that side and we all pulled for each other. Bill McKay, a medical student from Queen's University, was the best wing-forward I ever saw. To me, the unsung hero was the full-back, Dudley Higgins, who of course is a past president of the IRFU. You never had to look over your shoulder when he was on the team. He was such a great tackler he would stop a train.'

Did the players receive any reward for their unique achievement?

'The only thing we got was a photo of the winning team and the team crest!'

LEAVE IT TO MR O'BRIEN

Mullen's successor as Irish captain, the late Des O'Brien, had a very personal memory of him.

'I won my first cap against England in 1948. Karl came to me on the team bus and asked me if I would be a leader of the pack. I told him I didn't feel up to it because I didn't know any of the forwards as I was a London Irish player at the time. He said "We can soon fix that" and then he took me on the bus and introduced me to the forwards. Karl was a great player. The laws of the game were different then and he was very capable of winning a heel against the head when the ball was in the opposition's back row of the scrum. I would sum him up as great captain and an exceptional hooker.

'Of course, things were very different back then. We had none of the perks players have today. We wore our own club socks when we played for Ireland. The clubs liked that, as did we. Wales wore letters on their backs instead of numbers at the time. Team dinners after internationals were held in Mills restaurant in Merrion Row – just the team and half a dozen officials. Speeches were brief, as we all wanted to get to the three big dances being held from ten until three in the Gresham, the Metropole and the Shelbourne. We would be guests of all three. The night before a Dublin game, we would usually take the opposition team to the Gaiety Theatre. We had to pay for our own tickets! You were only given one jersey a season, no matter how many games you played. You could be dropped if you pinched a jersey after a game!

'In my first two years, the players were not allowed any tickets even to buy! Before the Scotland game in Dublin in 1949, Karl Mullen was offered two tickets to buy for his parents. The team decided no tickets, no game and there was quite a scene in the Shelbourne on the Friday night. Karl got his tickets and after that, the IRFU agreed with reluctance to let us buy two tickets each. Big deal!

'I was on the first team to take a plane to a match when we went to France. Our touring party amounted to 68, of whom 40 were alickadoos!

'The letter which informed me of my selection to play against South Africa in 1951 provides a fascinating insight into rugby sociology on many levels. It included the phrase "No room booked". As my mother lived in Dublin I was expected to take lodgings with her. After the 1949 "players' revolution", internationals were entitled to two tickets each but were given only two days to pay for them, which was incredibly difficult for a player like me based in London given the state of communications in 1951.

'We were the undisputed kings of wheeling the scrum. In an England game, we wheeled the scrum from our own line to their half. Another time, we wheeled our opponent's scrum seven times. Every time there was a scrum, you could see the fear in the opposition's eyes. Half of our training was spent practising dribbling. When the laws changed in the mid-'50s, the tradition of wheeling the scrum waned dramatically and the art of dribbling died completely. I really feel half of the game died with those skills.

'I found the secret of leading an Irish pack was to keep them under tight control from the start, otherwise they went off like a cavalry charge and died away in the last 15 minutes of each half. We had a very tight-set scrum that only timed the shove when the ball left the scrum-half's hand. We gave a stone a man away to the 1951 Springboks and yet we could shift them back two feet at every scrum. In those days, the hooker had to fight for the ball and two feet was all he needed.

'In the five years I played for Ireland, nobody had a wife or a motor car. We either walked or cycled. This gave us a natural fitness which players don't have today. I know this might sound like boasting but I think we were the fittest back row that ever played for Ireland. Jim McCarthy in particular had exceptional fitness. Our other colleague in the back row, Bill McKay, was a 400-yards sprinting champion and a boxing champion. The three of us played together fourteen times for Ireland and only lost three times.

'We had great leadership from Karl but we had amazing talent all round the field. The only adjective that fairly describes Jack Kyle is "genius". One of our favourite tactics was to deliberately starve him of the ball for 20 minutes and lull the opposition into a false sense of security. Then we fed him and they were destroyed. He was also in a class of his own when it came to kicking for touch.'

DOCTOR'S ORDERS

In August 2004, Karl Mullen was catapulted back into the media spotlight when his grandson, Cian O'Connor, won a gold medal at the Athens Olympics in showjumping. Long after his retirement as a player, Mullen was involved in one of the most famous incidents in Irish rugby. During a match he was attending, one of the great folk heroes of Irish rugby, Phil O'Callaghan was in the thick of the action.

Philo put out his shoulder in the match and the doctor was to experience O'Callaghan's tongue at first hand when he ran onto the pitch to give him medical care, kindly offering to put the dislocated shoulder back into position and warning him in advance that it would hurt. Apparently, Philo made a terrible fuss about the pain. Dr Mullen admonished him, saying that he had recently delivered a teenage girl's baby and that she had been tremendously brave in comparison.

Philo answered, 'I wonder what she bloody well would have said if you tried putting the f**kin' thing back in.'

40

THE UNCROWNED KING

A FAMOUS STORY IS TOLD ABOUT JACK NICKLAUS. WHEN HE WAS unquestionably the top golfer in the world in 1973, he was watching television when the immortal Secretariat won, in spectacular style, the final leg of American racing's Triple Crown: the Kentucky Derby, the Preakness and the Belmont Stakes. Secretariat became the first horse to win the Triple Crown in 25 years. As he watched the big chestnut absolutely demolish the opposition, tears rolled in steady streams down Nicklaus's cheeks. The famous golfer had no bet on the race but was transformed into a blubbering baby watching this magnificent horse. Puzzled and embarrassed by the depth of his emotion, he asked a friend for an explanation. His friend said, 'It's because you've spent your life searching for perfection and you finally saw it.' Those who were lucky enough to have seen Jack Kyle in full flight must have felt a bit like that.

Such was Kyle's impact during his 46-cap Ireland career that he literally defined the age: his glory days, when Ireland reached its rugby zenith in the late 1940s, were known throughout the rugby world as 'the Jackie Kyle era'. According to the American philosopher William James, the world is a theatre for heroism. Kyle made every pitch he graced a theatre of dreams, cutting a swathe through defences and leaving the opposition trailing in his wake. In full flight, he was poetry in motion. He loved the drama that was part of the most glorious chapter in Irish rugby history. As he reminisces about those days and his fellow internationals, the great moments of the 1940s and 1950s unreeling before the vivid mind's eye of memory, his voice betrays the nerve-tingling excitement.

'There is a big advantage in being a small country, if that isn't a contradiction in terms, in that it is difficult for good players to slip through the net because of the interpros, the matches between the combined provinces and the rest of Ireland, and the final trial. If you were any good at all, somebody saw you play somewhere!

'I was not a great tackler. If I'd had to play rugby as a forward, I would never have played the game! Our back row of Jim McCarthy, Bill McKay and Des O'Brien was so strong that I didn't have to bother too much with the normal defensive duties of a fly-half. McCarthy was like greased lightning, and an incredible forager and opportunist. I could virtually leave the out-half to our two flankers. I just stood back and took him if he went on the outside.

'I was doubly blessed in that I also had Noel Henderson playing alongside me in the centre. He was a marvellous defender, performing many of my defensive duties and I'm not just saying that because he became my brother-in-law!'

BIG BROTHER-IN-LAW

The unpredictable often happens in rugby. It was to be his brother-in-law that caused Kyle's greatest surprise.

'Noel caused a major shock one day at our team meeting. He was a very quiet man and was not normally very loquacious at those sessions. As was his custom, Karl Mullen concluded by asking if there were any questions. Noel asked, "What I would like to know, captain, is there any way of knowing will the out-half be taking his man for a change?"

'Noel had the good fortune to be the father of four daughters. I met the former Scottish centre Charlie Drummond once, who also has a lot of daughters. When I told him about Noel he said, "We're raising good stock for future rugby players." There's a man who takes the long-term view!'

Historically, there have been some serious misunderstandings when sports personalities have become involved in more cultural pursuits. I will resist the obvious temptation to make jokes about David Beckham's wife and her crimes against music – apart from to observe that her voice is a weapon of mass destruction. In 2001, Posh brought Becks to the ballet. He ran into problems afterwards when he was interviewed about the performance. When asked what he thought about the pas de deux, he replied that he enjoyed it because he too was a father of two. Jack Kyle, however, was cut from a very different cloth.

'One of the images a lot of people have of rugby players is that they are ignorant buffoons. On that Grand Slam side, Noel, Des O'Brien and myself had a great interest in poetry. It broke the tedium of many a train journey for us. I was particularly interested in the poetry of Yeats and I was also a great Patrick Kavanagh fan. We swapped poems and read poetry to each other. We even wrote our own poems. Mind you, if our rugby was of the same standard as our poetry, we would never have won the Grand Slam!

'When Des was with London Irish, a regular spectator at their games was the great poet Louis MacNeice. He often tried to talk to Louis in the bar afterwards about poetry, with no success. MacNiece always said, "I came here to watch rugby, not to talk about poetry."'

Incredibly, on 10 February 2006 Kyle celebrated his 80th birthday. There was more than a tinge of sadness on that day for an absent friend.

'Des O'Brien died on the previous St Stephen's Day. Jim McCarthy and his wife, Ronnie Dawson, Ronnie Kavanagh, James Nelson and myself went to Edinburgh for the funeral. Des was a superb back-row player, a delightful man and great company. His funeral was a celebration of a full and interesting life. He left word that there was to be a party after his funeral, and so we went back to his house and around the piano we sang many of the songs which he used to sing.'

Throughout his illustrious career, Kyle was showered with accolades. Did any of them have a special significance for him?

'Louis MacNeice was doing a radio broadcast here in Belfast one evening. He was asked if he could make one wish, what it would be. His answer was that he would love to play rugby like Jack Kyle. That's the compliment that meant the most to me.'

Kyle always enjoyed the good-natured banter between backs and forwards. He tells the story of the time Noel Henderson walked into a restaurant in Limerick, ordered a drink and asked the waiter if he would like to hear a good joke about rugby forwards. 'Listen, mister,' the waiter growled, 'see those two big guys on your left? They were both second rows for Shannon. And that huge fella on your right, he's the number 8 for Young Munster. And I'm the prop forward for Garryowen. Now, are you absolutely positive you want to go ahead and tell your joke here?'

'Hah, guess not,' Henderson replied. 'I wouldn't want to have to explain it five times.'

DIFFERENT TIMES

Kyle's clearest memory of the Triple Crown-winning side is of Jack Daly.

'At the time, we always faced playing the Welsh on their own patch with trepidation. In 1948, though, when we played them in Swansea, Jack sat in the dressing-room punching his fist into his hand, saying, "I'm mad to get at them. I'm mad to get at them. I'm mad to get at them." His enthusiasm rubbed off on the rest of us.

'You have to remember that it was such a different set-up then from today. We came down from Belfast on the train in the morning and in the afternoon we went for a training session, using the term loosely, in Trinity College. Johnny O'Meara might throw me a few passes and that would be enough for me. We used an interesting word a lot at the time: "stale", which I never hear now. Basically, we believed that if we trained too hard, we would not perform on the Saturday. It was probably an excuse for us not to do any serious work!

'I always felt that, just as a girl who is born beautiful can only enhance her looks a little bit, you can only achieve a limited amount in rugby by coaching. It's really a question of natural ability. I only dropped a goal once for Ireland. It was from a very difficult angle. If I had thought about it, I could never have attempted it. It was just instinctive. A lot of times, we were working on a subconscious level. On another occasion, I combined with Jim McCarthy for Jim to score a great try. I got a letter afterwards telling me it was such a textbook score we must have practised it on the training ground. Looking back now, it's amazing how few of the set moves we had worked out actually came off.'

CLIFF-HANGER

When asked about his most difficult opponent, Kyle eventually selects Cliff Morgan.

'I played against him frequently. Cliff was one of the great out-halfs. He was brilliant on the Lions tour of South Africa in 1955; they still talk about his performance on that tour. The problem playing against Cliff was that I never knew what he would do next. That meant I was unable to concentrate on my own game as much.'

Jack continues to keep in touch with the rugby community. He particularly admires the former Irish players who have gone on to use their fame to raise money for people in need, like Johnny Moloney, who has worked tirelessly to raise money for Outreach Moldova. This Irish-founded charity helps children in orphanages in Moldova, a country that is just five hours away from Ireland by plane but the poorest in Europe. Its primary goal is medical care, combined with appropriate humanitarian aid.

Former Ireland and Lions forward Bill Mulcahy tells one of the many stories about Jack Kyle.

'The classic tale about Jack concerns John O'Meara's first cap, when he was to partner Jack at half-back. He was naturally a bit apprehensive about partnering the unrivalled best player in the world and was debating how he would address Jack. Should he call him Dr Kyle or Mr Kyle? John travelled up in the *Cork Examiner* van and walked meekly into the team hotel. Immediately he walked in the door, the first person to greet him was Jack who said, "Congratulations, Johnny. Delighted to see you here. Where would you like me to stand on the pitch?" Who else would have shown such modesty?'

Kyle had some peculiar experiences playing rugby in Ireland. Shortly after the Grand Slam triumph in 1949, Jack drove down to Cork. On his travels, he arrived at a level crossing which was neither open nor closed but halfway across the road. He got out of his car, found the stationmaster and asked, 'Do you know the gate is halfway across the road?'

'I do,' replied the stationmaster. 'We are half expecting the train from Cork.'